North Carolina LIGHTHOUSES

The Stories behind the Beacons from Cape Fear to Currituck Beach

CHERYL SHELTON-ROBERTS & BRUCE ROBERTS
Foreword by Ray Jones

THE UNIVERSITY OF NORTH CAROLINA PRESS

CHAPEL HILL

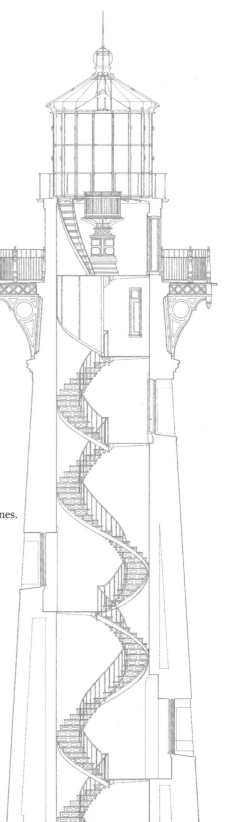

Cover photographs: (*front*) Bodie Island Lighthouse © Michael VerSprill; (*back*) an architectural drawing of the top half of Cape Hatteras Lighthouse by Judith E. Collins, courtesy of the Library of Congress Prints and Photographs Division.

Manufactured in the United States of America

The University of North Carolina Press has been a member of the Green Press Initiative since 2003.

Designed by Jamison Cockerham
Set in Scala, Brothers, and Kododa
by Tseng Information Systems, Inc.

LIBRARY OF CONGRESS CATALOGING-IN-PUBLICATION DATA
Names: Shelton-Roberts, Cheryl, 1950– author. |
    Roberts, Bruce, 1930– author. |
    Jones, Ray, 1948– writer of introduction.
Title: North Carolina lighthouses : the stories behind the beacons
    from Cape Fear to Currituck Beach /
    Cheryl Shelton-Roberts and Bruce Roberts ; foreword by Ray Jones.
Description: Revised and expanded edition. |
    Chapel Hill : The University of North Carolina Press, [2019] |
    Includes bibliographical references and index.
Identifiers: LCCN 2018040435 |
    ISBN 9781469641485 (pbk : alk. paper) |
    ISBN 9781469641492 (ebook)
Subjects: LCSH: Lighthouses—North Carolina—History. |
    Lighthouses—North Carolina—Pictorial works.
Classification: LCC VK1024.N8 S53 2019 |
    DDC 387.1/5509756—dc23
    LC record available at https://lccn.loc.gov/2018040435

To DAVID STICK, *whose research on North Carolina lighthouses and Outer Banks history opened doors for future historians. He brought to the forefront the value of our coastline, its lighthouses and lifesaving stations, and the captivating stories behind each of them.*

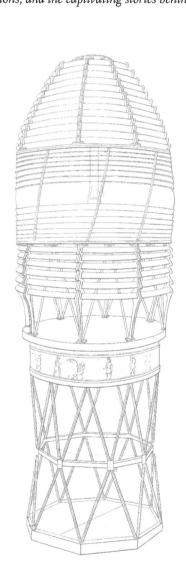
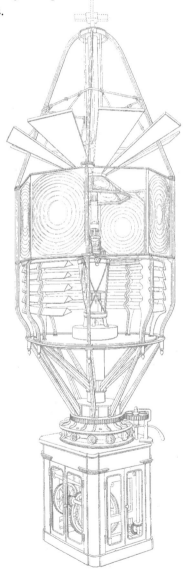

Contents

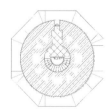
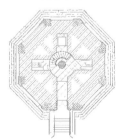

Foreword

Lighthouses call to us, not just from across the water but also from across time. Their primary purpose—to guide mariners—and their basic form—a structure with a light at the top—have changed little in more than 2,000 years. —RAY JONES, *The Lighthouse Encyclopedia*

Lighthouses are symbols of a history mysterious and far removed, yet they capture the imagination like little else because they are still part of us. They are tangible. We can touch and be touched by them, see what they see.

An extraordinary history runs through the lighted guardians that have watched over North Carolina's beautiful capes, sounds, and rivers for centuries, in part influenced by human history, but just as much dictated by the furtive nature of this part of the world. The Outer Banks define our state's outermost edge, but it is often hard to tell exactly where solid land ends and open water begins. Watching waves pound on the beach, it becomes obvious the land has only a tenuous hold—but also the ocean's grip on its own domain is slippery. The sandy isles and shallow waters create an enchanting and disorienting illusion, and they have taken a deadly toll for as long as sailors have worked these waters.

North Carolina's shore stretches an impressive 301 miles, and unlike other Eastern Seaboard states that trend gently northeastward, it thrusts far out into the Atlantic Ocean, slicing across our nation's vital north-south shipping lanes. A long, broken peninsula that appears to be coming unglued, these low-slung barrier islands are at many points invisible from the mainland, adding to the disorientation. They poked their heads above water thousands of years ago, dynamic in the extreme. The Banks have "perplexed scientists for centuries," says coastal geologist Stanley Riggs.

To the east of the islands lie three sweeping capes and gigantic sandy shoals: Cape Fear's Frying Pan Shoals near Wilmington, Cape Lookout and its shoals near Morehead City, and the knobby knee of Cape Hatteras and Diamond Shoals at Buxton stretch underwater for miles. At Hatteras, sea

OPPOSITE
This satellite view captures a section of North Carolina's slender stretch of barrier islands and one of its capes. Cape Lookout stretches a sandy finger menacingly into the Atlantic Ocean, with Beaufort Inlet to the west and Ophelia Inlet to the north. Ocracoke Inlet, northernmost in the image, opens into the vast Pamlico Sound. The milky aura along the barrier islands and concentrated at the capes comes from notoriously dynamic shoals that have caused hundreds of vessels to wreck. *Photograph courtesy of NASA.*

ix

captains had to choose between a longer and safer route east of the Gulf Stream or a quicker but riskier passage that made them roll the dice with the hidden shoals. Shipwrecks by the thousands litter the ocean floor.

North Carolina's lighthouse heritage begins, geographically at least, a few miles below the Virginia border. Rising above rolling sand dunes, the Currituck Beach Lighthouse was completed in 1875, the final link in lighting the state's entire coast. In the 1870s came an extraordinary lighthouse building boom—a series of projects so innovative that some historians have compared the overall effort to the U.S. space program. This bold undertaking gave North Carolina the best system of coastal towers and navigational lights in America.

To the south, near a once-important maritime passage called Oregon Inlet, stands the Bodie Island Lighthouse. A bit older than Currituck Beach, it is the last of three lighthouses erected here. Farther south, near where the island chain bends sharply to the southwest, the Cape Hatteras Lighthouse rises firmly rooted now half a mile from where it was built in 1870.

On Ocracoke Island endures the oldest North Carolina light still in operation, built in 1823. At the far southwestern corner of the Outer Banks, yet another brick giant illumines the night sky at Cape Lookout, constructed before the American Civil War and a model for its brethren up the coast. The very oldest and the very newest towers in the state are neighbors—Bald Head Island's 1817 "Old Baldy" and the 1958 Oak Island Light.

The story of North Carolina's beacons, like all of America's lights, is about rising and falling fortunes. Not much needed after World War II with the advent of modern highways and sophisticated technologies, they fell into disrepair. They needed benefactors to care for them and a new sense of purpose, and, happily, many of these irreplaceable pieces of history have now regained their rightful places of honor.

In this book are the soul-stirring stories of North Carolina's lighthouses and the people who built them, were saved by them, cared for them, and now love them in a whole new way. It is a history of darkest danger, nearly unfathomable courage—and, above all, dazzling light.

Ray Jones

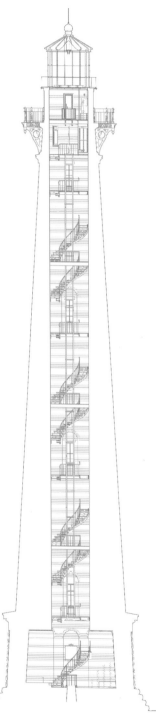

NORTH CAROLINA

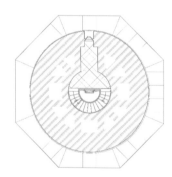

LIGHTHOUSES

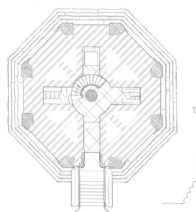

EXISTING NORTH CAROLINA
Lighthouses
and Date Tower First Lighted

1875
CURRITUCK
BEACH

1887
SECOND ROANOKE RIVER

ALBEMARLE SOUND

2004
ROANOKE
MARSHES
*(Built from original
1877 plans)*

1872
BODIE
ISLAND

64

Alligator River

2004
ROANOKE RIVER
*(Built from original
1866 plans)*

Lake Phelps

Mattamuskeet Lake

PAMLICO SOUND

12

1870
CAPE
HATTERAS

17

1823
OCRACOKE

Neuse River

70

12

1850
PRICE'S
CREEK

1958
OAK ISLAND

1859
CAPE
LOOKOUT

1818
BALD HEAD

Introduction

Lighthouses are endlessly suggestive signifiers of both human isolation and our ultimate connectedness to each other. —VIRGINIA WOOLF

In our courtship with the sea, lighthouses have given us romantic and legendary stories. Withstanding tempests and time, they collect nature's rhythms and set them to the music of wind and tide to which we are instinctively drawn, because in our chest beats the heart of an ancient mariner. Lighthouses call to us in tones of adventure and daring, of dignity and courage, of dutiful patience and purpose. They are there for all mankind; they know no bias. Lighthouses simply serve at our pleasure.

North Carolina has nine original, standing lighthouses. It is impressive that seven of these are listed on the National Register of Historic Places, with four of the seven situated, maintained, and protected within national parks.

Today, perhaps considered outmoded by GPS devices, lighthouses have remained useful, but there is more to the story than just bricks and mortar and their photogenic appeal. From early lighthouses, like the Pharos of Alexandria in Egypt, built in the third century B.C., to the tower we know today at Cape Hatteras, these structures have gained countless admirers for their striking architecture. Initially, their sole purpose was to send a signal to mariners seeking either a safe harbor or a secure route away from a dangerous coastline. Sitting comfortably in our homes, it is difficult for us to realize just how real the dangers were for those venturing on the sea. Death lurked in hidden shoals, shallow waters, and sneaky currents that could pull a ship into fatal hazards—this was an everyday affair for sailors and nautical passengers. However, transcending our understanding of their original purpose, we have discovered that there is something inherently sincere about lighthouses. Today, they are at the heart of heritage tourism as vessels of maritime history and lore; further, as history defines

OPPOSITE
North Carolina has nine original lighthouses guarding over 300 miles of low-lying barrier islands. In recent years, two full-scale reproduction lights have been created to revive history at the Roanoke River and Roanoke Marshes Light Stations in Plymouth and Manteo, respectively. *Created by Sally Fry Scruggs.*

Cape Hatteras Lighthouse is one of the most iconic towers in the world due to its admirable height, pushing 200 feet, and its black-and-white spiral daymark. It nearly became victim to erosion created in part by rising sea level. Shallow waters 15 miles offshore, created by Diamond Shoals, called for a warning light at this site beginning in 1803.

where past and present meet, these guardians have become monuments, prized as cultural resources.

In light of advancing technology, lighthouses have taken on life beyond their original purpose. Not only have they survived the continuum of automation, but their preservation has also become a rallying cry for those living on the coast and beyond. The most notable example is the Cape Hatteras Lighthouse. Nearly 130 years after it was built, the lighthouse was moved inland to save it from encroaching ocean waters. The relocation project became a lightning rod that pitted environmentalists against potential real estate developers, as well as local residents who had looked at this light in the same spot for generations. While the successful completion of this project in 1999 proved to be a pivotal investment in preserving a piece of American maritime history, it brought to the forefront the questionable use of groins and retaining walls—manmade structures to prevent sediment depletion—and other means to harden the coast that cause other environmental concerns. In addition, moving the lighthouse away from the edge of the sea addressed the elephant in the room: the reality of rising sea levels caused by climate change. Instead of losing its historical context as those who opposed the move claimed, this famous light has earned the distinct honor of being listed as a National Historic Landmark—something only eleven other American lights can currently claim. It also is a huge draw for tourists, enriching the economy of this small coastal community.

The history of North Carolina's lighthouses is essentially the history of our nation: lighthouses had to do with safety, yes, but arguably economic concerns were the reason for their construction. Owners of early colonial lights were predominantly businessmen in the Northeast, and each light was an investment for them, as shipping was the primary way to move goods. The process was risky at best, and a guiding light helped reduce the loss of ships, lives, and cargo, which in turn helped grow a vigorous economy. The first federal monies invested in our country's infrastructure in 1789 did not build a post office or courthouse; rather, they supported "the establishment and support of Lighthouses, Beacons, Buoys, and Public Piers." The new government took on the responsibility of marking North Carolina's three capes as soon as possible to increase safety and boost trade. Encouragement for economic trade and growth came with establishment of the 1794 Cape Fear Lighthouse to help direct maritime traffic twenty-six miles upriver to the growing port of Wilmington.

As structures that today could be dubbed American anachronisms,

An official U.S. Lighthouse Service seal was used on government lighthouse property. The logo marked items belonging to the service, including dinnerware that dressed a keeper's table, the warm blanket he used to fend off the cold, and his uniform cap. *From the personal collection of John Havel.*

Lighthouse Measurement Is Not as Simple as It Appears

Measurement of the height of any lighthouse is an approximate figure unless it is done by laser—and even then, the stated height is based on the starting and ending points, and those may vary depending on the source of the measurement. For instance, one source will give only the height of the brick column; others will measure from ground level to the tip of a lightning rod, while another measurement considers only the height at the "focal plane above mean water," which is the center of the lantern room at the level where a focused beam of light is emitted. Technically, the height of a lighthouse should include all parts that are permanent fixtures of the tower, including the foundation, lantern room, ventilation ball, and lightning rod.

lighthouses have remained simplistic in structure and role, almost stubbornly so. However, to those who admire them, lighthouses have become far more than directional guides: they are tangible reminders of our connections to the sea and how fortunate we are to have descended from hardy ancestors who survived incredible trips across poorly charted oceans when ships were little more than wooden coffins at the complete mercy of weather.

We have compiled nearly three decades of research and collecting in *North Carolina Lighthouses* for readers to study and enjoy. We have written a dozen books on lighthouses, and in this edition, we are offering the essence of the information and photographs that we have found most interesting and meaningful. This edition includes many new discoveries as well as images never before published.

This book's chronological and geographical layout illustrates the coverage of the various areas of the coast with lighthouses since 1794. In the final chapter, we discuss preservation efforts as well as new roles for North Carolina's lights, which include creating economic advantages for the communities surrounding them, as well as offering an off-the-grid experience on one of the Texas-oil-rig-style towers more than two dozen miles off the North Carolina coast. We do not hesitate to say that the subject of lighthouses continues to grow in popularity and enthusiasm.

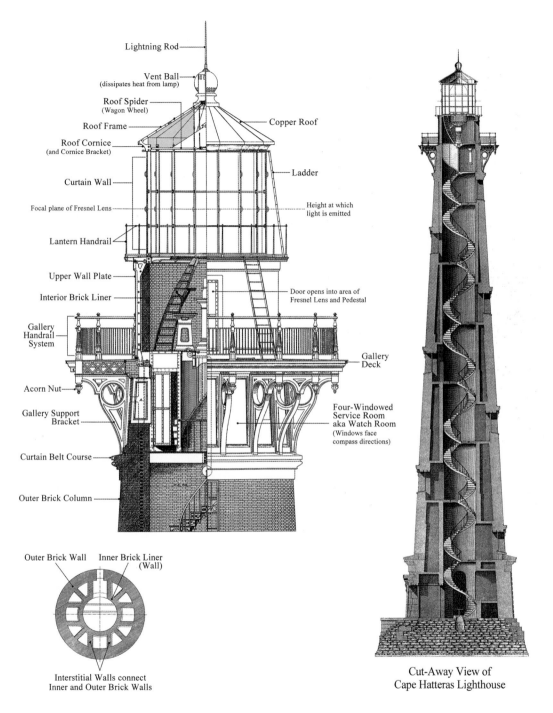

Lightning Rod

Vent Ball
(dissipates heat from lamp)

Roof Spider
(Wagon Wheel)

Roof Frame

Roof Cornice
(and Cornice Bracket)

Curtain Wall

Focal plane of Fresnel Lens

Lantern Handrail

Upper Wall Plate

Interior Brick Liner

Gallery
Handrail
System

Acorn Nut

Gallery Support
Bracket

Curtain Belt Course

Outer Brick Column

Copper Roof

Ladder

Height at which
light is emitted

Door opens into area of
Fresnel Lens and Pedestal

Gallery
Deck

Four-Windowed
Service Room
aka Watch Room
(Windows face
compass directions)

Outer Brick Wall   Inner Brick Liner
(Wall)

Interstitial Walls connect
Inner and Outer Brick Walls

Cut-Away View of
Cape Hatteras Lighthouse

Architectural drawings from the original 1869 Cape Hatteras Lighthouse architectural plans.
Graphic design by Virginia Howell; redrawn by John Havel (2017). *From the author's collection.*

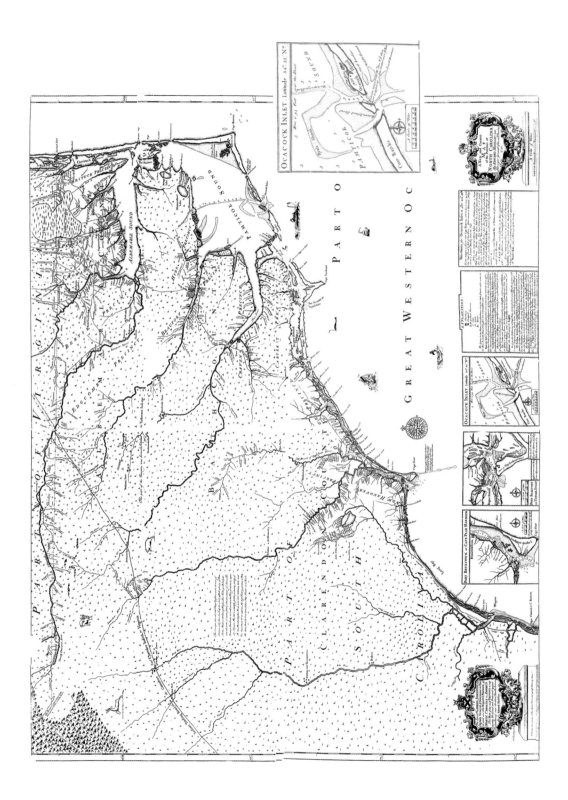

Lighting North Carolina's Coastline

1

On August 7, 1789, the First U.S. Congress passed its ninth act, our country's original public works legislation, and President George Washington signed it into law. Shipping was of such economic importance that Congress took on all responsibilities for building and maintaining lighthouses in this important act. It stated that "all expenses which shall accrue from and after the 15th day of August 1789, in the necessary support, maintenance and repairs of all lighthouses, beacons, buoys and public piers erected, placed, or sunk before the passing of this Act, at the entrance of, or within any bay, inlet, harbor, or port of the United States, for rendering the navigation thereof easy and safe, shall be defrayed out of the treasury of the United States." This act created the U.S. Lighthouse Establishment (USLHE), which operated as part of the national Department of the Treasury, and it also launched our federal government's commitment to safety at sea, as well as its full support of encouraging our national economy to grow on the backs of ships that transported people and goods to and from American shores. In 1988, the members of Congress and President Ronald Reagan recognized the 200th anniversary of the passing of this historic act and declared August 7 of every year to be National Lighthouse Day.

However, when the act passed, there was little consensus among the governing leaders of the twelve independent states that the USLHE was necessary. It was not until 1797 that federal officials negotiated the transfer of a dozen operating lighthouses to the USLHE and finalized settlements related to the lighthouses under construction.

NORTH CAROLINA'S EARLY LIGHTS

Cape Fear, Cape Hatteras, and Cape Lookout define the chameleon-like North Carolina coast, which comprises long fingers of barrier islands. Because of the tricky terrain, the waters off their shores have earned the sobering nickname Graveyard of the Atlantic. Cape Hatteras, known as

OPPOSITE
A New and Correct Map of the Province of North Carolina by Edward Moseley, Late Surveyor General of the Said Province ([London], 1733), includes bygone names, including Pamtico, now Pamlico, and Ocacock, now Ocracoke. It illustrates the humble attempt to provide guiding lights to sailors. Ocracoke Inlet lay adjacent to Beacon Island, on which two small lights were exhibited. The Cape Fear River is named "Waggomau [Waccamaw]" and Bald Head Island appears as "Barren Head," giving credence to the island's name originating from its topographical appearance. INSET: Detail of map showing Beacon Island in Ocracoke Inlet.

"the cape," and Diamond Shoals are the focal points of the graveyard, which have shaped the area's development and the destiny of people who sailed its waters. These three hazardous capes were the first sites marked with lights to either guide mariners into safe harbor or warn them away from their dangerous shoals that reached far out into the Atlantic.

According to the *Map of the Province of North Carolina by Edward Moseley, Late Surveyor General of the Said Province, 1733*, only two "beacons" (likely small lights on posts) composed the grand total of lights marking any of the local waters. Handwritten instructions on this map directed sailors to bring the two "range" lights into alignment to find the safe channel. At the time, these humble lights stood on Beacon Island, a small piece of land under British control about four miles southwest of Ocracoke Island. Obscured by other historical events and eventually forgotten, Beacon Island witnessed the Spanish invasion of Ocracoke in 1747 and the British blockade during the American Revolutionary War. (For more about this historic site, see chapter 3.)

After the United States won independence from Great Britain in 1783, the federal government immediately took on the task of providing lights for the East Coast's main ports and inlets. North Carolina received federal funds to build lighthouses to mark the entrances to the Cape Fear River and Ocracoke Inlet at Shell Castle Island, as well as a warning light at Cape Hatteras. For more than a century, lights would continue to pop up steadily along the Atlantic coast, with the U.S. government assuming both engineering and fiscal responsibilities.

LIGHTING CAPE FEAR

In 1794, North Carolina's first federally funded lighthouse—commonly defined as a tower with a light surmounted in an enclosed lantern room—was built to mark the mouth of the Cape Fear River, an area embracing Smith Island, of which Bald Head Island is part, and Frying Pan Shoals, for ships headed to Wilmington, the state's chief port city. This long, wandering, mighty river has shaped the area's history from the time Native Americans first lowered cypress canoes into its gently flowing waters, which they called "Waccamaw." They hunted on the island while keeping permanent settlements on the mainland long before pirates discovered the island's resources and used coastal alcoves as hideaways. As trade grew and commercial ships began frequenting the river area, the government added lighthouses, beacons, and light vessels along the river to encourage captains to sail inland to Wilmington and conduct business.

The federal government also undertook great efforts to light the way around dangerous Frying Pan Shoals, an underwater extension of Cape Fear just below the ocean surface outside the entrances to the river and inlets. Silt, mud, and sand wash down more than 6,000 stream miles of the Cape Fear River to the Atlantic Ocean, building up on both the outside and inside of inlets and causing channel blockages. As a result, the channels flowing around Frying Pan Shoals constantly change with each tide. The name "Cape Fear" was well earned as many ships encountered unplanned tragic stops on these shoals, never to be seen again. It is worth noting that in some instances, the cape was called "Cape Fair," which might have been a clever marketing technique to encourage colonists to move there, but anyone familiar with the hazards knew differently. Nevertheless, early settlers used the Cape Fear, Northeast Cape Fear, and Black Rivers for trading tobacco, timber, fur, and produce. Eventually, Wilmington became a point of entry for slaves to be auctioned to work on farms and plantations.

THE FIRST BALD HEAD ISLAND LIGHT

Planning for the first lighthouse on Bald Head Island began in 1783, but monies were not available for construction until 1784, when the North Carolina General Assembly levied an import duty on cargo coming into the Cape Fear River area. This tariff is how all twelve East Coast lights had been established between the years 1716 and 1788, by far the majority having been located in great shipping states of the Northeast.

In 1790, Benjamin Smith, Bald Head's owner and later the governor of North Carolina, granted ten acres for the construction of the lighthouse. The colonial government started building the tower because of the great need for a light to guide vessels into the Cape Fear River, and later the federal government took responsibility for the project.

A 1792 entry in Secretary of the Treasury Alexander Hamilton's financial ledger shows $4,000 earmarked for the Bald Head Island Lighthouse, which was completed in 1795. Abishai Woodward, or Abisha, as spelled on his gravestone, a carpenter from Connecticut, won the federal contract, and George Hooper of Wilmington supervised the construction. When Woodward first arrived on the scene, construction was well under way, leaving him no say regarding the poorly chosen site.

A series of letters bring to life details about the lighthouse, its contractor, the collector of customs who had a great deal of influence in all of the transactions, the commissioner of revenue who had an even greater influence, and lighthouse keeper Henry Long. In politely handwritten script, one letter tells of the difficulty in getting bricks to the construction site and other delays that hindered the project. Another letter describes bricks and other supplies being hauled from the Delaware River to Wilmington, where the materials were offloaded and then reloaded onto another vessel to make the long trip to the site. One missive contains Keeper Long's pleas to have lamp oil shipped in casks no larger than forty or fifty gallons so he could offload the precious oil and roll the cases to the lighthouse with less risk of damage. Another note contains architectural drawings, including the cistern that was designed to hold two types of lamp oil for winter and summer. And Keeper Long's correspondence to Timothy Bloodworth, collector of customs, complains that he had to use his own boat for transportation, which was often dangerous, and that his pay was not sufficient for all his responsibilities. Long also requested a kitchen be installed in the lighthouse.

The artist who drew this illustration of the 1794 Bald Head Island Lighthouse signed it simply "Kettle." It was built too near the eroding Cape Fear River's edge and was short-lived. *Lithograph courtesy of the State Archives of North Carolina.*

Keeper Long died in a hunting accident in late 1806—the kitchen would never be built—and the residents of the Wilmington community nominated one of their own to take his place, Sedgwick Springs. The U.S. attorney general, at the behest of President Thomas Jefferson, announced Springs's appointment as lighthouse keeper in January 1807.

Unfortunately, the lighthouse was erected too close to the edge of the Cape Fear River, allowing erosion to undercut the lighthouse foundation. In 1813, six years into Springs's appointment as keeper, Bald Head's lighthouse was razed from its foundations, a victim of shifting of sand and flowing water. Keeper Springs began a new tenure in 1817 with the completion of the replacement lighthouse, known today as Old Baldy.

The only known sketch of the first Bald Head Island Lighthouse, signed by an artist named "Kettle" in 1805, offers a rare glimpse of this first tower. The capricious behavior of nature undermined one of America's earliest lighthouses, but three more towers would be built nearby to carry the torch.

LIGHTING CAPE HATTERAS

Historically, the name "Cape Hatteras" has been synonymous with "danger" for mariners sailing around this point. Over a century ago, local residents recalled stories about forty or more sailing ships set waiting offshore for a breeze to quicken and safely carry them around the cape. Southbound vessels fought southwest trade winds to avoid the opposite-flowing Gulf Stream and the currents that could force them onto shore. They had to wait for favorable winds to carry them around the notorious Diamond Shoals. Working against the ships, these breezes often turned into raging storms and sent ships to a sure death on the shoals. Agitated waves broke in shallow waters twelve and fifteen miles offshore surrounding the shoals, reducing mighty vessels to mere sticks of wood, drowning crews and passengers, and sending valuable cargoes of sugar, molasses, and lumber to the unknown depths of the ocean floor. There was little help for ships in distress until the late 1880s, when the U.S. Life-Saving Service began providing rescue services along North Carolina's coast.

For ship owners, access to an open inlet was as good as cash in hand; better yet, it could be considered a door to a bank. British sea captains had long acknowledged that Ocracoke Inlet was a vital passage through the treacherous barrier islands to North Carolina's mainland ports. By 1828, Currituck Inlet had closed or shoaled to the point of being too risky to reach, leaving Hatteras and Ocracoke the only available inlets until Oregon Inlet opened in 1846—but safe passage through all of these inlets waxed and waned as nature took its course. Although there was never a true inlet where the Cape Hatteras Lighthouse was situated, thousands of ships passed by there on their way to somewhere else, and all too often they did not reach their destinations.

NATURE LAID THE COURSE

With all the danger that Cape Hatteras posed to mariners, why did they choose to pass by it at all? Simply put, they had to. A line drawn straight down a map of the East Coast shows that the cape defiantly elbows its way out into the Atlantic 300 miles farther east than Florida's northernmost coast, creating a huge obstacle. Mariners plied these waters for three reasons, all of them influenced by the Gulf Stream.

First, ships traveling from the Caribbean and other southern ports utilized the natural forces of the northerly flowing Gulf Stream and southwest trade winds until they reached Cape Hatteras. The natural flow of the Gulf Stream added about four miles an hour to a ship's daily progress—a tremendous time-saver for ships under sail power; however, at Cape Hatteras, the stream takes a slight northwest turn before resuming a clockwise flow while passing by Diamond Shoals. Many times, ships ran up on the shoals during clear weather with no forewarning of the hazard. The fortunate ones would continue onto northern ports at Norfolk, Baltimore, Philadelphia, and New York.

Second, northbound vessels headed to Europe passed by the cape before they turned east. Hitchhiking north on the Gulf Stream, akin to a river flowing within the sea, these ships sailed as far as Cape Hatteras and then used its clockwise flow back to Europe. Early Spanish explorers returning home learned quickly that they could save several days, even weeks, by taking advantage of the Gulf Stream current.

A third reason for oceangoing vessels to venture into the cape's lair involved a southerly, one-knot flow of cold water from the north that passes just offshore. Captains had to maneuver southbound ships to stay in the southerly flowing remnants of the Labrador Current, which pressed them dangerously close to Diamond Shoals south of Bodie Island.

If the warm Gulf Stream and the cold Labrador currents remained parallel to one another, weather conditions would remain calmer, with smoother transitions between the seasons, but this was more often the exception than the rule. The two currents do battle constantly as their courses wander into one another at the cape and create dramatic waves akin to sparring stallions. The results include fog and sudden storms with robust winds and mountainous waves, while the warm waters of the Gulf feed the fury of hurricanes birthed off the western coast of Africa or the Caribbean coast, driving the engines of powerful and unpredictable storms.

Some of the lucky foreign shipwreck survivors decided to stay on these barrier islands, build homes, and start families. American Indians were the only natives to the coast, and all others were Virginia colonists or shipwrecked souls who decided they had traveled far enough and would tempt fate no more.

To help ships safely navigate Diamond Shoals, Tench Coxe, commissioner of revenue, reported that mariners asked for a light at Cape Hatteras. In 1794, Secretary of the Treasury Alexander Hamilton requested

a "first rate light" at the cape, and President Washington encouraged the construction of a lighthouse.

GUARDIAN OF STONE: THE FIRST CAPE HATTERAS LIGHTHOUSE, 1803

In 1794 Congress began debating about a site for this lighthouse. In 1798 federal officials procured a deed for four acres from William, Jabez, Mary, and Aquilla Jennette, for which they were paid fifty dollars. Joseph Jennette, their deceased father, left guardianship to his wife, Christian, as listed in the 1790 census, and the couple's four children later married, creating a dynasty of lighthouse keepers at Cape Hatteras that spanned nearly a century.

Although the land for the Cape Hatteras light had been secured, it took another year to finalize the land transfer and begin construction. The nationwide search for the right architect and builder to design and construct the tower proved to be as challenging as procuring the building site. Hiring a contractor who was willing to brave the harsh elements, deliver

Shipwrecks along the coast of North Carolina pronounced the lighting there crushingly inadequate. Cold waters flowing north to south clashed with the complex tropical Gulf Stream at Cape Hatteras to birth strong storms, frequently packing hurricane-force winds. On this coast, a sailor's cards were stacked against him during the age of sail until the early twentieth century.

the needed materials, and take on erecting this light while simultaneously erecting one to mark Ocracoke Inlet at Shell Castle Island proved a difficult task. Fortunately, Henry Dearborn, a Massachusetts congressman who later was secretary of war in Thomas Jefferson's cabinet from 1801 to 1809, expressed interest in building both lights. The U.S. Treasury Department made appropriations for both lighthouses for a total of $38,450. As they had offered John McComb, a well-known architect, $37,500 for Cape Hatteras alone, this seemed like a good deal.

Due to multiple delays, Dearborn did not start construction on the Cape Hatteras Light until 1799. How much time he spent on the two sites is not known, but we do know that the work was arduous: materials had to be off-loaded from boats, bricks had to be hand carried through the sand to the site, and workers suffered from a "mosquito-borne illness," likely malaria. Finally, in 1802 the first Cape Hatteras Lighthouse rose from the bare sand alongside a two-story keeper's quarters and a vault with nine cedar cisterns that could hold 200 gallons of oil each. Keeper Adam Gaskins was on site, and everything was ready to go, but it would take another long year before eighteen sperm whale oil lamps, arranged in three tiers on a revolving platform, were installed. Finally, in 1803 the light shone across Hatteras Island and reached toward the Graveyard of the Atlantic.

From its inception, the Cape Hatteras Lighthouse stood in a class of its own among the other twenty-seven existing American lighthouses. It was a coastal light meant to warn mariners to stay away from the shoreline, rather than a harbor light meant to bring ships into port. Its early Federal-style octagonal tower, built of sandstone and brick, measured 26.5 feet at the base and tapered upward 90 feet. The keeper climbed the interior wooden stairs to reach the 12-foot-tall birdcage-type lantern mounted at the top of the tower. Some people considered it a homely edifice, though it must have been a beautiful sight for passing mariners.

Until the mid-nineteenth century and even later, mariners had few reliable sailing charts and no dependable and affordable ship's chronometers to determine longitude—measurements were still largely done with sextants. Many captains were left to navigate using the lunar distance method or by "dead reckoning," a deserved term for mariners guessing where in

The 1803 Cape Hatteras Lighthouse was a humble Federal-style octagonal tower made of dark sandstone. It was America's first coastal warning beacon that replaced a welcoming harbor light. *Drawing by Mike Litwin from the author's collection.*

the world they were at any given moment. A light in the night could be a lifesaver.

FOR ALL ITS GREATNESS, A DIM DEBUT

It was clear from the beginning that Hatteras had serious problems, including eroding sand around the foundation due to relentless wind. Even more alarming, its light was too dim to reach out over the shipping lanes. During these early years of illumination, federal lighthouse engineers experimented with different lighting apparatuses, and improvements in all types of illumination became a priority, a practice that continues to this day. The very early keepers often used a "pan lamp," a pan similar to a cake tin filled with whale oil and covered with a lid with holes through which wicks protruded. Ironically, the brightest light a pan lamp produced was when it malfunctioned and burned the lantern room.

In 1782, a Swiss inventor named Ami Argand devised a system utilizing a hollow circular wick that burned more brightly because of increased airflow around the flame. Later, sometime between 1812 and 1815 Winslow Lewis, a noted American lighthouse engineer and seaman, devised his own lighting system, which incorporated a modified Argand lamp with a parabolic reflector and offered somewhat better illumination. Though the Lewis system was an improvement over the pan lamp, ship captains were still generous with complaints.

"The worst light on the coast," said one U.S. Navy captain about Hatteras. Another stinging review in a Philadelphia newspaper by a steam packet captain noted, "There was *as usual*, no light to be seen from the lighthouse." Finally, a North Carolina newspaper ran a number of complaints from merchants and captains about the light, angering USLHE administrator Stephen Pleasonton, who believed the article implied that the keeper often let the light go out.

Cape Hatteras had a tall order to fill: its beam of light needed to reach at least fifteen miles to illuminate the dangerous Diamond Shoals, and a 90-foot tower with dim lamps could not do the job. Pleasonton was unconcerned with the fact that, although Lewis told him that the light could be seen up to thirty miles out to sea, there was not a grain of truth in his claim. Lewis was the low-bid contractor of the early nineteenth century, and we know now that builders could have erected taller towers, but Pleasonton allowed only a certain amount of money per lighthouse site.

A grouping of Argand oil–fed lamps backed by reflectors were arranged on a chandelier to form a lighting system. The more lamps burning simultaneously, the brighter the light; however, keepers dealt with fitful lamps that often malfunctioned and poor-quality silver reflectors. It took decades for Congress to order the replacement of this obsolete system and the installation of Fresnel lenses. *Drawing from* Illustrated London Times, *January 5, 1884, courtesy of Thomas A. Tag, technical adviser for the U.S. Lighthouse Society.*

The Cape Hatteras Lighthouse could not be successful due to its original height and finicky lamps; instead of a new lighthouse, Pleasonton continued to do only what was needed to keep the mariners' complaints at a minimum.

At least the steam packet captain's complaint led to the refitting of the lantern with eighteen Argand lamps—only sixteen were reported lighted in the official USLHE Light List printed by the government—and new reflectors in 1835. Within five years, however, the collector of revenue reported to Pleasonton that the lighting system was almost useless. USLHE officials accused the primary keeper, Isaac Farrow, of either damaging the lamps and reflectors or neglecting his duty. Evidently, it never occurred to Pleasonton that the Lewis lighting system was inferior; he just demanded that the keeper be removed. Although Farrow was not fired and remained at Hatteras, he died two years later, before all the confusion was settled. Though the light received good reviews from passing captains shortly thereafter, captains' and keepers' complaints of a weak light at Hatteras dogged the USLHE for years afterward. The Lewis system was also inefficient. It used a great amount of oil to provide mediocre illumination. What Pleasonton did not understand—or refused to—was the fact that the cost of the superior Fresnel lenses, about $12,500 during that time, would be offset within one year by the amount of oil saved from dropping the Lewis system, an estimated $3,500 worth of oil for each light.

With continued public outcry, a radical change was in order. Had Cape Hatteras and its light display been a play on Broadway, it never would have gotten past opening night.

LIGHTING OCRACOKE INLET

Construction on North Carolina's second official lighthouse began about 1798. The North Carolina General Assembly began making plans to build on Ocracoke Island about 1770, when it procured land to erect the tower, but the state government did not move forward on the idea before the federal government assumed building lighthouses in 1789.

Shipping merchants John Wallace and John Gray Blount established a flourishing industry on the south side of Ocracoke Inlet on Old Rock Island (which they gave a more regal title, Shell Castle Island), about a half mile long and 60 feet wide, made of oyster shells. It included a warehouse for storing cargo awaiting transshipment, a gristmill, and a windmill. In May 1794 the federal government, still new to the lighthouse business, decided to place the light where business had already formed on Shell Castle Island. Appropriation for the tower came on July 10, 1797, and Blount and Wallace deeded the land for the lighthouse, stipulating that on the site "no goods should be stored, tavern kept, spirits retailed, merchandise carried on, or person reside on for the purpose of pilot or lighter vessels."

The small lot, 70 by 140 feet, proved to be large enough to accommodate a tower 55–60 feet tall, a keeper's quarters, and a 200-gallon oil vault made of three cedar cisterns. Completed and lighted around 1800, Ocra-

Shell Castle Island, formerly known by its unassuming name, Old Rock Island, was established on a heap of oyster shells by 1803. The lighthouse was built for the transshipment business on neighboring Portsmouth Island for goods bound for Ocracoke Inlet and mainland ports. *Photograph of "Blount pitcher" courtesy of State Archives of North Carolina.*

coke's first lighthouse is said to have been fitted with a single oil-burning "spider lamp," a parabolic-shaped reservoir with several burning floating wicks, which provided light that was neither efficient nor very bright.

In 1818 lightning sparked a fire that destroyed the tower and keeper's dwelling—the combination of an open flame in unreliable lamps, fuel stored inside a tower, wooden stairs, and human error resulted in the burning of countless lighthouses. Lightning posed a threat as well, because lighthouses were the tallest structures on any of the islands and lightning rods had yet to be commonly used. Fire plagued many lighthouses until the late 1800s, when keepers began storing oil outside the tower, iron steps replaced wooden ones, and cleaner-burning lamps were installed.

Following the demise of the Shell Castle Island Lighthouse, the island became a quarantine area, and the once lively port became a ghost island remembered only on a painted pitcher.

LIGHTING CAPE LOOKOUT

Congress appropriated monies for the first Cape Lookout Lighthouse in 1804. The following year, Carteret County residents Joseph Fulford and Elijah Pigott provided the federal government a four-acre site at the cape.

Henry Dearborn of Boston, David Geston of New York, and Brian Hellen of Beaufort, North Carolina, placed a public announcement in the Saturday, December 22, 1810, issue of the *Boston Patriot* looking for contractors. According to the *Patriot*, the lighthouse was to be "a wooden tower ninety-three-feet tall from ground level to the bottom of the lantern room and its octagonal walls formed a 'pyramidal' shape that were to be 3 feet thick with a 55-foot diameter sloping upwards to 14 feet and surmounted by a lantern room." The lighthouse was to be painted with three coats alternately white and brown with a brick well interior.

The outer wooden tower and inner brick well have been described by scholars as two towers, one nestled inside another. The exterior had the stripes, though they were red and white. Records do not show what Benjamin Beal Jr., Duncan Thaxter, and James Stephenson of Boston actually built, but the light made its appearance in 1812.

BRIGHTNESS NOT ITS FORTE

Like the light at Cape Hatteras, the light at Cape Lookout proved to be disappointingly dim. In 1817, Winslow Lewis wrote, "Cape Lookout Lighthouse. Situated on Cape Lookout, on the coast of North Carolina. The Lantern is 95 feet above the sea, and contains a fixed light. This light can be seen without the shoals, which extend out from it; but vessels passing them in the night, ought rather to trust to the lead than the light. The light-house is painted in horizontal stripes, alternately red and white, and appears at a distance like a ship of war with her sails clewed up, and was often taken for such during the late war."

"Trust to the lead" meant for mariners to cast a line with a lead weight to find the water's depth. The thirteen lamps that made up the lighting apparatus were not bright enough, and Lewis, the man who installed the lighting system, emphasized the danger of the changing shoals and warned that the light should not be the sole factor in navigating the quicksand-like Cape Lookout Shoals, which extend nine miles from the cape. The lighthouse was fitted with the same system of lamps and parabolic silver reflectors for the duration of its service.

Upon the completion of the Cape Lookout Lighthouse, the shoals of all three of North Carolina's dangerous capes were marked with lights, albeit

In 1812, Cape Lookout hosted a 93-foot-tall lighthouse that was two towers in one. The inner brick structure supported the stairs, while the outer octagonal wooden tower was painted brown and white as a daymark for mariners. *Drawing courtesy of the National Park Service.*

modestly so. The natural order of things would have been to construct additional lights along the coastline, but persistent erosion had undermined the foundation of the 1794 Bald Head Island Lighthouse at Cape Fear, and the USLHE had to see to repairs before new lights could be constructed.

For more information on all North Carolina lighthouses, see the Outer Banks Lighthouse Society website, at https://www.outerbankslighthouse society.org.

Engineers of Independence

In addition to trained troops to fight the British at the onset of the Revolutionary War in 1775, General George Washington most needed engineers to build bulwarks, roads, bridges, and ground defense protection. In Washington's opinion, the country would never be truly independent until it had its own engineers. But the colonial states had no schools for engineers; indeed, Washington's two favorite engineers were Rufus Putnam and Henry Knox, both self-educated. The general had to otherwise rely on French engineers—it would have been British engineers, had the fledgling nation not been at war with England at the time.

To meet the demand for homegrown military leaders, West Point Academy was founded in 1802 as a school for military training and engineering. President Thomas Jefferson appointed Secretary of War Henry Dearborn to begin the academy. Dearborn had been a Revolutionary War leader and the man responsible for the construction of Shell Castle Island and Cape Hatteras Lighthouses. Many of its graduates were future wartime leaders and heroes, including during its early years Robert E. Lee, George Meade, Peter C. Hains, Danville Ledbetter, and W. H. C. Whiting, to name only a few. These men blazed trails westward into unknown territories, built infrastructure, were leaders in the Mexican-American War and American Civil War, and designed and built lighthouses. History also knows Hains for hatching the brilliant idea to paint lighthouses for daytime identification on North Carolina's lighthouses; for instance, black-and-white bands said "Bodie Island," and black-and-white spirals said "Cape Hatteras."

Ushering in a new age of scientific technology were other West Point and Naval Institute graduates. These included Superintendent of Coast Survey Alexander Dallas Bache; his brother Richard Bache, a champion for adoption of the Fresnel lens lighting system in America; and Hartman Bache, another Bache brother and member of the Coast Survey, along with their first cousin, George Mifflin Bache. A. D. Bache would later join his close friend Joseph Henry, secretary of the Smithsonian Institute and chairman of the U.S. Lighthouse Service, as two of President Lincoln's top picks to form the National Academy of Sciences in 1863.

Coast surveying provided mariners with up-to-date maps and provided the government with a guide for selecting new lighthouse sites. However, it was risky business. Among those who lost their lives performing this service were George Mifflin Bache, who perished in a gale off Cape Hatteras on September 8, 1846, and Richard Bache, who drowned on the West Coast surveying a site for St. George's Reef Lighthouse in 1850. All four Baches were great-grandsons of Benjamin Franklin, a pioneering scientist and inventor himself, who created the first map of the Gulf Stream. These were some of the great minds that influenced a backward and failing U.S. Lighthouse Establishment and turned it into the best in the world as the U.S. Lighthouse Board.

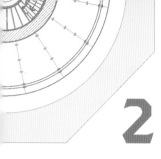

2

The Second Bald Head Island Lighthouse and Other Cape Fear Lights

In 1815, more than 100,000 bricks lay in a heap where the Bald Head Island Lighthouse had once stood on the banks of the Cape Fear. For years erosion of the bank had dogged the tower, known then as the Cape Fear Light. On January 20, 1815, Wilmington's collector of customs, Robert Cochran, informed U.S. Treasury secretary A. J. Dallas that every effort had been made to save the old lighthouse "from being wash'd away by the encroachment of the Sea; in order to save the materials it became necessary to pull it down." As many bricks as possible had been salvaged to be incorporated into a new tower to guide ships from the Atlantic Ocean into the mouth of the Cape Fear River.

Local pilots who were experienced in steering vessels safely into the river and others who were familiar with the waters around Bald Head Island gave their opinions on the ideal lighthouse location that would be both safe from erosion and convenient for landing construction materials. Cochran wanted the light to be raised to 100 feet and a new keeper's house built, along with a vault for oil. Keen on recycling building materials, the USLHE ordered that the old lantern room, except for the glass, be put back into service.

Completed and lighted in 1818, the second Bald Head Island Lighthouse stands 110 feet tall and looks much like its predecessor. One of the few surviving early Federal-style octagonal lighthouses, it is the oldest standing tower in North Carolina. It greets visitors with a stone plaque over the door that states, "AD 1817," the year the site was established on the southwestern part of Bald Head Island, placing it on the southeastern bank at the main entrance to the Cape Fear River. Unlike contemporary octagonal lighthouses built of stone, the second Bald Head Island Lighthouse is a brick tower—transporting stones to the site by ship was too difficult and expensive, and few skilled bricklayers lived in the area. Experienced Connecticut bricklayer Daniel S. Way served as the construction contractor and used the salvaged bricks to build a tower whose lifetime has spanned more than two centuries—but none of this happened effortlessly.

As soon as Way arrived on Bald Head Island, he found that the old bricks and other salvaged materials had to be carted a mile to the new building site, not just a few yards as he had originally thought. In a letter dated December 27, 1816, he stated that not only would it require extra expense to have the bricks relocated, but also the new building materials required for the project would cost twice as much as he had budgeted. In addition, he found conditions on the island different from what he expected, and he incurred "other additional expenses to[o] tedious to name." He had kept his bid low because it was a "publicks" work, but he discovered that it was indeed too low, and he claimed he had already spent more than he had been advanced by Wilmington's collector of customs, Robert Cochran. "Unless [the] government makes me some allowance, myself and numerous family must be reduced to penury and want." At this point, he claimed he had spent $3,000 for materials. While the amount that Way bid is not well known, it is documented that the final cost for the second light on Bald Head Island totaled between $15,000–$16,000. Way's complaints were forwarded to Commissioner of Revenue Samuel H. Smith. Cochran

Old Baldy has been the focal point of Bald Head Island for 200 years. This photograph was captured by a drone while the lighthouse was undergoing extensive restoration in 2017. The tower is surrounded by marshland, with Harbour Village and the Bald Head Island Marina in the background. *Photograph by Tyler Finkle, courtesy of International Chimney Corporation, Inc.*

The Second Bald Head Island Lighthouse

In 1893 U.S. Lighthouse Board engineer Herbert Bamber visited East Coast light stations such as Old Baldy to survey and document each part. His legacy includes not only several lighthouses he planned and built but also the majority of the earliest extant photographs of the state's light stations. *Photograph from the personal collection of John Havel.*

wrote to Smith and suggested that Way had bid too quickly and reminded him that there had actually been two other bids, although higher, from men more familiar with the island and the requirements involved in moving the old bricks and raising a new tower. Smith, however, backed Way, and he received more money to complete the project.

Winslow Lewis, who signed his letters "Superintendent for fitting U.S. Lighthouses," ordered the new tower's lighting system, a fixed light consisting of fifteen individual 21-inch whale-oil-fed, hollow-wick lamps backed by parabolic silver-coated reflectors and arranged on a metal chandelier-type pedestal. Lewis also ordered that the tower's stairs be constructed of local yellow pine (he disapproved of stone stairs, again, due to the expense of transporting and moving them), and he introduced using tin oil butts, in lieu of an oil vault, and storing them in the lower part of the lighthouse. The old oil from the first tower proved to be substandard, and Lewis ordered it to be distributed elsewhere—he wielded a great deal

U.S. Lighthouse Service History in Brief

There were three distinct organizational periods in American lighthouse history: the U.S. Lighthouse Establishment (USLHE), from 1789 to 1852; the U.S. Lighthouse Board, from 1852 to 1910; and the Bureau of Lighthouses, from 1910 to 1939. In some cases the collective term "U.S. Lighthouse Service" was used to include a broad span of time of the organization. Different names used in this book for the Lighthouse Service attempt to relate to the period of history to which it refers, but especially to the third phase of the organization.

U.S. LIGHTHOUSE ESTABLISHMENT (USLHE), 1789–1852

The federal government took control of fifteen colonial lighthouses as soon as the USLHE organized in 1789. Initial control of navigational aids was held by Secretary of the Treasury Alexander Hamilton. When Albert Gallatin became secretary in 1801, he took over control until 1820, when he was succeeded by the first "fifth auditor" of the treasury, Stephen Pleasonton. These early years of lighthouse business were less than smoothly run, with the USLHE being handed off to various congressional offices. Further, few improvements in technology were made during the fifth auditor's thirty-year career, and towers made of brick and cut stone averaged only 60 feet in height—more often than not too short for its light to be visible enough to be of help. Despite the downside of these early attempts to give guiding lights to mariners, it was at least a beginning to shedding light on the state's dangerous capes and inland water hazards. But Pleasonton refused to purchase and install Fresnel lenses that would most improve the lighthouses' effectiveness. Due to the lenses' initial high cost, it would be more than a quarter century before Congress demanded the purchase of these revolutionary optics. (For more information on this subject, see chapter 4.)

U.S. LIGHT-HOUSE BOARD, 1852–1910

Four reports influenced an important reorganization of the USLHE. A critical report during the late 1830s by U.S. Navy lieutenant William D. Porter to Congress through the secretary of the treasury complained of poor-

The Second Bald Head Island Lighthouse

quality work on existing lighthouses. This was followed by a report of the congressional Committee on Commerce in 1842 that said everything was just fine, which stirred further investigation. Then, just one year later, a third and very different report by I. W. P. Lewis to Congress documented poor structural quality and placement of existing American lights and the insufficient attendance to keeping lights. Finally, in 1851 U.S. Navy lieutenant David D. Porter, lighthouses' most ardent fan and critic, gave Congress a biting review of poorly placed towers, naming many that were of inferior construction quality.

Porter's report led to the creation of a nine-member Light-House Board in 1852: seven members were military and two were civilians with expertise in science. Army and navy secretaries attended to the routine management of navigational aids. The board divided the country into twelve districts, with the coast of North Carolina in the fifth district. Each district had an appointed inspector "charged with building the lighthouses, with keeping them in repair, and with the purchase, the setting up, and the repairs of the illuminating apparatus." This effectively removed all responsibilities from the collector of customs in an attempt to eliminate political influences in these decisions. The finest materials available were used, towers soared to 150 feet and more in height, and Fresnel lenses tripled the intensity of each light. The board made a set of standard plans available to engineers and contractors to choose from and improve if needed. It also made noteworthy improvements in foghorns, lightships, screwpile lighthouses, and buoys, as well as the color schemes for daytime identification of each tower. Electric power, which was first used in the Statue of Liberty in 1886, ushered in a new era that would eventually put keepers out of a job.

A list of the Lighthouse Board's members reads like a Who's Who of America. For a list of all members, see http://www.joshism.net/light houses/LHboard.html or http://uslhs.org/history/board-members.

BUREAU OF LIGHTHOUSES, 1910–1939

By 1910, the U.S. Bureau of Lighthouses maintained a total of 11,713 navigational aids of all types. The government put a new spin on the federally run service by turning over responsibilities to knowledgeable civilians to give continuity to its operations. At this time, the bureau was run by one presidentially appointed, progressive administrator, George Putnam, formerly of the U.S. Coast and Geodetic Survey (now the National Geodetic Survey). Carefully screened civilians were chosen to be district inspectors, later known as district superintendents. Lights were outfitted with new technology, keepers were given raises, a retirement plan was begun in 1918, and written communication with employees in the field was established—to the commissioner, people *were* the Lighthouse Service. Putnam retired in 1935, and the personable Harold King took over until July 1, 1939, when the Lighthouse Service merged with the U.S. Coast Guard, which took over aids to navigation. In 2000, the National Historic Lighthouse Preservation Act provided a mechanism for the dispersal of federally owned light stations to federal, state, private, and nonprofit interests.

The majority of records of the Lighthouse Service are held in the National Archives in Washington, D.C., in Record Group 26.

of influence for more than thirty years while he won lighthouse contracts under the supervision of Fifth Auditor Stephen Pleasonton.

OLD BALDY IN MODERN TIMES

One can immediately see and feel the passage of time at the second Bald Head Island Lighthouse. The mottled tones of the rough exterior stucco make the tower look older than it is and evoke the familiar identity it carries today as Old Baldy. Surrounded by the quiet marshland, the omnipresent scent of salt air, and the quietude that can be experienced only on an island, it is difficult to walk away from this place without tucking away into memory a bit of this area's history.

During Old Baldy's years of service, the U.S. Lighthouse Service turned the light off and on depending on changing conditions of the inlets through the barrier islands to the mouth of the Cape Fear River and the presence of other lights in the area. Lighthouse officials decommissioned Old Baldy in 1866, when the third light at Federal Point took up position at New Inlet, the north entrance to the river. Beginning in 1870, however,

An olden plaque over the Bald Head Island Lighthouse entry states its establishment date. The light was activated in 1818. Daniel S. Way was in charge of construction, which included moving salvaged brick from the razed 1794 tower to be incorporated into this lighthouse.

the Army Corps of Engineers closed New Inlet by installing "the Rocks" (a gigantic rock jetty also known as the New Inlet Dam) to block all of the breaches caused by small inlets into the river. Closing off these shoaling areas increased the flow of water into the mouth of the Cape Fear River and effectively created a natural scouring action. Not long after Old Baldy was closed, lighthouse administrators deactivated the third Federal Point Lighthouse in 1880 and put Old Baldy back into action with a fourth-order Fresnel lens as a range light paired with a ship's lantern suspended on a pole, and later a buoy, to lead river traffic into a dredged channel of the river. In 1883, Old Baldy's flash characteristic was changed from a fixed white light to a red light flashing every thirty seconds. The Lighthouse Service kept the light active until it was deactivated for the last time in 1935. Left to its own fate, the light continued as a distinct daytime maritime aid. During World War II, Old Baldy was equipped with a radio beacon to aid in defending North Carolina's shoreline.

Today, the nonprofit Old Baldy Foundation (OBF) owns, maintains, and preserves the second Bald Head Island Lighthouse, which is listed on the National Register of Historic Places. The OBF extensively restored the tower in 1990 and reopened it to the public in April 1995, offering visitors self-guided tours of the structure. The organization completed another restoration in 2017 in honor of the light's 200th anniversary. In addition, the

The Second Bald Head Island Lighthouse

One of Herbert Bamber's photographs of the Bald Head Island Light Station offers a view of the modest keeper's quarters, with the lighthouse in the background in 1893. The keeper on the porch with two children (at right) is deduced to be James "Sonny" H. Dosher. *Photograph courtesy of the H. Bamber Collection, Outer Banks History Center.*

OBF has built a reproduction of the 1850s keeper's quarters near the tower and invites the public to experience life on the island during that era. Also on view are exhibits about the history of Bald Head Island, Middle Island, and Bluff Island, which compose the island complex referred to on old sea charts as Smith Island.

Although officially decommissioned generations ago, the old tower bears the scars of time and remains a justly famous icon of the island and its history. In 2009 the OBF purchased all of the available parts of the first-order Fresnel lens that lighted the 1903 Cape Fear Lighthouse. The OBF currently owns the lens framework, the pedestal, and about a third of the prisms, including seven bull's-eye panels. Unfortunately, an antique dealer had purchased the lens and sold the prisms as souvenirs. The OBF hopes to recover all of the prisms and assemble them in a new building that will house a museum and exhibit area.

Old Baldy stands near the boundary of the temperate and semitropical climate zones, where flora and fauna live together as in no other place, making it a treasure trove for botanists. A quaint chapel in a shaded arbor near the lighthouse offers this Gaelic blessing:

Bald Head Island Lighthouse

LOCATION Bald Head Island
NEAREST TOWN Southport, N.C.
COMPLETED
    1817 and activated 1818
TOWER HEIGHT 110 feet
STEPS TO LANTERN ROOM 108
BUILDING MATERIALS
    Brick coated with stucco
DESIGN/PAINT SCHEME
    Multicolored stucco
OPTIC Currently a decorative
    light; unofficial private
    aid to navigation
STATUS Historic site, oldest
    standing lighthouse
    in North Carolina
ACCESS Lighthouse reached
    by passenger-only ferry;
    open seasonally for climbing
    with entrance fee
OWNER/MANAGER
    Old Baldy Foundation, Inc.
FOR MORE INFORMATION
    Old Baldy Foundation, Inc.
    P.O. Box 3007
    Bald Head Island, N.C. 28461
    (910) 457-7481
    www.oldbaldy.org

Deep peace of the running wave to you,
Deep peace of the flowing air to you,
Deep peace of the quiet earth to you,
Deep peace of the shining stars to you,
Deep peace of the gentle night to you,
Moon and stars pour their healing light on you,
Deep peace of Christ the light of the world to you.

THE FEDERAL POINT LIGHTHOUSES

In 1761, New Inlet opened after a hurricane dredged out the shallow channel on the north side of the entrance to the Cape Fear River. It provided an alternate route to the Port of Wilmington, serving as a shortcut for southbound traffic that allowed ships to avoid the dangerous Frying Pan Shoals before entering Old Inlet. The flow of tides in and out of New Inlet brought sandy shoals that perpetually shifted and required experienced pilots to navigate safely through them. Bald Head Island Lighthouse, today known as Old Baldy, was too far away to help locate New Inlet, and mariners called for a light to be built closer to the channel.

The First and Second Federal Point Lighthouses

Although these lighthouses were once part of what is now a well-known site at the Fort Fisher State Recreation Area, their history is elusive. Much of what is known about the first Federal Point Lighthouse has been discovered by the Federal Point Historic Preservation Society. Various reports that have been pieced together over time have revealed that it was built on the east side of the Cape Fear River by Benjamin Jacobs as a conical, 40-foot brick tower that bore a white plaster exterior. Its eight whale-oil lamps provided a light that served well to mark the entrance to the river at New Inlet for twenty years, until it was destroyed by fire on April 13, 1836.

Old Baldy is one of eleven Federal-style octagonal towers built in the United States between 1792 and 1817. It is the only one built of brick, because the U.S. Lighthouse Establishment chose to use the most readily available construction material to keep expenses within reason.

The USLHE hired Hiram Stowell to reconstruct the first Federal Point Lighthouse, which also came to be known as Confederate Point, and to build a small keeper's house. The original design of this lighthouse had an 18-foot diameter at its brick base that tapered to 9 feet at the lantern room and housed eighteen whale-oil-fed lamps. Nearby was a small brick keeper's house. However, during the mid-1840s, the tower and keeper's quarters were remodeled, as depicted in a painting by George Tate during

The second Federal Point Lighthouse marked Cape Fear River's New Inlet entrance at the tip of Federal Point. Col. William Lamb, Confederate commander, watched for blockaders from a platform built against the lighthouse. Capt. George Tait of the Fortieth Regiment, North Carolina Troops, painted this scene in 1863 shortly before the lighthouse was intentionally pulled down. *Painting courtesy of the State Archives of North Carolina.*

the early days of the Civil War. When the second Federal Point Lighthouse began operating in 1837, the USLHE shut off the light in Old Baldy and painted the tower black to distinguish it from the new lighthouse, which stood approximately eight miles to the north. In 1863, Confederate forces took down the second Federal Point Lighthouse tower to give Fort Fisher's guns free range of fire across New Inlet to destroy any Union blockader coming too close to the fort. The Confederate soldiers used the bricks to construct the Mound Battery fortification, and Col. William Lamb turned the keeper's house into his war headquarters (see chapter 7).

After the war, much of this historic site's history lay hidden until November 2009, when a group with the North Carolina Office of State Archaeology and staff members of the Fort Fisher State Historic Site excavated what appeared to be the bases of the first two Federal Point Lighthouses—since the second light was reportedly positioned at the same site, presumably both lights' foundations are located there. The team uncovered remains with measurements almost identical to known building plans for the original 1816 light. Excavators recovered the foundations, and now only these remains, along with a sketch and a painting, survive to help us appreciate the critical role these lighthouses played as sentinels for Wilmington, one of North Carolina's major ports.

The Office of State Archaeology and staff of the Fort Fisher State Historic Site dug what they identified as the foundation of the first Federal Point Lighthouse, presumed also to be the foundation of the second lighthouse. In the background is Confederate Point Monument at Fort Fisher, site of the keeper's quarters of the first and second Federal Point Lighthouses. *Photograph courtesy of the State Archives of North Carolina.*

The Third Federal Point Lighthouse

After the Civil War ended, the Lighthouse Board ordered the critical light at Federal Point to be rebuilt, buying back the site from the landowner who had reclaimed the property during the war. Completed in the spring of 1866, the 45-foot-tall, two-story white lighthouse looked like a big clapboard residence with a lantern in the center of its roof. It stood on iron pilings and featured a fourth-order Fresnel lens in its lantern room to shed much-needed light over New Inlet.

In just three years, the new lighthouse needed repairs, and the unattended repairs worsened before a man-made obstacle ended the tower's short tenure. When the Army Corps of Engineers constructed the Rocks, a man-made rock jetty to close New Inlet, the third Federal Point Lighthouse lost its purpose. The federal government abandoned it at the end of 1879, and the lighthouse burned in 1881 while former Keeper Taylor was using it as a residence. Records indicate that the North Carolina Aquarium at Fort Fisher, one of the North Carolina's main coastal attractions, is believed to be situated on this historic site.

The third and final 1866 Federal Point Lighthouse stayed active until the Army Corps of Engineers intentionally closed New Inlet in 1880. The keeper occupied the structure until it burned the following year. This is one of the earliest extant photographs of a North Carolina lighthouse. Note the fourth-order Fresnel lens in the lantern room. *Photograph courtesy of Cape Fear Museum of History and Science, Wilmington, N.C.*

RANGE LIGHTS DOT THE DARK CAPE FEAR RIVERSIDE

In 1807, Robert Fulton launched a new mode of traveling on water when his steamboat, officially called the *North River Steam Boat* and nicknamed the *Clermont,* paddled up the Hudson River in New York. By 1818, steamboats regularly carried passengers and cargo along the Cape Fear River between Fayetteville and Wilmington. In 1819, President James Monroe took the steamboat *Prometheus* down the Cape Fear River from Wilmington to Southport. The president and his entourage traveled only downstream since the *Prometheus* was quite slow traveling upstream—its engine was incapable of matching the river's opposing currents—and this historic trip proved to be a harbinger of things to come.

By the 1850s, vast numbers of vessels, sometimes as many as ninety at a time, loaded, unloaded, or waited for space at the docks in Wilmington. Often rows of ships two vessels deep docked at the wharves, and ships wait-

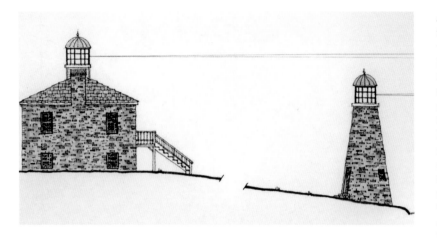

ing to load or unload cargo occasionally moored miles downstream. Mariners made the best of the time they spent waiting for space at the dock—they designated a tree about two miles south of the port as the "dram tree," and as legend tells it, when a ship safely reached this point, every sailor onboard enjoyed a dram (or perhaps more) of spirits.

The Lighthouse Service implemented a clever plan to mark safe passage from the Atlantic Ocean to the Wilmington docks: with an appropriation from Congress starting in 1848, they erected a series of lighted beacons to guide ships past some of the more dangerous shoals. Lighthouse officials wanted to avoid stranded vessels since they clogged shipping lanes and took a great deal of effort to dislodge and get moving again. Between 1849 and 1855, three pairs of range lights at Oak Island, Price's Creek, and Upper Jetty were completed. For range lights, the rear light stood taller than the front light; consequently, when a pilot positioned his ship so the lights lined up one over the other, he knew he had safely reached a channel away from menacing shoals. Lighthouse officials expected not only increased commercial shipping but also fewer stranded ships. For six years before the outbreak of the Civil War, pilots could confidently navigate their ships safely up and down the river due to these range lights.

On the west bank of the Cape Fear River north of Southport, Price's Creek Range Lights guided ships through a narrow river channel. The brick keeper's house, which served as the rear range light, had a wood tower in the center. It held a sixth-order Fresnel lens raised 35 feet above the ground. A 25-foot-tall brick tower, which also emitted a gleaming light from a sixth-order Fresnel lens, stood by the river at Price's Creek and

Price's Creek, near Southport, is the only river light still situated in its original location. Built as a range light, it paired with a keeper's house to its rear; both housed sixth-order Fresnel lenses. They marked a channel through a hazardous shoal area near the juncture of the Cape Fear River and New Inlet channels. *Photograph by Robert D. DaVia.*

served as the front range light. Hanson Kelly Ruark served as keeper during the Civil War, and his daughter, Mary Catherine Ruark, shared a prized story with generations of her family about standing at Price's Creek when she was nine years old, watching and listening to two battles at Fort Fisher across the river.

The ruins of the humble front range light tower, which served as a Confederate signal station throughout the conflict and now stands on private commercial property, can be seen from the Fort Fisher–Southport ferry just before it docks on the west side of the river. The tower is historically significant for three reasons: it is the only river light still standing on the Cape Fear River, it is one of only two extant river lights, and it is the only original range light in North Carolina.

Farther north, near the lush Orton Plantation, a beacon was established on Orton's Point in 1849 to forewarn of the marshy point with a sixth-order Fresnel lens. Stories from plantation owners who fondly recalled watching the light while sitting on their homes' big front porches have been passed down through the generations. Another warning light from a sixth-order Fresnel lens shone in a 25-foot lighthouse on Campbell's Island at the edge of a marshy area that was to be avoided by vessels, about six miles south of Wilmington.

In 1851, the USLHE, during its final days before being reorganized, stationed a light vessel at Horse Shoe Shoal (also known as Horseshoe Bend or simply the Horse Shoe) that evolved to a fog-bell channel marker near Southport between New Inlet and Price's Creek. It marked a hazardous shoal in the channel near the intersection of the Cape Fear River and New Inlet channels.

In 1855, the Lighthouse Board placed the last of the Cape Fear River range lights at Upper Jetty on the east side of the river about three miles south of Wilmington. A sixth-order Fresnel lens on top of the keeper's house served as the front range light, and another one on an open framework about 800 feet behind the house served as the rear range light.

The Lighthouse Board built these important river lights during a time of prosperity with all intentions that their operation would continue indefinitely, but this was not the case. To save money following the Civil War, the board ordered Jeremy Smith, the acting Union lighthouse engineer and inspector, to discontinue and abandon all Cape Fear navigational aids. The board decided to replace them later with post lights, pole-mounted brass lanterns that could burn for six or seven days before being refilled. They also established an initial network of approximately two dozen post lights to illuminate the twenty-six winding miles upriver to the Port of Wilmington; in the 1900s, they increased the number of lights to nearly three dozen. The lighthouse officials hired lantern keepers, also known as lamplighters, who were based in Southport and Wilmington and made rounds by boat to refill the lanterns.

After the rebuilding of the Oak Island Range Lights in 1879, efforts were made to chase the ever-changing safe channel in the Cape Fear River. At least one of the lights was placed on rails and moved as the channel shifted due to shoaling. It was critical that mariners be guided across the hazardous Western Bar safely into the river. *1893 photograph courtesy of the H. Bamber Collection, Outer Banks History Center.*

THE OAK ISLAND RANGE LIGHTS

All the grand towers that have shed light across the dark Cape Fear River for two centuries formed integral parts of a network of tall and short lights, as well as light vessels, buoys, and myriad other markers, including "tubular lanterns." As early as 1849, there were range lights on Oak Island near the present location of Fort Caswell and the Oak Island station of the U.S. Coast Guard (USCG). While Bald Head Island Lighthouse marks the east side of the Cape Fear, Oak Island marks the west side at the southern Old Inlet off the Atlantic Ocean into the river, to help mariners safely cross the shoals. Constant efforts were made to deepen the channel to 26 feet and

encourage the business of deeper-draft vessels. Widening and deepening port channels are akin to building wider interstate roads to accommodate heavier traffic.

According to the 1849 official U.S. Light Service Light List, two brick towers, 27 and 37 feet tall, respectively, surrounded by low sand hills, served as the first Oak Island Range Lights. Over the years they were used, they varied from a white light to a red warning. Built just before a newly reorganized Lighthouse Board embraced advancing technology, each of the towers held ten whale-oil lamps, with 14-inch bowl-shaped parabolic reflectors behind each lamp in the old Winslow Lewis lighting style. The 1856 Light List shows that the towers had been refitted with fifth-order Fresnel lenses, and a fog bell, struck by machinery, had been added in 1855 to guide mariners venturing through the shoals.

The constantly changing channel into the entrance to the Cape Fear River required ongoing evolution of the Oak Island Range Lights, which was alternately used for two decades with the Bald Head Channel beacon beginning in 1874. At that time, the front light had been changed to an open-frame wooden pyramid painted brown resting on a brick base, and the rear light was mounted on the keeper's house. These range lights were rebuilt in 1879 after the Lighthouse Board delayed construction while waiting for the restless channel to settle down, which it never did. For years, the lights were moved on tramways to chase the best river entrance channel. According to the 1880 Light List, a two-story keeper's house, probably retained from the original set of range lights, stood a bit to the southwest of two open-frame wooden towers, which were painted white and exhibited a fixed, nonflashing red warning, replacing the standard white light. On July 15, 1889, the Lighthouse Board recorded in its annual report and on a Notice to Mariners that an updated network of lights was activated to help demark crossing the bar into the river and to accommodate changes in the Cape Fear River channel: the New Channel Range Lights, the Bald Head Shoal Channel Range Lights, the Oak Island Range Lights, bell buoys, and post lanterns.

Starting on October 11, 1893, a storm lasting two days undercut the brick foundation of the keeper's quarters at the Oak Island Range Lights. That natural disaster, coupled with complaints from mariners about the range lights being insufficient to mark the shifting, shoaling bar, motivated the board to discontinue the beacons in 1894. Mariners needed a taller lighthouse to avoid Frying Pan Shoals and to find an entrance to the river.

The Oak Island history of storm and stress reminds us that in lighthouse building, one must remember that nature will have her say.

FOR A COASTAL LIGHT, TALLER IS BETTER

In the 1890 "Annual Report of the Light-House Board to the Secretary of the Treasury for the Fiscal Year Ended June 30, 1890," for the fifth district in North Carolina, a first-order light was called for at "the pitch of Cape Fear." The plea noted that the discontinuance of the third Federal Point Lighthouse a decade earlier had left the area virtually dark, since the Bald Head Island light could serve only as a harbor light due to lack of height and its inland position. No action was taken for several years.

Then, at the turn of the twentieth century, the channel into the Cape Fear River changed drastically, resulting in the need for a coastal light to mark safe passage through Frying Pan Shoals, which extended approximately thirty-six miles offshore, so vessels could safely enter the mouth of the river. In 1903, the U.S. Lighthouse Board constructed Cape Fear Lighthouse at the end of Federal Road on the southeastern tip of Bald Head

OPPOSITE
The U.S. Lighthouse Board traditionally exhibited new technology at world events, and keepers coveted assignments to guard and interpret these exhibits. In 1901, the first-order Fresnel lens destined for the Cape Fear Lighthouse was displayed at the Pan Am Exhibition; subsequently, it went to the 1902 St. Louis Expo. Lens expert Thomas A. Tag has identified a "blower siren" fog signal (middle right) with its air tank and engine and a multi-horned Hamilton-Foster Fog Signal (middle left), along with various models of offshore Florida Keys lights. Note the chariot wheels the lens turned on to provide flashes of light; later, in 1920 while operating in the lighthouse, the lens floated in a bath of mercury. The light dominated Bald Head and Oak Islands for over half a century. *Photograph courtesy of Thomas A. Tag, technical adviser for the U.S. Lighthouse Society.*

The Lighthouse Board built the 1903 Cape Fear Lighthouse to warn of Frying Pan Shoals more than thirty miles off Bald Head Island. Its first-order Fresnel lens displayed six flashes of light each minute. Some sources state that the tower was made of steel, which is an alloy of iron with a lower carbon content, for strength. *Photograph courtesy of the David Stick Collection, Outer Banks History Center.*

Island. The board appropriated the hefty sum of $70,000, in two $35,000 increments, to build the lighthouse, as navigating Frying Pan Shoals had proved as dangerous as Diamond Shoals off Cape Hatteras. The stark skeleton tower, painted white, rose approximately 160 feet out of the sand, and its spider-web-like bracing and eight tremendous supporting columns made it an imposing structure. The black ironwork of the lantern room housed a first-order Henry LePaute Fresnel lens illuminated by an incandescent oil-vapor lamp.

Charles Norton Swan, known as Cap'n Charlie to islanders, lighted the lantern for the first time in August 1903, and he remained the keeper until he retired in 1933. Cap'n Charlie, whose eyes were "as deep blue as the sea he loved," came from generations of seafaring men, and his father also had worked for the U.S. Lighthouse Service.

As a perfect example of the U.S. Lighthouse Service and the U.S. Life-Saving Service working together as "sister services," the Cape Fear Lighthouse's three keepers kept constant vigil for shipwrecks. The surfmen and light keepers' families were especially close and kind to anyone in need of help. As told by David Stick in *Bald Head: A History of Smith Island and*

These graceful cast-iron spiral stairs ascended through the central column of the Cape Fear Lighthouse to a cast-iron lantern that supported the two-ton first-order Fresnel lens. The spiral stairway emulates nature with its nautilus-shell-like pattern. *Photograph courtesy of the State Archives of North Carolina.*

Cape Fear, if a wreck were spotted, the lighthouse keepers immediately used signal flags to send out the alarm to the Cape Fear Life-Saving Station's surfmen, pilots in Southport, and tugboat companies.

One such story of a rescue, detailed in Ethel Herring's *Cap'n Charlie and Lights of the Lower Cape Fear,* involved a wealthy Dr. and Mrs. Hearst from New York, whose unfortunate incident luckily had a happy ending. The couple were sailing several miles northeast of the island when Mrs. Hearst tumbled and fell from their yacht. Dr. Hearst threw her a life preserver and dragged her to shore but was unable to pull her safely onboard. Severely weakened, Mrs. Hearst had to be carried to Cap'n Charlie's house, where his wife, Marie, cleaned and cared for the bedraggled Mrs. Hearst. The lifesaving crew and Cap'n Charlie helped Dr. Hearst right his boat, and the couple paid their tremendous gratitude by writing letters of accolades and sending generous Christmas gifts to the children of the keepers and surfmen.

Sheafe Satterthwaite, former professor with the Center for Environmental Studies at Williams College in Williamstown, Massachusetts, spent time with Cap'n Charlie and his family in Southport in 1958. He recorded the old keeper recalling his experiences at Cape Fear Lighthouse:

> We kept it burning and kept it in good repair all those years. There were only eleven days the light didn't burn. That was during the World War I when the [German] submarines came over there. . . . The light came from France. At that time we didn't know how to make that kind of [Crown] glass. It has prisms, and they magnify. It was 87,000 candlepower and burned [kerosene] oil. Later it had a mantle light—oil pressure, you know. It had a six-inch mantle. The light was on exhibition at the World's Fair in Chicago. It was brought right here from there and put in the lighthouse.

The USCG used dynamite to destroy Cap'n Charlie's light in 1958. He told Satterthwaite, "It kind of hurt me when they blew up my light." The stalwart tower resisted destruction—Cap'n Charlie was holding her up, some say—and it took several blasts to finally bring her down. The USCG passed the light on to an updated style of lighthouse it had built on neighboring Oak Island. Cap'n Charlie received the front door as a souvenir.

Bald Head Island, Cape Fear, Federal Point, and Oak Island Lights: Timeline

1795 First Bald Head Island Lighthouse, aka the first Cape Fear Lighthouse, built.

1813 First Bald Head Island Lighthouse razed due to erosion by the river.

1816 Establishment of first Federal Point Lighthouse, located on the east side of the Cape Fear River in an area known today as Fort Fisher.

1817–18 Second Bald Head Island Lighthouse, aka Old Baldy, built; many bricks and lantern room come from first tower.

1836 First Federal Point Lighthouse burns down.

1837 The USLHE hired Hiram Stowell to build the second Federal Point Lighthouse.

1849–55 Range lights established along Cape Fear River to Port of Wilmington.

1854 U.S. Lighthouse Board first uses first-order lightships to mark Frying Pan Shoals; the fleet is active until 1964.

1863 Second Federal Point Lighthouse taken down by Confederates to give clear range of fire from Fort Fisher and the Mound Battery.

1863–65 Old Baldy surrounded by Fort Holmes; 1,100 Confederates stationed and living at the fort, a key factor in saving the lighthouse from destruction during the Civil War.

1866 Third Federal Point Lighthouse established and Bald Head Island Lighthouse darkened. Cape Fear range lights, except those on Oak Island, which are rebuilt on wooden platforms, discontinued.

1879–80 Bald Head Island Lighthouse reactivated after New Inlet closes; third Federal Island Lighthouse abandoned.

1881 Third Federal Point Lighthouse burns down.

1883 Old Baldy's fixed white light changed to red flash every thirty seconds.

1893 Old Baldy's flashing red light changed to white flash every thirty seconds.

1894 Oak Island Range Lights discontinued.

1903 Cape Fear Lighthouse established on the ocean side of Bald Head Island. Old Baldy changed to a fixed white light from a fourth-order Fresnel lens; its name officially becomes Bald Head Lighthouse.

1935 Old Baldy deactivated permanently as an official aid to navigation; Fresnel lens removed.

1941 Radio beacon installed on the Cape Fear Lighthouse tower to help airplanes and ships get their bearing.

1958 Cape Fear Lighthouse demolished by USCG; new Oak Island Lighthouse established.

1963 Old Baldy privately bought; later given to the Old Baldy Foundation, a private nonprofit organization.

1964 Frying Pan Shoals Light Station, a Texas-oil-rig-style lighthouse, built; *LV-115/WAL-537* lightship discontinued.

1979 Frying Pan Shoals Light Station automated as Frying Pan Tower.

1985 Old Baldy Foundation takes over maintenance and preservation of the lighthouse; light turned on again as an unofficial aid to navigation.

2000 A reproduction of the 1850s keeper's house completed at Old Baldy; houses the Smith Island Museum.

2004 Oak Island Lighthouse and property deeded to Town of Caswell Beach; its light is still operated by USCG; the nonprofit Friends of Oak Island Lighthouse (FOIL) forms; USCG abandons Frying Pan Tower, scheduled for demolition.

2006 In summer, FOIL assembles volunteers and allows access to the Oak Island Lighthouse tower; remains accessible today.

2010 New 1,000-watt halogen bulbs replaces 1,000-watt incandescent bulbs in the Oak Island Lighthouse; Richard Neal buys Frying Pan Tower for $85,000, with ongoing restoration as an operating bed-and-breakfast.

2017 Old Baldy marks 200 years of light with celebrations all year.

Today "Pirate invasion" of Bald Head Island held annually to celebrate National Lighthouse Day (officially August 7).

Three U.S. Marine helicopters rather than cranes did the job of heavy lifting in the assembly of the Oak Island Lighthouse. One helicopter did the exact placement of the aluminum lantern room under guidance from the others. *Photograph courtesy of the State Archives of North Carolina.*

THE LIGHTS OF OAK ISLAND

In 1958, nineteen years after the USCG assumed responsibility for America's navigational aids, the service built a commanding 153-foot-tall lighthouse in Caswell Beach on Oak Island, using twentieth-century engineering knowledge to sink 70 feet of foundation into bedrock to support the thin, tubular, rigid lighthouse with walls a mere 8 inches thick. It was a tall tower to fill a tall order: warn mariners of Frying Pan Shoals offshore. The base of the Oak Island Lighthouse was composed of two dozen concrete-

The Oak Island Lighthouse was created by pouring reinforced concrete into a tall, cylindrical mold, one section at a time. Color was infused into the concrete to reduce future, costly repainting. The adjacent USCG base, which is still responsible for maintaining the light is an essential part of the Oak Island Light Station. *Photograph courtesy of the David Stick Collection, Outer Banks History Center.*

filled steel pilings anchored 67 feet into the earth's crust. Thirty feet wide at its base, the massive tower is reinforced by a 3-foot-deep octagonal concrete base. From there, the tower stretched 153 feet into the skies over Oak Island.

To establish a color for each section, the first 40 feet was the natural gray of Portland cement. The next 50 feet was poured with white Portland cement and white quartz aggregate, creating its white color. The top 52 feet was a gray Portland cement with black coloring added in the mixing process. The Marine Corps, using helicopters, installed the 11-foot-tall aluminum lantern, and the lantern room originally housed eight high-intensity, 480-volt mercury arc bulbs that could flash 1.4 million candlepower. When bad weather rendered the visibility of the light below nineteen nautical miles, the USCG increased it to 14 million candlepower, making it into quite a spectacular sight.

Currently, two banks of four lights each burn 1,000-watt quartz (halogen) bulbs. With parabolic mirror reflectors, this still produces a powerful light. For economic reasons, the paint was mixed directly into the concrete; in fact, the primary paint scheme permeates the wall and is more sharply defined inside the tower than outside due to the years of abrasive wind and sand. To ease the labor of carrying equipment up the 131 ship's ladder steps that ascend in sections upward at a sharp angle, rather than traditional spiral stairs, a bucket lift large enough to hold tools and other equipment runs right up the center of the shaft on a cable attached to an electric motor under the lantern room. Like bookends, the ancient Old Baldy humbly stands on one side of the Cape Fear River while every ten seconds the modern, huge Oak Island Lighthouse sends out four flashes of light in four seconds, followed by six seconds of dark.

Oak Island Lighthouse

LOCATION Oak Island
NEAREST TOWN Caswell Beach, N.C.
COMPLETED 1958
TOWER HEIGHT 153 feet
ELEVATION OF FOCAL PLANE ABOVE SEA LEVEL
   169 feet (lighthouse sits on a rise of ground)
STEPS TO LANTERN ROOM 131 ship's ladder steps
BUILDING MATERIALS Reinforced
   concrete; aluminum lantern
DESIGN/PAINT SCHEME Cylindrical
   bands of black, white, and gray
OPTIC Cluster of 1,000-watt halogen bulbs;
   range of visibility, 19 nautical miles
FLASH CHARACTERISTIC Group of four
   1-second white flashes every 10 seconds;
   one of the most powerful lights operating
STATUS Active aid to navigation
ACCESS Open to the public seasonally
   and by reservation
OWNER/MANAGER Beacon operated by
   U.S. Coast Guard; Town of Caswell Beach
   owns property; restored and maintained
   by the Friends of Oak Island Lighthouse
HISTORY AND TOUR INFORMATION
   Friends of Oak Island Lighthouse
   1100 Caswell Beach Rd.
   Caswell Beach, N.C. 28465
   www.oakislandlighthouse.org
FOR MORE INFORMATION
   North Carolina Maritime Museum at Southport
   204 East Moore St.
   Southport, N.C. 28461
   (910) 457-0003
   ncmaritimemuseumsouthport.com

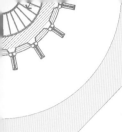

3 Ocracoke Island Lighthouse and Its Neighbors

Some suggest the lighthouse has outlived its own usefulness, but those who so speak must never have sat on the docks at Ocracoke on a summer evening and felt their very souls permeated by peace and good will.
—DAVID STICK, *Cape Hatteras National Seashore, 1964*

While other North Carolina lights faded into history, including Shell Castle Island Lighthouse and Beacon Island Lights that once marked Ocracoke Inlet, the familiar Ocracoke Lighthouse looks much as it did two centuries ago, still surrounded by small homes lined with white picket fences that paint an idyllic scene. The village of Ocracoke, which is tougher than it appears, grew through shipping and fishing and has earned the nickname the Nantucket of the South.

Historian Philip Howard, a native of Ocracoke Island and an avid researcher of the island's history, has found more than four dozen variations of the name "Ocracoke." He notes that the name is undoubtedly of early Native American origin, with the first known recorded spelling as "Wococon" on John White's 1585 map of the North Carolina coast. Although the island was uninhabited at that time, the name seems to derive from the tribe of Woccon Indians who lived in eastern North Carolina and frequented the Outer Banks seasonally to feast on the fish and shellfish that were plentiful in the area. In his book *Place Names of the Outer Banks*, Roger Payne speculates that "Wococon" could be an Anglicized corruption of the Algonquian word "waxihikami," which means "enclosed place, fort, or stockade." To date, the earliest record of the current spelling "Ocracoke" that Howard could locate is documented on an 1852 Coast Survey map by A. D. Bache.

Ocracoke Inlet made it possible for ship captains to reach inland ports, but at times it hindered more than helped their safe passage. Water flowing into the "outlet" from the Atlantic Ocean carried sand, and water flowing out of the inlet from Pamlico Sound carried silt from runoff originating hundreds of miles inland, resulting in a channel that constantly changed

in depth. Ships that drew more than 8 feet of water risked grounding. These dangers impeded development of commerce around the inlet and at mainland ports, negatively affecting the local and state economies. For centuries, captains had sought a deep-water inlet to reach North Carolina's port towns, including Plymouth, Bath, Edenton, Washington, Elizabeth City, Brunswick, Swansboro, and Wilmington.

In 1715, the North Carolina Provincial Assembly passed "An Act for Settling and Maintaining Pilots at Roanoke and Ocracoke Inlet," which assigned boat pilots to the area and provided land for docks and modest living quarters. These pilots gained employment by guiding vessels across "the bar," the shallow water formed by shoaling at the threshold of Ocracoke Inlet and the Atlantic Ocean.

Once large ships cleared the bar, they faced a maze of shallowly shoaled areas before they found a secure place to moor. To ensure continued safe passage, government officials also hired pilots of smaller vessels, called "lighters," to guide ships to Portsmouth Village, where cargo was then loaded onto ships bound for international ports.

This lightering, also called transshipment, gave birth to "Pilot Town," later renamed Ocracoke Village. Like many coastal communities, Pilot Town never lacked for names—it was also known as Port Bath since so many ships traveling through the inlet carried cargo destined for Bath on the mainland. Ship captains trusted and depended on the pilots who lived in Pilot Town for the safekeeping of their vessels, passengers, and cargo.

Numerous fishermen also chose to settle in Pilot Town, along with the people who took pride in salvaging and selling whatever they could save

Salvors worked a wreck scene on the north end of Ocracoke Island following a deadly storm in 1898. Islanders sold the salvaged goods or built their homes with valuable ships' timbers. The same storm destroyed a bluefishing fleet off Cape Hatteras; for days wreckage, including bodies, washed up on the Outer Banks. The storm had such great impact that it was covered by the *New York Times*. *Photograph courtesy of the State Archives of North Carolina.*

The 1823 Ocracoke Lighthouse, situated at the end of a white picket fence, is one of the best photo subjects on the Outer Banks. Miles of these picket fences wind along and around island homes, as well as the light station. Utilitarian as well as decorative, they demark personal property, protect property from free-range animals, and guard fishing gear.

from wrecked ships. Remnants of ships and their cargo provided Ocracokers with a broad range of necessities. Many Ocracoke Island homes, many still standing to this day, were built from lumber that washed ashore. Everyday items, from bananas to shoes, often floated in as flotsam and kept the islanders in relative comfort.

Ocracoke Island is now in Hyde County and part of the Cape Hatteras National Seashore, while Portsmouth Island is located in Carteret County and part of the Cape Lookout National Seashore. They both are part of the National Parks of Eastern North Carolina. Both islands have long been associated due to their proximity and also being two lucrative nexus points of commercial shipping. The relatively small amount of money North Carolina's government paid to Pilot Town pilots pales in comparison to the potential financial loss of commercial ships and their valuable cargoes.

The keepers' quarters near the Ocracoke Lighthouse completes an idyllic scene. The quarters were given a second story in 1897 to allow more room for the keeper and his family. In 1929 an assistant keeper's position was added, which called for another addition to create a double keeper's quarters. Today it is used by National Park Service staff. *Photograph by Diana Chappell.*

A NEW LIGHTHOUSE FOR OCRACOKE INLET

Around 1770 private owners deeded land to the North Carolina General Assembly for a lighthouse on Ocracoke Island, but the state government failed to build the tower before the federal USLHE assumed responsibility for all lighthouses. In 1794 federal officials chose to build the lighthouse on nearby Shell Castle Island instead of Ocracoke. However, disaster struck in 1818, when lightning sparked a fire that destroyed the Shell Castle Island Lighthouse (see chapter 1).

Congress did not approve funds to replace the burned lighthouse until about 1822. By that time, the main channel in Ocracoke Inlet had shifted, and lighthouse officials decided to build the new lighthouse on Ocracoke Island—ironically, they chose the same site the state's colonial government had chosen more than fifty years earlier. The federal government appropriated $20,000, and lighthouse officials purchased two acres for $50 from Jacob Gaskill on December 5, 1822, to complete the project. Noah Porter of Massachusetts built the tower and keepers' quarters for $11,359.35, notably under budget but with some obvious flaws.

Ocracoke Island Lighthouse

LOCATION Ocracoke Island
NEAREST TOWN Village of Ocracoke,
  within walking distance
COMPLETED 1823
TOWER HEIGHT 65 feet
ELEVATION OF FOCAL PLANE ABOVE SEA
  LEVEL 75 feet (sits on a slight rise)
STEPS TO LANTERN ROOM 80
BUILDING MATERIALS Brick coated
  with stucco and whitewashed
DESIGN/PAINT SCHEME Solid white
OPTIC Fourth-order Fresnel lens;
  range of visibility, 14 miles
FLASH CHARACTERISTIC
  Steady white light
STATUS Historic site on National
  Register of Historic Places
ACCESS Not open to the public on a
  schedule, but site can be visited each
  day; lighthouse reached by ferry
OWNER/MANAGER
  National Park Service
FOR MORE INFORMATION
• Cape Hatteras National Seashore
  1401 National Drive
  Manteo, N.C. 27954
  (252) 995-4474
  www.nps.gov/caha/index.htm
• Ocracoke Preservation Society
  P.O. Box 491
  Ocracoke, N.C. 27960
  (252) 928-7375
  ocracokepreservation.org

The 65-foot-tall whitewashed, conical tower supports a black-iron lantern room. It sits quietly at the end of a picket fence, with one side of the lighthouse more steeply sloped than the other and the lantern room off-center. Some historians know it as the "old style" lighthouse of the Stephen Pleasonton and Winslow Lewis era of construction, popular during the early to mid-nineteenth century.

The humble keeper's quarters measured 34 by 20 feet, with two rooms downstairs and a fireplace in each room. Stairs led up to "chambers," which historians have interpreted as either one or three bedrooms. The attached "porch," which measured 14 by 12 feet, had brick walls plastered on the inside and two windows. The porch likely served as a kitchen area since the contract description called for a chimney with an iron crane, trammels (hangers), and hooks with an oven of "middling size" on one side and a sink with a gutter to run through the brick wall. An outhouse and freshwater well provided the limited conveniences available at that time.

The tower originally housed fifteen lamps fitted with oil burners and 16-inch reflectors that revolved on a chandelier-type tier, installed by Winslow Lewis. Lighthouse officials did not document the first lighting of the lamps, which sent out a revolving red flash every two minutes at 75 feet above sea level. The keepers first used whale oil and later kerosene to light the lamps.

As with most construction projects, things didn't go as smoothly as planned. After his final inspection, District Inspector Bullfinch went so far as to pressure village residents to reject the government's lighthouse. He claimed that Porter had neither graduated the walls by lathing the interior, revealing the contractor's lack of experience, nor used soapstone for the deck, using freestone instead. Porter also used Carolina pine instead of Georgia pine, which was considered an inferior wood. There were even complaints that the keeper's house had poor framing.

In February 1824 letters and replies from both the "fifth auditor" of the U.S. Treasury, Stephen Pleasonton, and Winslow Lewis, the lighting apparatus contractor for this lighthouse as well as dozens of other American lights, whom Pleasonton relied on for advice, supported Porter, arguing he had fulfilled the lighthouse contract with what they thought was honest, hard work. Pleasonton even agreed to pay Porter not only the remaining money owed him but also the interest he incurred on money he had to borrow to complete the lighthouse. Lewis also pointed out that Porter had been frugal and spent far less than Congress had appropriated for the light station.

However, the modern viewer sees a tower that is a bit skewed and has some lumps in the exterior—which the residents complained about years ago—but the fact that it has endured and survived all kinds of weather for almost two centuries, including severe storms, proves that it was built well enough. Its irregularities only add to its character.

Shipping had been shuffling in and out of the area for nearly a century when the "new" 1823 Ocracoke Lighthouse arrived on the scene, a youngster beckoning business for mainland ports of the state. Until the 1840s, some 1,400 ships entered Ocracoke Inlet each year, averaging more than forty sets of sails each day. It must have been nothing short of a glorious sight.

Ocracoke remained a lively center of trade, as did the neighboring transshipment stopover at Portsmouth Island, until nature interrupted and altered the course of many ships as well as people's lives. In 1846, a hurricane opened Oregon and Hatteras Inlets to the north. Hatteras Inlet was deep enough that it became the preferred entry point to Pamlico Sound and mainland ports, and as a result, business at Ocracoke fell dramatically, reducing the torrent of business to a trickle there and on Portsmouth Island.

Several changes occurred over more than a century at the Ocracoke Lighthouse. By 1849 the original octagonal lantern room, called a birdcage-style lantern, was removed and a round one added to accommodate a smaller arrangement of ten brass lamps and 21-inch parabolic reflectors instead of the original fifteen lamps. The apparatus revolved to produce a

The original birdcage-style lantern room in the Ocracoke Lighthouse was changed out by 1849 for the one seen today to house a smaller arrangement of ten Argand-type lamps with 21-inch reflectors. A fourth-order Fresnel lens was installed in 1854, but it was damaged in 1911 and replaced with the first incandescent oil-vapor lamp. This was replaced by another fourth-order lens, shown here, sometime after 1927. *Photograph taken with a special fish-eye lens by Laddie Crisp Jr.*

Dangerous Encounters

Most sailors who frequently traveled this coastline had at least one close call due to either extreme weather or running aground on fickle shoals pushed around by prevailing winds, currents, and tides. The guidance of the Ocracoke Island Lighthouse has reassured many captains, but on the night of October 9, 1837, the captain of the elegant steam packet *Home* hoped only to get near enough to the lighthouse so that he could find help for his passengers before his ship broke apart.

"Mr. Hunt, we little thought this would be our fate when we left New York," Captain Carleton White remarked to his chief engineer. "I hope we may all be saved." Meanwhile, there was deafening noise as waves overwashed the *Home*'s beautiful decks and rabid waves ripped its hull into three pieces just six miles northeast of Ocracoke Island Lighthouse. Passengers on the deck were clinging to anything they could and screaming while they prayed that, with a bit of luck, which mariners always tried to carry with them, they could reach safety near the lighthouse.

The ship's captain had been aware of a storm in the Caribbean headed for Texas, but he didn't realize that the storm had torn across Jamaica and Central America, entered the Gulf of Mexico, ricocheted like a bullet off the Texas coast, and headed for the coast of North Carolina. Unwittingly, the captain steered for Cape Hatteras, where the *Home* initially encountered "Racer's Storm" and took on water. Panic began. Captain White decided not to beach the ship but, rather, to clear Wimble (near Chicamacomico, described as a stretch of sand, shells, and mud, south and east of Cape Hatteras) and Diamond Shoals. If they were blessed, the captain intended to head for the lee of the nearest harbor at Ocracoke. But such good fortune was not to be. She ran aground about six miles north of the island, dumping panic-weary passengers into a churning sea just 100 yards offshore. Ocracoke's beacon reached out in vain as the doomed people pleaded for escape in a lifeboat or with a life preserver.

Though the packet had been elegantly appointed—one of its greatest selling points—there were only two life preservers aboard. The fierce waves dashed two of her three lifeboats to pieces as they were lowered over the side, and the third simply dumped passengers into an angry sea that claimed approximately ninety lives that night. Ocracoke villagers helped as much as they could and opened their homes to the forty survivors, but the next day they heard unbearable reports of bodies washing ashore.

Soon after this horrific disaster, Congress approved legislation requiring every ship to carry a life preserver for each passenger.

flash of light every two minutes. As part of its modernization program, in 1854 the Lighthouse Board fitted the lighthouse with a fourth-order Fresnel lens made by Sautter, Lemonnier and Company of Paris, France. The light became "fixed," or nonflashing, at that time, and the lantern's distinctive ten sections of trapezoid-shaped panes of glass became part of its historic character.

An assistant keeper's position was created in 1897, surely a welcome event at the light station because keeping a light station alone presented many impositions to a solitary keeper. To accommodate the new keeper, a second story was added to the keeper's quarters. And in 1899 new fourth-order lamps were installed.

Then, in 1911, Ocracoke received the first incandescent oil-vapor lamp installed in the Lighthouse Board's fifth district. The lamp was too large for the lens and overheated, destroying the fragile mantle and cracking seven lens prisms. Archived Fresnel lens records are incomplete, and it is known only that a replacement fourth-order lens made by F. Barbier and Company (also known as Barbier and Fenestre) was installed sometime after 1927. Its base is stamped 1890, but no definite installation year has been found to date. In the late 1920s an incandescent oil-vapor lamp was still in use, but within two years it was electrified by a Delco battery-generator system beginning October 29, 1929.

During the Civil War, the light became a highly sought-after prize. Confederate forces removed the lens so the light could not aid the Union navy in its blockade of the southern coast, but fortunately they did not destroy the tower. This marked the first interruption in service in the light's history. Jeremy Smith, acting lighthouse engineer, was one of the busiest Lighthouse Board employees during the Civil War. He was in charge of the fifth district and saw firsthand the damage the war wrought on North Carolina's lights. He traveled along the North Carolina coast in the

Ocracoke Lighthouse's current lantern room houses the early style of trapezoidal glass panes. A wreath is traditionally placed outside the lantern room at Christmastime to lend a festive spirit.

schooner *Lenox* that often was based out of Beaufort, the coaling station for the Union blockaders. We can follow his progress in refitting lights with Fresnel lenses and ordering needed repairs from Cape Hatteras, Ocracoke, Cape Lookout, and beyond thanks to his clear penmanship in frequent letters to the Lighthouse Board. (For more information on the tower's fate and lens reinstatement, see chapter 7.)

According to records kept at the Cape Hatteras National Seashore, the lighthouse was cemented and covered with a special whitewash in the 1860s. The recipe for the stucco-style coating contained a half bushel of quicklime mixed with boiling water (called "slake lime," a mortar-like substance), a peck of salt, a half pound of powdered whiting (also called calcium carbonate), three pounds of ground rice in boiling water, and a pound of glue. Workers whipped up this brew many times, coated the tower heavily, and according to "Instructions to Light Keepers," let the mixture stand for several days. The instructions also stated, "Keep the wash thus prepared in a kettle or portable furnace, and when used put it on as hot as possible, with painters' or whitewash brushes." This formula not only gave the lighthouse a bright-white appearance but also served as a fire retardant. When workers reapplied the whitewash in 1906, the records do not give the exact recipe—they only document that applying it was a messy job involving six barrels of lime and paint. Letters from Keeper Tillman

Ocracoke and Area Lights: Timeline

1585 In June, Sir Richard Grenville's flagship *Tiger* stranded in Ocracoke Inlet trying to reach Roanoke Island with Sir Walter Raleigh's colonists; possibly offloads Spanish mustangs, ancestors to island horses.

1715 The North Carolina Provincial Assembly passes "An Act for Settling and Maintaining Pilots at Roanoke and Ocracoke Inlet."

1733 Two lights on Beacon Island noted on colonial sea chart.

1800 Shell Castle Island Lighthouse completed and lighted around this time.

1803 First Cape Hatteras Lighthouse completed and lighted (first authorized in 1794 but not completed until 1803).

1810 Census states Shell Castle "outpost" populated by eighteen whites and ten enslaved people of African descent who are considered skilled watermen and boat pilots.

1818 Lightning sparks a fire that destroys Shell Castle Island tower and keeper's quarters.

1822 May 7, Congress authorizes $20,000 for an Ocracoke Island Lighthouse to mark the inlet and Silver Lake; December 5, $50 paid to Jacob Gaskill for land for the station.

1823 Ocracoke Lighthouse built and lighted.

1824 January 14, contract for fitting Ocracoke's lamps completed.

1828 Currituck Inlet closed, increased business at Ocracoke Inlet.

1837 October 9, wreck of the *Home* near Ocracoke.

1846 Hurricane opens Oregon and Hatteras Inlets, diminishes business at Ocracoke.

1854 Ocracoke Island Lighthouse refitted with fourth-order Fresnel lens.

1855 Beacon Island Light built as range with Ocracoke Channel light vessel.

1859 March 3, Congress orders a short-range light placed in front of Ocracoke Island Lighthouse; Beacon Island Light and lightship discontinued by 1860.

1862 Confederate forces take Ocracoke's fourth-order lens; but Union forces restore it in 1863.

1897 Assistant keeper position established at Ocracoke Lighthouse; second story added to original quarters.

1899 Modern fourth-order lamps, specially designed for a Fresnel lens, ordered for Ocracoke Lighthouse and one installed.

1904 April 23, Notice to Mariners announces three beacons at Teach's Hole Channel, Ocracoke Inlet, and buoys at Cockle Shoal Swash Channel no. 8 and Swash Bar no. 9; keeper hired to tend the beacons, which have to be moved often due to shifting channel.

1917 Telephone connected to the light station from Hatteras Island in network of light stations and lifesaving stations.

1929 Another section added to keeper's quarters at Ocracoke Lighthouse; light electrified October 29, 1929, under Keeper Joe M. Burrus.

1933 Hurricane submerges Beacon Island.

1944 Hurricane damages Ocracoke Lighthouse; wooden stairs removed, replaced with ladders.

1946 USCG automates light at Ocracoke Lighthouse; Burrus, the last U.S. Lighthouse Service keeper, transferred.

1950s Metal stairs connected to interior wall at Ocracoke Lighthouse removed; central metal spiral stairs installed; exterior stucco and whitewash removed and fresh applied; NPS enters agreement with USCG to use light station as base of operations.

1954 Last keeper, Clyde Farrow, leaves the now fully automated Ocracoke Lighthouse.

1977 Ocracoke Light Station entered in the National Register of Historic Places.

1999 Ownership of tower transferred from the USCG to NPS.

2009–10 Restoration efforts begin November 13, 2009; tower completed and relighted March 3, 2010.

Smith reveal it was a five-day job for him and two hired laborers to apply two coats of whitewash to the tower's exterior "cement recently put on" and the interior. Smith complained that he had a hard time finding anyone who would help him for only a dollar a day, adding that a man could gather and sell clams for more money. The government reluctantly allowed Smith twenty dollars for the job and "to expand if absolutely necessary."

Later, in 1929, lighthouse officials installed electrical power and gave the Ocracoke Lighthouse an electric light with 8,000 candlepower that still produces a fixed beam visible for fourteen miles. As the power often fails during severe storms, officials outfitted the light with a battery backup.

THE U.S. COAST GUARD ERA

During World War II, the USCG station at Ocracoke posted lookouts around the clock. On January 23, 1942, as stalking German U-boats attacked Allied vessels near the North Carolina coast, lookouts reported that the British tanker *Empire Gem* was burning—she was loaded with more than 10,000 tons of precious petroleum headed to Britain when the German submarine *U-66* torpedoed her. Coastguardsmen traveled for four hours to reach the scene and found nothing but a huge burning mass. The Hatteras Inlet Lifeboat Station crew had reached the scene moments before the USCG and rescued two survivors, the captain and radioman. The rest of the British crew, fifty-seven men, died in the tragedy. Months later, on May 11, 1942, the German *U-558* sank another British ship, the HMT *Bedfordshire*. A small cemetery sits along a shaded lane in Ocracoke Village, serving as a reminder of the British military men who gave their lives just off the state's shores.

A local family donated the land for the site where Sub-Lt. Thomas Cunningham, Telegraphist Second Class Stanley Craig, and two unidentified British seamen were laid to rest. The residents of Ocracoke Village then donated the small cemetery to the British government, and each year the British town of Plymouth sends a Union Jack to fly over the graves, as part of an annual ceremony. A nearby plaque reads, "If I should die think only

A small, shaded piece of Ocracoke Island is forever England. On May 11, 1942, the HMT *Bedfordshire* was sunk by the German U-boat *U-558* just off the island's shore. An annual event is held to honor the British seamen who sacrificed their lives to protect America.

From the late eighteenth century until the mid-nineteenth century, Ocracoke Inlet was a center of a lively shipping trade. Skilled navigators, known as pilots, guided ships safely into the inlet and kept the passage unblocked by stranded vessels. Ocracoke was known for many years as Pilot Town. Pictured here is Silver Lake, formerly "Cockle Creek," where shallow-draft vessels still take refuge. *Photograph by Mark Riddick of Ice Cube Photo.*

this of me. That there's some corner of a foreign field that is forever England." The USCG maintains the graves and assists in arrangements for the annual ceremony. Every year, on the Friday closest to May 11, representatives of British and American military participate in a memorial service on the small plot of British soil on Ocracoke Island.

As technology allowed the USCG to fully automate the lighthouse, the last keeper, Clyde Farrow, left the station, and family life ended there in 1954. The lighthouse continued to operate, received restoration work that was completed in 2010, and has remained an island symbol through today.

A U.S. Life-Saving Service station—part of the USCG since 1915—has stood on the island since 1904. In 1939–40 the USCG ordered a new station and boathouse to be built on the old site. Today, the discontinued Ocracoke Coast Guard Station has received a facelift and for several years has served as the North Carolina Center for the Advancement of Teaching, Ocracoke Campus.

BEACON ISLAND LIGHT AND LIGHTSHIP

More than a century after the original post-type lights on this island were first recorded on a nautical chart in 1733, the Beacon Island Light was finally designated an official lighthouse in Carteret County on the 1853 U.S. Lighthouse Board Light Lists. It housed ten lamps of the old lighting system. The newly organized board did not purchase enough Fresnel lenses to refit it with a sixth-order lens until 1855, when it served as a range light with the Ocracoke Channel Light Vessel, a yellow-hulled, two-masted ship with a fog bell.

The light was short-lived, however, as mariners were forever chasing the position of a safe channel through Ocracoke Inlet. As a cost-saving measure, the Lighthouse Board suggested discontinuing the beacon and lightship. Instead, Congress approved a mere $750 on March 3, 1859, to build a short light in front of the Ocracoke Lighthouse to serve the same purpose as a range light. Both the Beacon Island Light and lightship disappeared from the Light List by the early 1860s.

During the Civil War, Confederate troops garrisoned on Beacon Island

Ocracoke Island Lighthouse and Its Neighbors

at Fort Ocracoke (Fort Morgan or possibly Fort Morris), then named "Fort Okrakoke," that stood next to the lighthouse. The fort's existence was short-lived, as Union forces chipped away at coastal defenses along the barrier islands. Reports indicate that the Union eventually took the fort and damaged the lighthouse in the process. Even though the tower was still standing in 1862, its light was darkened.

Without even the help of a lightship at the inlet entrance, the Ocracoke Lighthouse was left to do the job alone. Beacon Island, in southeastern Pamlico Sound near Ocracoke Island, was once considered a natural estuarine island called a "high salt marsh." The National Audubon Society protected and managed the area for its valuable nesting site for brown pelicans, first recorded in 1928, as well as colonial-nesting birds. In 2014, Hurricane Arthur hit the island hard and reduced its size to less than eight acres—today the island is barely visible. Once a site of protected conservation, it serves as a reminder that rising tides are a threat to those who build near waterways.

Ocracoke Island has also withstood its share of storms over the past two hundred years. Today it is a peaceful place to walk around the village and Silver Lake, take a boat ride, bike, and soak up the history that speaks to us in quiet voices from a different time.

M. Wesley Austin, Ocracoke Island Lighthouse Keeper

The 1823 Ocracoke Island Lighthouse has served as a watchdog over the inlet, which witnessed strong storms long before they were given human names. In an interview at her home on Ocracoke Island, Ruby Garrish, daughter of Ocracoke Lighthouse Keeper Wesley Austin, remembered the storm of 1913: "The waves were terrible. The boats washed up on the island and over the fences around the lighthouse. It was terrifying. Papa told me to run to the lighthouse and stay there. Momma and my sister were there and some other islanders. It took a long, long time to recover from that storm." Another hurricane that islanders recall with a headshake, as if it were a memory of unbelievable dimensions, is the storm of 1944. Arriving during the best fishing season, it sank all the boats in the harbor and took away men's yearly earnings, flooded their homes and sent people to seek refuge on any high ground they could find. Some even arrived at the light-house in a boat and went high into the tower for safety.

"Miss Ruby," as the islanders on Ocracoke knew her, was born on January 27, 1906, in the double keepers' house at the Currituck Beach Lighthouse in the village of Corolla. She was the second youngest daughter of Keeper Wesley Austin's eight children. Her "Papa" had transferred from the Cape Hatteras Light Station, where he had served for eight years. There, his career progressed as he worked his way up the roster from third to first assistant despite that he had a palsy, which he consciously controlled and didn't allow to interfere with his work. So well regarded was his work as keeper that he won the prized "efficiency award" for the best-kept light station in his district during the early 1920s.

Miss Ruby's uncle, Captain Benjamin Baxter Dailey, won the gold Congressional Life-Saving Medal in 1884 for leading the rescue of the *Ephraim Williams*. "We called him 'the Hero' in the family," she proudly recounted. Among these island communities, it was common for lighthouse and lifesaving station keepers' families to intermarry; in fact, one family might produce four or more keepers who joined one or both services. The USCG has remained a traditional career since it absorbed both the U.S. Life-Saving Service and the Revenue Cutter Service in 1915. When Ocracoke Island boys enlisted during World Wars I and II, they were taken directly to train others because they had grown up handling boats in storms.

Miss Ruby also spoke about "Uncle Walter." Her grandfather was James L. Barnett Jr., and his brother was the celebrated Captain Walter Barnett, who was in charge of Diamond Shoals Lightship *LV-71* when a German submarine sank it in 1918 (see page 190).

She enjoyed the island lifestyle since Ocracoke Village offered a community with neighbors, a school, and stores to buy groceries. "I remember we played tag in the lighthouse yard, and marbles. There were children who lived all around the lighthouse, and I had friends to play with even though we were on an island. We loved when the mail boat arrived each day if the weather was good. Everybody gathered and talked."

Miss Ruby also remembered the visits of the U.S. Lighthouse Service tender *Holly* and the coal, oil, and wood it brought. The inspector often came on this trip and gave Captain Austin the top score for a keeper's job well done. Captain Austin had to keep accurate records even for the lamp oil used for lights in the keeper's home. "He also raised his own beautiful vegetable garden, and we had chickens. How did he live and send me to school and raise eight children? He had to pay my high school tuition," she stated incredulously. In the 1920s, Keeper Austin's annual pay at a class 2 light station had reached $1,400 (with $240 deducted for living quarters) due to improvements made by Lighthouse Service Commissioner George Putnam, who also won congressional approval to set up a retirement system for keepers in 1918. Keeper Austin retired on September 30, 1929, with more than forty-five years of service and just one month before the light was electrified under the keepership of Joe M. Burrus.

"We didn't have a Christmas tree at Christmas, but we hung our stockings at the mantel." The Austins celebrated the holiday for its traditionally religious meaning. A small gift of fruit or something handmade was a mere second thought.

The Garrish, Austin, and Barnett families suffered a big loss in 1917. Ruby's brother Monford Lambert Austin joined the USCG Cutter Service in February at the age of seventeen, following in the tradition of his heritage. Only two weeks passed before Monford was called to duty to rescue victims from the steamer *Louisiana* near Ocean City, Maryland. The young Monford, along with a friend from Ocracoke who had joined the service with him, drowned in this valiant rescue attempt in foul weather and heavy seas.

"Papa?" Ruby summed up about her father: "I was very proud of my daddy. He was a good father. I loved him. As a lighthouse keeper, he got a lot of respect. He gave me good training. He always went to church, and he took us with him. It was an inspiration to me to love the church and love people. You get to know others and have good friends. Sometimes we need each other."

Fresnel Lenses Refocus Tower Lights

OPPOSITE
By 1822, Augustin Fresnel's first lighting system was composed of eight circular bull's-eye flash panels that refracted light from a four-concentric-wick lamp and focused it at the lens's center. Next, he attached eight trapezoidal lens panels in a fan shape at a 25-degree angle above and behind the main bull's-eyes to catch about one-quarter of light that would otherwise be lost. Finally, he added four rings of small mirrors below the main bull's-eyes to bounce light from the lamp and reflect it outward horizontally. This prototype produced a flash by turning on small, five-inch-diameter wheels. *Photograph courtesy of Thomas A. Tag, technical adviser for the U.S. Lighthouse Society.*

As night descends on the coastlines of America, piercing beams of light from Fresnel lenses break through the darkness and illuminate the land and water around them. Housed in lantern rooms that crown tall towers, these magnificent groupings of prisms capture light rays and efficiently focus them into a single shaft that can reach up to 16 nautical miles (nearly 22 statute miles). Some of these lenses have served in American lighthouses for about 150 years; today, the only North Carolina lighthouses to still have their original lenses are Currituck Beach, Bodie Island, and Ocracoke. Impressive as it is that anything could last this long and still provide excellent service, the story of the man who designed these lenses is even more so and shows that greatness can be achieved in the midst of the most difficult circumstances.

Augustin Jean Fresnel was born in Broglie, France, on May 10, 1788. His father, Jacques, was an architect and building contractor, and his mother, Augustine Mérimée, was a well-educated daughter of an estate's overseer where Jacques worked. During the 1794 French Revolution, the family moved to Mathieu, north of Caen, where Augustin learned strict work ethics that shaped his brief but highly productive life.

Augustin and his younger brother, Léonor François, were schooled at home before attending the École Centrale (Central School) in Caen. At the age of eight, Augustin still had not mastered his own native language, and ironically, he never mastered Latin or English, the two main scientific languages of the time. His natural genius for engineering and math, however, earned him acceptance into the École Polytechnique, the academy for higher education and research, which hosted the greatest mathematicians and mechanical engineers of that era, including Jean-Baptiste Biot and François Jean Arago. After graduation, Augustin took time to travel and think creatively before working with brother, Léonor, in the Corps des Ponts et Chaussées, the equivalent of the U.S. Army Corps of Engineers, where both of them rose to high positions as civil engineers.

During his thirty-nine years, Augustin suffered from symptoms of what probably was tuberculosis, yet he created remarkable inventions that changed lighthouses worldwide, and he envisioned futuristic theories. Arago, an outstanding French scientist, sparked Augustin's interest in light and optics, and Augustin subsequently began working on defining light in terms of waves instead of the accepted 150-year-old Newtonian theory of light as particles. He explored new theories, including defining heat, light, and electricity as part of the same energy source, differing only in "vibrations"; working with and enhancing the findings of his close friend and supporter André-Marie Ampère, whose electrodynamic molecular model was the hot item of the day; devising a system using a windup clockwork mechanism that allowed each lighthouse to display a distinct pattern of flashes to help identify them at night (called a "flash characteristic"); studying double refraction to further improve the efficiency of his lens design; continuing the evolution of the design, construction, and location of lighthouses; and experimenting with mediums of light, including human hair. Amazingly, he was doing all this with only a candle or a wick-burning lamp as light source. He also denounced Napoleon and found himself under house arrest more than once for his outspoken allegiance to the Royalist forces.

Augustin's friends saw him as a refractory man studying refraction, a serious workaholic, and a strict Puritan with the highest standards. Using simply the natural spirit of light and glass, he studied controlling light and how it could be magnified exponentially. He was curious about how light reflected and what happened when it was reflected infinitely, crossing its own path.

Augustin has always been known as a physicist, but to give him justice one must call him an inventor and philosopher as well. He worked by candlelight during cold, damp nights arranging mirrors, endlessly repositioning prisms, and taking meticulous notes until well after midnight. After sleeping for a few hours, he would rise to resume his experiments and work on his signature lighthouse lens. He conducted his experiments while he was on abbreviated breaks from his government civil engineering job or during forced moments of refuge ordered by Napoleon. Whenever he was called back into service by the Corps des Ponts et Chaussées, he had to respond, leaving his research until he could beg furloughs from his

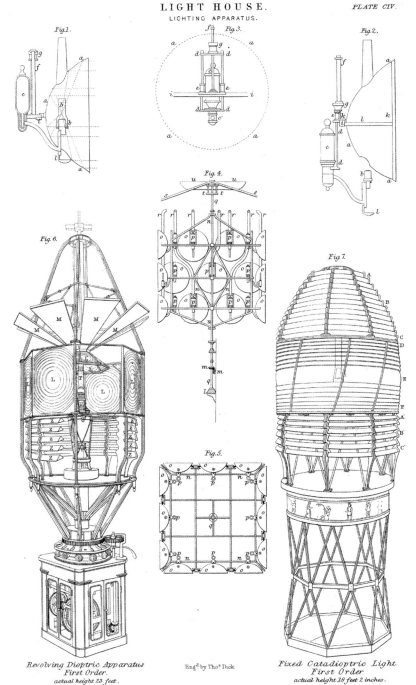

The evolution of American lighting systems is summarized here. The top row illustrates an early whale-oil-fed lamp backed by a silver reflector. At the center is the chandelier arrangement of several of these lamps. At the lower left is a Fresnel lens design with five lower rows of prisms, although it retains its upper bank of reflectors. The central eight bull's-eyes form a dioptric system; adding prisms below to reflect and refract light is a catoptric system. Combined, they create a catadioptric lens (lower right). The adoption of Fresnel lenses changed the appearance of American lighthouses: birdcage-style lanterns were taken down and rounded lanterns were built to better accommodate the new lenses. *From the author's collection.*

Fig. 1.

Fig. 3.

Fig. 2.

Fig. 4.

Fig. 6.

Fig. 7.

Fig. 5.

Revolving Dioptric Apparatus
First Order.
actual height 23 feet.

Eng.d by Tho.s Dick.

Fixed Catadioptric Light
First Order.
actual height 18 feet 2 inches.

A virtual twin to the first-order Fresnel lens originally housed in the 1903 Cape Fear Lighthouse, the Destruction Island Lighthouse lens is on display at Westport Maritime Museum in the state of Washington. A perfected lenticular system, it has twenty-four flash bull's-eye panels, with lower and upper banks of prisms that redirect light by refraction and reflection at the bull's-eyes' centers, called the "focal plane," creating brilliant spears of light. All together, it weighs approximately six tons. *Photograph by Joe Cocking for the Lighthouse Lamp Shop.*

superiors. Eventually, Augustin got his wish and began working full time for the French Lighthouse Service, which gave him the time and freedom to complete his experiments and make his lens design not just a dream but a reality.

Augustin also studied diffraction—when light spreads after passing through a narrow aperture or hole—and as part of his obsession to prove the wave theory of light, he studied the dark and light bands around the

After Augustin Fresnel's death in 1827, his brother, Léonor, continued to improve the lens design. The upper banks of mirrors were replaced by prisms that both reflect and refract light back to the center of the lens to be focused and intensified by bull's-eye panels to create an improved version of the catadioptric lens system. Less than 10 percent of light emitted from a lamp was left unused. *High-dynamic-range panorama produced by merging five fisheye images, by Laddie Crisp Jr.*

edges of shadows. He dreamt of a source of light intense enough to muscle rays through the dense prisms he designed to intensify the light, which would produce light bright enough to be seen over the dark coastal waters. Unfortunately, this powerful source of light, produced by the incandescent oil-vapor lamp, was not invented until the 1880s, far too late for Augustin, who died in 1827. Augustin's brother, Léonor, continued in his footsteps, and although he supervised the perfection of the Fresnel lens, scholars recognize Augustin as the primary inventor. Léonor's final version of the Fresnel lens substituted prisms for all of the upper and lower banks of mirrors in Augustin's model.

Until the 1820s, lighthouses used a reflecting or "catoptric" lighting system, with a mirrored surface behind the flame; groups of these reflecting surfaces were used in numbers proportionate to the amount of light needed to reach the horizon. In 1822, Augustin designed a reflecting sys-

Fresnel Lenses Refocus Tower Lights

Fresnel used eight of these bull's-eye lenses in his original design. Each refracted light in both vertical and horizontal directions to form focused beams of light. Lens expert Thomas A. Tag identified major manufacturers of Fresnel lenses, including Soleil in Paris (1720s), followed by Francois; Francois Jr. left for St. Petersburg, Russia, to work there. Others were Henry Lepaute in Paris; Sautter, Lemonnier and Company of Paris; Barbier and Fenestre of Paris; Chance Brothers in England; Stone-Chance in England; and Wilhelm Weule in Germany.

tem using prisms to bend or refract light, called a "dioptric" system. Merging the two lighting systems gave the world the "catadioptric" lenticular system, where a lens gathers, magnifies, and focuses the light at the central belt of prisms of a lens and emits it at the focal plane.

Lighthouses equipped with Fresnel lenses were much more visible to passing ships and helped make traveling by ship much safer. There was no place in greater need of these magnificent light enhancers than the southern coast of the United States, which has no headlands or prominent landmarks to orient mariners. The year 1854 was a very good year for North Carolina's lights, as seen in the Notice to Mariners.

Each time a light-house was built, a new lens installed, a flash pattern changed, or a light discontinued, a Notice to Mariners appeared wherever a mariner might see it. These official documents of the U.S. Lighthouse Service are continued today by the USCG in its annual Light List through its Navigation Center, Department of Homeland Security. *From the author's collection.*

NOTICE TO MARINERS.

CHANGES OF LIGHTS

AT

CAPE HATTERAS, BODY'S ISLAND,

AND

OCRACOKE,

(COAST OF NORTH CAROLINA.)

IN conformity to the notice to Mariners, issued from the Office of the Light-House Board at Washington, under date of December 1st, 1853, notice is hereby given that the proposed changes will take place simultaneously at the three above-named Light-Houses on the night of the first of June next, (1854.)

CAPE HATTERAS.

The Cape Hatteras Light will be a FIRST ORDER FRESNEL FLASHING LENS, exhibiting, in every 20 seconds of time, a brilliant white flash of 8 seconds duration, followed by a total eclipse of 12 seconds duration.

At the distance of 14 to 18 miles the duration of the flash will be somewhat less, and that of the eclipse proportionably greater.

The height of the tower from the ground to the top of the lantern is 140 feet.

The color of the tower from the ground to the height of 20 feet is GREY, and the remainder RED.

The tower is placed about 2 miles from the point of the Cape, on the southward and eastward extremity of a long ridge of white and naked sand, backed by woods.

The space of about 2 miles, between the Light-House and the pitch of the Cape, is a low flat and bare sand beach, very little above extreme high water.

The light will be 150 feet above the level of the sea, and should be seen, in good weather from a position 15 feet above the water, at the distance of about 19 nautical or 22 statute miles.

The approximate position of the Cape Hatteras Light-House, as determined by the Coast Survey, is—Latitude 35° 15′ 11″ North, Longitude 75° 30′ 33″ West from Greenwich.

BODY'S ISLAND.

The Body's Island Light, about 32 nautical miles to the northward of Cape Hatteras, will be changed at the same time (June 1st, 1854) to a FOURTH ORDER FRESNEL FIXED WHITE LIGHT, varied by alternate red and white flashes.

This light will be 50 feet above the level of the sea, and the white flashes should be seen, in good weather, from a position 15 feet above the water, at the distance of about 13 nautical or 15 statute miles; the fixed light not quite so far as the white flashes, and the red flashes at a less distance than the fixed white light.

The approximate position of Body's Island Light, as determined by the Coast Survey, is—Latitude 35° 47′ 20″.5 North, Longitude 75° 31′ 20″ West from Greenwich.

OCRACOKE.

The Ocracoke Light, about 23½ nautical miles to the southward and westward of Cape Hatteras Light-House, will be changed at the same time (June 1st, 1854) to a FOURTH ORDER FRESNEL FIXED WHITE LIGHT.

This light will be 75 feet above the level of the sea, illuminate the entire horizon, and should be seen, in good weather, from a position 15 feet above the water, at the distance of about 14½ nautical or 16 statute miles.

The approximate position of Ocracoke Light-House, as determined by the Coast Survey, is—Latitude 35° 06′ 31″.6 North, Longitude 75° 58′ 27″.4 West from Greenwich.

By order of the Light-House Board,

D. P. WOODBURY,
Captain of Engineers.

April 15, 1854.

Fresnel Lens Orders

ORDER	RADIUS (mm. / in.)
Hyperradial*	1,330 / 52.3
Mesoradial*	1,125 / 44.2
First order	920 / 36.2
Second order	700 / 27.6
Third order	500 / 19.7
Three and one-half order*	375 / 14.7
Fourth order	250 / 9.8
Fifth order	187.5 / 7.4
Sixth order	150 / 5.9
Seventh order*	100 / 4.0
Eighth order*	75 / 2.9

*These sizes were developed in the mid- to late 1800s and were extensions of Augustin Fresnel's design. The seventh- and eighth-order lenses were used almost exclusively in Scotland. American lighthouses predominantly used first- through sixth-order lenses. The large first-order lenses were reserved for coastal beacons, second and third orders for the Great Lakes and West Coast, and the smaller sizes in harbor lights. (Chart courtesy of Thomas A. Tag.)

5

The Second Cape Lookout Lighthouse

The 1859 Cape Lookout Lighthouse, the second tower built at the cape, stands in solitude on South Core Banks. Looking west, the light watches over Lookout Bight, Back Sound, Harkers Island, Barden Inlet, and Core Sound, with the vast Atlantic on its easterly side. According to historian David Stick, signs of inhabitants date to approximately 3000 B.C. It is likely that these people, who explored and lived at least part time in the area, were indigenous people who banked fires in sand dunes as guides.

In the early sixteenth century this area of the Outer Banks, now preserved and maintained as Cape Lookout National Seashore, formed the center of local maritime activity for European explorers and future settlers. Lighthouse keepers, lifesaving surfmen, boatwrights, pilots, fishermen, net makers, whalers, and other hardy, determined people left the mainland for Cape Lookout and the adjacent barrier islands by boat to make their living from the sea. Over time, harsh storms and subsequent changes in the landscape forced these self-reliant islanders to pack their boats and take root on islands behind "the banks," which provide at least a modicum of shelter from the fierce ocean waves and wind.

THE SECOND TOWER'S BEGINNING

This second tower was the result of failed attempts to improve the 1812 tower. U.S. Navy lieutenant David D. Porter reported in 1851 that the light remained "nearly impossible to find."

Not giving up, the Lighthouse Board had the tower refitted with a first-order Fresnel lens and improved lamps in 1857, trying to provide a brighter light, but the tower still proved to be too short to shine a strong caution across Cape Lookout Shoals, where it was desperately needed. The Lighthouse Board published a list of thirty-eight towers they recommended be elevated. The Cape Lookout Lighthouse was number fifteen on the list, but its outmoded construction (an interior brick tower with a wooden outer frame) would not accommodate added height. This called for a new light-

NOTICE TO MARINERS
(No. 43.)

CAPE LOOKOUT LIGHT-HOUSE

COAST OF NORTH CAROLINA

FIXED LIGHT.

Official information has been received at this office from Captain W. H. C. Whiting, Corps of Engineers United States Army, that the new lighthouse at Cape Lookout has been completed.

The tower is the frustum of a cone. It is built of brick, and is surmounted by an iron lantern painted black.

The color of the tower is red, and the focal plane is 156 feet above the level of the sea.

The keepers' dwelling, which is a part of the old tower, is painted in red and white horizontal stripes.

The illuminating apparatus is a catadioptric Fresnel lens of the 1st order, showing a *fixed light* of the natural color which should be visible in ordinary weather a distance of 22 nautical miles.

The position of this light-house, as given by the Coast Survey, is:

Latitude 34° 37' 20" North.
Longitude 76° 30' 41" West of Greenwich.

The new light-house will be lighted for the first time at sunset on Tuesday, the first day of November next, and will be kept burning during that and every night thereafter until further orders.

By order of the Light-house Board:

W. B. FRANKLIN,
Secretary.

TREASURY DEPARTMENT,
Office L. H. Board, September 19, 1859.

Cape Lookout started its life as a fixed light. Its first-order Fresnel lens was replaced by a DCB-224 rotating aero beacon in 1975. Today, it has a solar-powered multitier LED optic. *From the author's collection.*

house, the best that could be built, and the board placed it on their top-ten list in importance to aiding mariners. Instead of destroying the old red-and-white striped lighthouse, the board kept it in place as a daymark, and ruins of the old tower's stone foundation remain to this day near its taller companion. (For more information about the 1812 Cape Lookout Lighthouse, see chapter 1.)

The second Cape Lookout Lighthouse is one of the coastal sentinels built between 1857 and 1859 by the finest engineers of the day. Many of these men graduated from West Point Academy and served as members of the Army Corps of Engineers.

The 1859 lighthouse reaches an impressive 163 feet into the azure skies over South Core Banks and Cape Lookout Shoals, an area named "Promontorium Tremendum" (Horrible Headland) on sixteenth-century maps. This ominous nametag proved to be well deserved since the shifting shoals, which are part of the Graveyard of the Atlantic, lurk just under the ocean's surface and can reduce water depth to only a few feet in unexpected shallows. Mariners frequently found themselves shipwrecked on the shoals, facing an unplanned burial at sea, before they spotted Cape Lookout.

In addition to providing a warning beacon, the Cape Lookout Lighthouse also serves as a welcoming light that beckons mariners to the protective lee of Lookout Bight, a hook of sand that extends from the cape and holds the waters of Core and Back Sounds like a cupped hand. Historically, Lookout Bight served as a convenient rest stop midway between the major ports at Charleston, South Carolina, and Norfolk, Virginia. During World War II, a submarine net across Lookout Bight protected Europe-bound Allied warships anchored in the sound from marauding German U-boats.

Many documents related to the 1859 Cape Lookout Lighthouse are missing or may have been lost to fire. Now preserved at the National Archives, the existing indexed letters (containing minimal details of the original documents), along with a few other surviving documents, give tantalizing clues about the construction of the lighthouse. For example, in a letter dated April 28, 1858, Capt. W. H. C. Whiting, then serving with the Army Corps of Engineers based in Wilmington, wrote of "the non-necessity for pilings," indicating that the tower possibly rests on a pine timber grillage.

Although Whiting's signature is on the plans for the new lighthouse, questions have been raised about exactly who is to be credited with building it, the same question asked at other American light stations. A surveyor, a designer—if not the district engineer—a draftsman, a superintendent of construction, and the Lighthouse Board were all involved in approving plans at various stages of development. But the consensus among engineers surveyed is that whoever put his name on a set of plans and was given the responsibility for their execution staked his reputation on the project and deserves a great deal of the credit.

An artist's rendition of what the second Cape Lookout Lighthouse would have looked like prior to being painted with its classic black-and-white "checkers," known today as "diamonds." *Drawing by Mike Litwin from the author's collection.*

Whiting's plans utilized the most modern architectural logic of the time in the tower's successful design, which added enough height to send a blaze of light across Cape Lookout Shoals and rise above the morning mist or fog. Its conical style offers less resistance to wind, its double-wall brick construction tapers from 8 feet at the base to 2 feet at the top to provide insulation and strength, and its iron lantern room accommodated the first-order Fresnel lens from the old tower.

Changes to the light station included repurposing the old tower as a daymark, along with renovations that converted the old veteran into living quarters for the head lighthouse keeper and his two assistants.

In 1873, the Cape Lookout Lighthouse received its black-and-white checkered pattern, commonly referred to as "diamonds." The black diamonds face north-south, while the white diamonds face east-west, creating a unique and easily identified daytime visual for this tower. That year the Lighthouse Board also added a larger keepers' quarters, although it proved to be too small to house three keepers and their families. The keepers wanted to have their families with them, but the cramped living space inevitably caused problems.

Scattered across original documents in the National Archives are letters written by Principal Keeper A. G. Hooper to the board in 1906 to let officials know that he and his son, plus two assistant keepers, the wife of one of the assistants, and the wife's "servant girl," were all sharing one house. Hooper had strong words with the assistant keepers and wanted the board to order the "girl" to leave because "we have to use the same hallway." There were arguments among them over Keeper Hooper's son's attraction to "the girl," and it disturbed the dynamics of the house's residents. One of the assistant keepers left that year, and the other left the following year. Finally, responding to years of keepers' complaints about crowded living conditions, in 1907 the board added a new principal keeper's quarters that comfortably housed an entire family. Hooper continued serving as the principal keeper at the Cape Lookout Lighthouse until he transferred to the Ocracoke Light Station in September 1909. While arguments could complicate personal friendships, all lighthouse keepers knew that they must continue to carefully tend the light—retaining their jobs and the safety of everyone sailing near Cape Lookout depended on it.

The influence of the Cape Lookout Lighthouse's presence is witnessed in one nearby community's taking the name "Diamond City." First chartered in 1723, a whaling community had existed across "the Drain" from

In 1873, the tall coastal towers in North Carolina received a special daymark pattern to give each its daytime identity, with the exception of the Currituck Beach tower, which was left unpainted. Uniquely designed, the centers of Cape Lookout's white diamonds point east-west while the centers of the black diamonds point north-south.

Cape Lookout Lighthouse

LOCATION South Core Banks Island

NEAREST TOWN Beaufort, N.C.

COMPLETED 1859

TOWER HEIGHT 163 feet

ELEVATION OF FOCAL PLANE ABOVE SEA LEVEL 150 feet

STEPS TO LANTERN ROOM 201 "pie-wedge" steps

BUILDING MATERIALS Double-wall brick construction
  with cast-iron stairs and lantern room

DESIGN/PAINT SCHEME Black and white diamonds
  (called "checkers" in 1873 when painted)

OPTIC DCB (directional code beacon) aero
  beacon; range of visibility, 19 nautical
  miles; solar powered in 2017

STATUS Active aid to navigation

ACCESS Open to the public seasonally and
  generally Thursday through Sunday; tickets
  can be purchased near the lighthouse

OWNER/MANAGER Beacon operated by U.S. Coast
  Guard; property owned by National Park Service

FOR MORE INFORMATION
  Cape Lookout National Seashore
  131 Charles Street
  Harkers Island, N.C. 28531
  (252) 728-2250
  www.nps.gov/calo/planyourvisit

FOR INFORMATION ON LOCAL HERITAGE,
  DIAMOND CITY, WATERFOWL HUNTING
  TRADITION, AND MUCH MORE
  Core Sound Waterfowl Museum and Heritage Center
  www.coresound.com

FOR INFORMATION ABOUT HORSE WATCHING WALKS
  National Park Service
  Foundation for Shackleford Horses
  www.shacklefordhorses.org

the light station on the eastern part of Shackelford Banks. It finally organized with a population of several hundred people around 1885; however, it would soon disappear primarily due to the destructive 1899 "San Ciriaco" hurricane. Many of those with local origins stayed in the area by settling several other communities, including the "Promised Land" in Morehead City, by floating their humble abodes across the sound and building new foundations, many of which still stand.

NATURE RULES

The Depression brought lean times to the entire country, and the Outer Banks were no different. In 1933, a category 3 storm wreaked havoc on the communities on the barrier islands. The force of wind and waves opened Barden Inlet and separated the once contiguous Shackleford and South Core Banks.

As a result of that powerful hurricane and other storms, as well as the increasing use of motorboats that allowed faster trips for transferring people and supplies to and from the island, human presence dwindled on the banks, and these barrier islands evolved into a pristine example of a coastal wilderness area.

On March 10, 1966, President Lyndon Johnson authorized Cape Lookout National Seashore within the NPS as one of the most diverse and

No roads or bridges touch South Core Banks Island. When keepers and their families lived in the house, there was light glowing only from oil lamps. In 1933, generators supplied electricity to lights. There is a quietude about the island that is found in few other places.

complex ecological areas of the Outer Banks. Officially established in 1976, this national seashore stretches a remarkable fifty-six miles from Ocracoke Inlet in the north to Beaufort Inlet at the south, with undeveloped barrier island throughout. Cape Lookout now serves as a global model demonstrating that barrier islands are dynamic ribbons of sand, moving and changing to ensure its own preservation. Its natural state provides an answer to a hotly debated subject: allowing barrier islands to remain dynamic versus hardening the coast with groins and continuous oceanfront

Cape Lookout Lighthouse: Timeline

1804 Congress authorizes lighthouse at Cape Lookout.

1810 Specifications for construction and request for bids appear on the front page of the *Boston Patriot*.

1811 Construction contract awarded to Benjamin Beal Jr., Duncan Thaxter, and James Stephenson of Boston.

1812 First Cape Lookout Lighthouse, a brick tower inside a wooden frame, lighted; according to USLHE Light List, height at lens is 93 feet, with overall height of 107 feet; President Madison appoints James Fulford keeper at $300 per year.

1845 Captains report difficulty seeing the light produced by thirteen whale-oil lamps.

1851 Lighthouse in need of serious repairs, which are attempted; sand builds up against keepers' house; complaints from seafarers mount.

1857 Congress appropriates $45,000 for a new lighthouse; first-order Fresnel lens requested from Sautter, Lemmonier and Company of Paris, France, by this time, but there is no record that it was installed.

1859 New tower completed; first-order Fresnel lens installed in the new tower, lighted on November 1; two assistant keepers appointed; old tower left as daymark and converted to keeper's quarters.

1861 Confederates remove first-order Fresnel lens and store it at state capitol in Raleigh for safekeeping.

1863 Union forces retake the area and install third-order Fresnel lens.

1864 Confederate raiding party blows up part of the iron spiral stairs in the new tower; the third-order Fresnel lens survives; light put back into service; wooden stairs temporarily replace damaged sections of stairs.

1867 Original first-order Fresnel repaired in France and reinstalled; temporary wooden stairs replaced by cast-iron stairs as soon as iron becomes available after the Civil War.

1873 Tower painted with distinctive diagonal black-and-white "checkers" (diamonds); kerosene (mineral oil) replaces whale oil to fuel the lamp; assistant keeper's quarters built; now serves as a museum to the public—first floor depicts the quarters as it looked in 1900.

1879 Final year the old (1812) tower appears on the official Light List as a daymark.

1904 Lightship placed on Cape Lookout Shoals to add warning of the hazard.

1907 Third house built to house primary keeper until tower automated in 1950; sold to Dr. Graham Barden Jr. in 1957 and moved about a mile from the lighthouse.

1914 Revolving panel installed on the outside of the lens, changing the light from fixed to flashing; an incandescent oil-vapor lamp, able to produce a brighter light, installed.

1933 Generator-powered radio beacon and electric lights installed in the lighthouse; lightship removed until World War II; an extreme September hurricane opens Barden inlet and separates Shackleford Banks from Core Banks.

1939 USCG takes responsibility for the lighthouse from the Bureau of Lighthouses.

1950 Lighthouse automated by electricity—keepers no longer needed.

1966 Cape Lookout National Seashore established; lighthouse and property transferred to NPS; USCG maintains the light.

1972 October 18, light station listed on the National Register of Historic Places (NRHP)

1975 First-order Fresnel lens removed from tower and replaced with an aero beacon.

1978 November 29, Portsmouth Village listed on the NRHP.

1989 February 1, USCG station complex listed on the NRHP.

1997 February 13, Congressman Walter B. Jones Jr. introduces H.R. 765, Shackleford Banks Wild Horses Protection Act.

2000 June 30, Cape Lookout Historic District listed on the NRHP.

2003 Cape Lookout Lighthouse transferred to NPS and appears on U.S. postage stamps as one of five in the Southeastern Lighthouses series.

2010 July 15, after being restored, lighthouse opens for regular but limited seasonal public climbing.

2017 In May, in a move to function off the grid, solar power panels installed to power keepers' quarters, lower section of lighthouse.

2017 September USCG, Station Fort Macon, changes out the DCB 224 aero beacons for LED lights to economize running of the Cape Lookout Light Station.

development. These forever-wild ribbons of sand at Cape Lookout National Seashore show firsthand that the only way to sustain the health of barrier islands is to leave them unhardened and undeveloped and allow them to move as wildly and freely as the Shackleford Banks horses.

Cape Lookout National Seashore

Cape Lookout National Seashore includes Shackleford Banks as well as Core Banks, a landscape broken into northern and southern barrier islands by New Drum Inlet, Portsmouth Village, and dozens of islets within the glimmering waters of Core, Back, and Pamlico Sounds. Untouched by bridges or paved roads, the land preserved within the national seashore has never supported a large population. These slender barrier islands feature predominantly empty beaches punctuated by low-lying dunes and large areas of salt marshes along the sounds. Some of the only remaining native grasses of the eastern United States grow here. Dune grasses anchor precious sand along windblown beaches and marshland waters, while marsh grasses provide nurseries for shrimp, clams, crabs, and a wealth of fish and waterfowl.

Wind, wave action, and tides with underwater rivers of natural currents keep the barrier islands a dynamic system that is perpetually in flux. Like a living creature, the islands slowly heal from wounds caused by harsh gales; natural storm-caused overwash allows soundside sand to build up while it can reduce the beachside by as much as 30 feet within a year. Due to the east-west lay of the land on Lookout Bight, an estimated 1,000 feet of beach eroded between the lighthouse and the sound from 1940 until 1979. Unfortunately, ongoing erosion that has waxed and waned over many years

This is an original 1893 cyanotype of the Cape Lookout Lighthouse by U.S. Lighthouse Service engineer and photographer Herbert Bamber. According to historian John Havel, Bamber developed prints while on location on 8-by-10-inch glass plates. He sent them to his Baltimore superiors, but he kept one cyanotype copy for his own. *From the author's collection.*

continues to threaten the keepers' quarters. Park officials are making plans to evaluate the historical value of the structures within the national seashore, including the Cape Lookout Lighthouse, and decide how to protect them from climate change.

At one time thick forests covered the barrier islands, but over the years trees have disappeared from virtually all of the Outer Banks, except for remnants of maritime forests, including Guthrie's Hammock on Shackleford Banks. A few magnificent stands of ancient live oaks and cedars huddle together in protective groups here and there. The islanders who settled and worked here cut many of the native trees to build houses and boats—little did they realize that by cutting the trees, they were taking away the very support from under their feet. Other forces constantly at work include time, tide, and saltwater spray that cause the death of forests on one side of a dune as new vegetation takes root on the protected side. A natural process called succession repeats itself within beach environments: like a slow-crawling creature, whatever tenacious vegetation takes root near the high-tide line grows, trapping sand until it is suffocated by it. Sand continues to build, spills over, spreads out, and moves until it hits

The National Park Service is studying ways to protect historic properties in danger from sea level rise. At the Cape Lookout Light Station, soundside erosion threatens with the impact of seasonal storms. Barrier islands naturally erode on one side while accreting on the other—overwash is a natural process, and this mobility is critical to the health of an island. But sometimes man-made structures unwittingly end up in harm's way. *Photograph by Courtney Whisler.*

something else upon which to build. This is the birth of a sand dune that will live out its life until it is eventually eroded away, but given space to continue its life, its protected side will begin to migrate to find something else to grip, anchor to, and accumulate more sand.

The Cape Lookout National Seashore Administration performs a balancing act to allow visitors to enjoy the rich history and scenery of "the Banks," as locals call the area, and still protect the creatures and plants that make this a unique place on our planet. Visit the Cape Lookout Lighthouse website for more information about visiting, activities, special sites, and climbing the light itself. See also the Core Sound Waterfowl Museum and Heritage Center's website or plan a visit. The center is adjacent to the Cape Lookout National Seashore's headquarters; immediately nearby is a soundside hiking trail and a ferry terminal that carries visitors to South Core Banks Island, the lighthouse, and Shackleford Banks.

The Shackleford Banks Horses

Wild horses have a long history on the Outer Banks, dating back to the seventeenth century. With mane and tail flowing in the omnipresent wind, a wild horse is an iconic symbol of the famed wild spirit of the North Carolina coast.

Four herds of feral horses currently reside in protected areas along an approximately 160-mile-long stretch from Cape Lookout to Corova, north of Corolla near the Virginia border. Locals have long called them "Bankers" or "Banker ponies," after the Outer Banks themselves. DNA testing indicates Spanish horses, traded in Europe as well as in parts of North America during the Spanish Colonial Period, are related to the Banker ponies. Gus Cothran, a geneticist with the University of Kentucky, performed DNA tests on the Banker ponies on the Shackleford Banks horses, and results show that least some horses are indeed descendants of Spanish horse bloodlines and that they are genetically closer to horses than to ponies, mainly due to their larger size. In 1493, Christopher Columbus brought Spanish steeds on his second voyage to the New World for breeding purposes. As Spanish ships passed various parts of the Outer Banks, horses were driven ashore on the barrier islands and left to survive on their own.

On the southern Outer Banks, these rough-coat wild horses still run free on Shackleford Banks and are one of the few wild horse species today in the United States. To keep the Shackleford Banks horses truly wild, NPS personnel do not treat them as pets, and their diets are not supplemented—the horses continue to adapt to eating seagrass, sea oats, and various grasses growing in the "swales" (areas between dunes) where they are protected from salt spray and grow prolifically. According to Sue Stuska, Cape Lookout National Seashore wildlife biologist, the horses are picky

Shackleford Banks horses are believed to have been on the island for centuries. Explorers offloaded horses to lighten their laden ships while providing transportation on the island when needed. The wild horses are protected legislatively and are cared for by the National Park Service and the Foundation for Shackleford Horses, Inc. Visitors are asked not to feed them because human food can be fatal to them. *Photograph by Cheryl Burke of the* Carteret County News-Times.

about what they eat and have favorite watering holes, swales, and areas where they enjoy resting. During the heat of summer, groups of horses linger on the beach to catch the onshore winds that both cool them and keep bugs away.

Each of the nineteen groups of Shackleford Banks horses has its own social strata, with at least one alpha stallion and one alpha mare with young foals. The stallion fiercely defends his harem of mares, which appears to be a full-time job. When a young male is old enough, usually at three years of age, he joins one of about four bachelor groups and waits his turn to form or join another group and earn a more respected status within the hierarchy. NPS horse personnel periodically use birth control darts to keep the horses on the island at a reasonable number and prevent extreme competition for food, as well as to give a mare a break if she has foaled too often. In addition, NPS personnel regularly inspect each horse to ensure that all of these beautiful creatures are healthy and well fed.

The federal Shackleford Banks Wild Horses Protection Act, passed in 1998, requires an annual report on the status of the herd. In April 1999, the NPS and the Foundation for Shackleford Horses signed a memorandum of understanding for joint management of the island's horses. For information about horse watching walks, contact Cape Lookout National Seashore or the Foundation for Shackleford Horses.

The ribs of an old sailing ship rest near the Cape Lookout Lighthouse. A shipwreck can be unearthed by a strong storm, only to be covered again in a subsequent storm. Traveling these barrier islands was risky, which could explain why sailors were very superstitious. Luck, weather, and skills of the skipper were all that stood between a sailor and an untimely death at sea.

THE HEROIC RESCUE OF THE
SARAH D. J. RAWSON CREW

In addition to being a sanctuary for wildlife, Cape Lookout is the site of one of the most dramatic sea rescues in North Carolina maritime history. In the nineteenth century, three lifesaving stations, sometimes called lifeboat stations, whose head surfman was also called "keeper," guarded the coast that now makes up the Cape Lookout National Seashore. Portsmouth Life-Saving Station, built in 1894, sat on the northeast end of the island; the Core Banks Life-Saving Station, often called the Atlantic Station, was built in 1896 about halfway between Ocracoke Inlet and Cape Lookout; and the Cape Lookout Life-Saving Station, built in 1888, was located about one and a half miles southwest of the lighthouse. Dozens of rescues took place at the three stations, but one of the most memorable took place at the Cape Lookout Life-Saving Station in 1905.

With Atlantic waters around 45 degrees Fahrenheit in February, hypothermia was one of lifesaving surfmen's greatest foes. A human body loses heat in water about twenty-five times faster than in air, and cramps,

When a shipwreck was spotted, surfmen with the U.S. Life-Saving Service tried to save every person they could reach. As shared by historian James Charlet, there was one event near Creed's Hill Life-Saving Station during which Keeper Patrick Etheridge gave the command to launch the lifeboat. One of his men protested that they would never make it back. Etheridge retorted, "The Blue Book says we've got to go out and it doesn't say a damn thing about having to come back." Surfmen's efforts were not to cease until all attempts at rescue had been made. *Photograph courtesy of the David Stick Collection, Outer Banks History Center.*

coupled with exhaustion, are ready companions in a cold sea; muscles stop working, and sleep overtakes the victim. This would make any rescue difficult enough, but making the situation even more difficult were the facts that the Cape Lookout lifesaving crewmen were suffering from influenza at the time, and they had to row several miles in three and a half hours in cold, heavy seas to reach the three-masted schooner *Sarah D. J. Rawson* caught on Cape Lookout Shoals. In addition, mountainous waves were pounding the foundered ship to pieces, and the lifesaving crew and their surfboat faced the risk of being hit by the *Rawson*'s now-buoyant cargo: tons of raw timber en route from South Carolina to New York. Under these seemingly impossible circumstances, the crew put their surfboat into the water and defiantly pushed their way to the imperiled sailors.

Lifesaving station keeper William H. Gaskill and his eight crewmen who manned the oars of their surfboat anchored near the wreck the best they could. These men, most of whom had fallen ill, had to wait more than twenty-one hours for the tide, wind, and waves to become more favorable in order for them to execute a rescue during daylight. During those long hours, they could not sleep for fear of hypothermia, and they had no food—all they had were their oil coats, which they later gave to the freezing and exhausted men they saved. They didn't return to the safety and warmth of their station until late the following afternoon.

The Cape Lookout Life-Saving Station crewmembers who participated in the station's most famous rescue were Keeper William H. Gaskill, Kilby Guthrie, Walter M. Yeomans, Tyre Moore, John A. Guthrie, James W.

Fulcher, John E. Kirkman, Calupt T. Jarvis, and Joseph L. Lewis. On April 12, 1905, each surfman received the prestigious Gold Lifesaving Medal for outstanding bravery in rescuing six of the seven crew members from the wrecked *Sarah D. J. Rawson*. Sadly, one member of the crew had been washed overboard and swallowed by the high sea immediately after striking the shoals and before rescuers reached the ship.

No honor can be too great for the selfless men who worked for the U.S. Life-Saving Service. Today, members of the USCG carry on the noble tradition of the lifesaving surfmen by risking their own lives to rescue anyone in danger on America's waters.

On a New Year's Eve, a stormy winter sky serves as a dramatic backdrop for this view of the Cape Lookout Lighthouse across Core Sound.

6

The Third Bodie Island Lighthouse

From the north entrance of the Cape Hatteras National Seashore at Nags Head, Highway 12 ribbons down the barrier island through long stretches of wide, uncluttered, wave-swept beaches to the east, while Roanoke Sound lies to the west. About six miles south, the tall, slender tower of the Bodie Island Lighthouse reaches heavenward. It is one of three lighthouses that have stood guard over this part of the Atlantic Coast, and it represents the overall saga of the U.S. Lighthouse Service and the myriad challenges of illuminating America's shores.

During the 1700s, Bodie Island was a true island, known and pronounced as "Body's Island" in old Lighthouse Service records, but over the next hundred years of storms and other natural changes in the landscape closed the inlets that separated it from the northern beaches of the Outer Banks, turning this stretch of land into a peninsula.

In 1837, 1st Lt. Napoleon L. Coste made an initial survey of the southeastern coast aboard the cutter *Campbell* to recommend new lighthouse sites. He started on the Florida coast and worked his way along Georgia and South Carolina, noting where he recommended new lights to be built: "Bodie Island is the next place, and one of great importance. More vessels are lost there than on any other part of our coast. . . . It is my opinion, that, by the erections of a light-house on it, much property would be saved, and navigation of the coast facilitated." More requests for a lighthouse came from Capt. Charles Skinner and then U.S. Navy lieutenant G. N. Hollins late in 1838. Their pleas were heard but not acted on for nearly another decade.

That same year, Congress asked the USLHE to build a tower on or near Bodie Island to prevent ships from running up on Diamond Shoals thirty-five miles to the south. These shoals, which extend fifteen miles into the Atlantic, form one of the most dangerous obstacles for clear passage on the East Coast. The son of the last Bodie Island Lighthouse principal keeper, John Gaskill, who grew up at the lighthouse, points out that guiding a sailing ship is not like steering a car—it takes a considerable amount of time

Former North Carolina state senator Marc Basnight requested a boardwalk and viewing stand at the Bodie Island Light Station. They provide visitors an opportunity to see the entire light station from a distance but close enough to appreciate the details. Occasionally, at high tide, a reflection appears in a nearby estuarine area brimming with wildlife that serves as a protective barrier between the lighthouse and the Atlantic Ocean.

Name Game

Numerous variations of the Bodie Island Light Station's name appear in documents from the NPS, USCG, and records of the Geographic Naming Board dating back to 1838. In addition, variations of the name, including Body, Bodie, Boddie, and Boddy might appear within a single nineteenth-century document found in Record Group 26 at the National Archives, a vast group of documents dedicated to the U.S. Lighthouse Service. Obviously there was much confusion regarding the actual spelling of the name. So which is it? The final answer: Bodie Island, pronounced "body," and here are the facts.

In 1891 the Geographic Naming Board canvassed knowledgeable people about the origin of the name "Body" to determine a final name that was based on fact, not hearsay. The spelling of "Body's Island," which appears on the marble plaque inside the lighthouse, came from island residents' pronunciation of the owner's name. Nathan Boddie, an English clergyman from Essex County, England, settled in the area sometime in the 1740s or 1750s. As was accepted at the time, branches of the family altered their name to "Bodie" after they moved farther south, and it appeared with this spelling for generations.

When Professor Mason of the Smithsonian Institute was consulted about which spelling to accept, he decided to weigh an explanation from a family descendent, Congressman N. W. Boddie of North Carolina. "Bodie Island" was the final decision because it not only agreed with the opinion of a descendant of Nathan Boddie but also removed the association with unpleasant image of "bodies washed ashore." While this decision cleared up the spelling, it created confusion about the pronunciation. The consensus is to pronounce it "body" but spell it "Bodie," since its orthography is from a family name, not a human corpse.

to change sails and gain a good wind from the right direction to make needed steering adjustments. It took planning and maneuvering to turn a sailing ship running close to shore at Bodie Island farther out to sea. Even so, once northbound ships passed the Cape Hatteras Lighthouse, captains needed a light at Bodie Island to help them keep a safe bearing well off the coast and out of the opposite-flowing cold current—or else risk disaster.

Skillfully assembled sailing ships with their massive timbers were no match for the power of storms. Too often, ships ran upon shoals and were destroyed by merciless waves. Pictured is the wreck of the schooner *Laura A. Barnes* (lost 1921) at Coquina Beach near Bodie Island.

Fifth Auditor Stephen Pleasonton wrote Collector of Customs Thomas H. Blount at his office in Washington, North Carolina, that the "Lighthouse Act passed by Congress July 7, 1837, appropriated $5,000 for the Boddy's Island light" including $100 to purchase four acres of land. USLHE officials were assigned the job of purchasing land for the lighthouse, but it proved surprisingly difficult to find a site with a clear property deed on a sparsely populated island during the mid-nineteenth century. Years went by and these plans only collected dust; however, historical documents indicate that after five years had passed and Blount had not been able to procure a deed, he again wrote Congress. This time, he represented growing public concerns about the number of ships and amount of cargo being lost in the vicinity of Bodie Island: "There is no part of the Coast of the U.S. which requires a Light House more than Body's Island—'tis in the direct route of all going North or South & of all foreign vessels bound into the Chesapeake, & when there during the last summer, there were fifteen wrecks in sight at one place, & within the last month, a Brig bound into Norfolk was wrecked there worth more than would have built the light house."

Ongoing problems with obtaining the land and getting the building materials to the construction site delayed completion of the first lighthouse for nearly ten years. The lighthouse was finished in late 1847, and, according to a letter to Pleasonton from Collector of Customs James K.

Hatton, its light was activated as early as January 22, 1848, but certainly by March 13, the date of Hatton's letter. It stood on the south bank of Oregon Inlet, which a hurricane had opened just a year earlier and separated Bodie Island on the north side of the inlet from Pea Island on the south side. Francis A. Gibbons oversaw the construction of the 54-foot tower that housed fourteen whale-oil-fueled Argand lamps and 21-inch silver reflectors.

Unforeseen problems, however, literally undermined the lighthouse from the first day of construction. In the name of economy, lighthouse officials did not adequately investigate the composition of the soil at the site to determine if it was stable enough to support a tower, and the building plans neglected to anticipate a heavy foundation on soft ground. Years earlier, even the parsimonious Pleasonton admitted that to build a light tall enough with a revolving light would require a total of at least $12,000 — but $5,000 would have to do. Blount was unfamiliar with lighthouse construction and ignored Gibbons's recommendation for a sturdy base. Without a solid foundation, the lighthouse kept leaning more and more until the revolving chandelier of lamps was thrown out of sync and rendered useless. Making matters worse, swift erosion of Oregon Inlet's shoreline undercut the tower's tentative footing, which forced the Lighthouse Board to abandon the first Bodie Island Lighthouse in 1858, leaving more than 100 miles of coast between Cape Henry, Virginia, and Cape Hatteras, North Carolina, in total darkness. Mariners plying these waters were at the mercy of a compass and charts that were woefully inaccurate due to the ever-changing shoals along the Outer Banks.

THE SECOND BODIE ISLAND LIGHTHOUSE

By 1858, the Lighthouse Board recognized the need to replace the old tower and completed a second lighthouse on Bodie Island, this time on the north side of Oregon Inlet. Keeping its promise to build only the finest structures in its quest to make American lights the best in the world, the lighthouse officials ordered topographical engineer Lorenzo Sitgreaves to oversee design and construction of this tower. Sitgreaves spent the 1850s mapping the western territory through Arizona and executing delayed lighthouse contracts on Lake Superior. The board instructed him to use the highest-quality materials available, including a stone foundation on seventy piles driven into the earth. They also charged him to order 300,000 bricks and to fit the iron lantern room with a third-order Fresnel lens, an anomaly for this coastal position because, beginning in 1852, the board made it standard to fit tall coastal lights with first-order lenses. The largest order used in the continental United States, it had the capacity to cast a light 19 nautical miles seaward. In a letter dated October 1, 1858, to district headquarters, Sitgreaves wrote that he had repaired the old keeper's house and would reuse the facility. He also stated that there would be a newly constructed second house for an assistant keeper.

Plans for this lighthouse are housed in the National Archives; official U.S. Lighthouse Service Light Lists state that its height to the focal plane was 83 feet and its height above sea level measured 90 feet. Sitgreaves wrote the fifth district superintendent at Baltimore headquarters on July 19, 1858, that his estimate for a new tower (with some excess built in) was $19,525.19. Weather and lost supplies delayed construction, but when it was completed and activated on July 1, 1859, it was regarded as a fine structure. Sitgreaves only had to pull down the failed 1847 tower to complete the project. The final cost of the light station project is recorded as $22,000 in the National Archives.

Soon after completion, the Civil War began, and the new tower became a prize both sides sought. It never saw its third birthday. It was destroyed by Confederates in an attempt to keep it from being an advantage to Union troops, and once again, darkness embraced this stretch of perilous coast. (For more information about the second Bodie Island Lighthouse during the Civil War, see chapter 7.) After the war ended, in an effort to stabilize the nation's economy and help revive maritime trade, Congress began repairing and rebuilding lighthouses across the coast.

The short-lived second Bodie Island Lighthouse was built during the golden era of lighthouse construction during the 1850s. A hallmark of this era was double-wall brick construction, which yielded superior towers at lower costs. This new building model called for space to be left between two conical brick walls, which meant that fewer bricks were needed. It also provided a stronger structure, a necessity when a 150-foot-tall tower had to support a six-ton lens.

THIRD TIME'S A CHARM

Federal funds provided $150 for a new fifteen-acre site north of Oregon Inlet, purchased from John B. Etheridge. Completed in 1872, the third

The Third Bodie Island Lighthouse: Timeline

1837 Lt. Napoleon Coste, commander of Revenue Cutter *Campbell*, explores coast south of the Chesapeake; calls for new light on or near Bodie Island or Pea Island. $5,000 appropriated initially and later increased.

1838 Congress asks for light in same area as also recommended by U.S. Navy lieutenant G. N. Hollins.

1846 Hurricane opens Oregon Inlet, splitting Bodie Island into two parts.

1847 March 3, First Bodie Island Lighthouse authorized by act of Congress and $12,000 appropriated; exact lighting date thought to be spring 1848.

1854 U.S. Lighthouse Board installs fourth-order Fresnel lens; tower at least one foot out of plumb; revolving lens malfunctions.

1858 First Bodie Island Lighthouse abandoned; Congress appropriates $25,000 for new tower; completed 1859, with third-order Fresnel lens and height at sea level 90 feet.

1861 Retreating Confederates remove Fresnel lens and later destroy tower.

1871 June 13, fifteen acres purchased from John B. Etheridge and wife for $150 to replace destroyed lighthouse; work begins in November.

1872 October 1, new lighthouse shows fixed white light; October 19, duplex keepers' house completed; wire screen installed to protect lantern glass from geese hitting lantern.

1873 Lighthouse painted with black and white horizontal bands.

1874 Third assistant keeper's job, held temporarily by keeper's wife, eliminated.

1877 Lightning strikes tower, causing minor vertical cracks; keeper on stairs feels jolt that temporarily numbs lower half of his body.

1878 Bodie Island Life-Saving Station built one mile north of lighthouse; Pea Island Life-Saving Station (historic, African-descent crew) completed on south end of Pea Island (for more information, see www.peaislandpreservationsociety.com/projects).

1895 Oil removed from storage room at bottom of tower and stored in sheet-metal oil house for safety.

1897 2,200 square feet of new wooden walks put down; 360 square feet of old walks replaced.

1898 Telephone installed connecting lighthouse and lifesaving stations.

1900 With three keepers living in the 1873 house, repeated requests for second keeper's quarters submitted to the Lighthouse Board over five years; never granted because no contractor answered bid for $7,500.

1912 Incandescent oil-vapor lamp installed, increases candlepower more than five times.

1920s "Call bell" installed in keepers' quarters to notify if lamp malfunctions.

1922 Second assistant keeper position eliminated; salaries of remaining two keepers increased.

1932 Generator-charged banks of batteries installed; powered flash controller turns electric light bulb on/off.

1939 President Franklin Delano Roosevelt assigns USCG to assume lighthouse responsibilities.

1940 Keeper Vernon Gaskill Sr. leaves light station; Keeper Julian Austin Sr. stays to close it down; May 22, lighthouse automated, unmanned, operated by Nags Head Coast Guard.

2000 July 13, lighthouse transferred from USCG to NPS.

2005 April 25, USCG transfers Fresnel lens and lamp operation to NPS.

2006 Studies and restoration funding completed: $100,000 restoration of first-order Fresnel lens that was removed and stored; ironwork and interior brickwork restoration begins; funding to complete tower restoration denied through 2008.

2009 July 11, lighthouse goes dark for duration of two phases of restoration.

2009–10 Omnibus budget bill includes complete restoration of lighthouse; 1879 Bodie Island Life-Saving Station, 1916 boathouse, and 1925 USCG station moved to entrance of lighthouse complex.

2013 April 18, relighting ceremony held; tower opened for climbing in spring; Outer Banks Lighthouse Society hosts reunion for keepers' descendants, introducing its book on keepers.

U.S. Lighthouse Board engineer Herbert Bamber visited the Bodie Island Light Station in 1893 and photographed Principal Keeper Peter Gregory Gallop with his assistant keepers—John Shannon is the only one identified to date. Keepers did not live in the lighthouse; it was strictly a workplace. *Photograph from the personal collection of John Havel.*

Bodie Island Lighthouse soars a little over 167 feet into the sky. William Fuller Hatsel served as its first principal keeper from 1872 until 1878. His wife, Rebecca, briefly filled in as third assistant during 1874, after which this position was eliminated. That same year, Keeper Hatsel was visited by Nathaniel H. Bishop, a naturalist who traveled the East Coast and kept a diary, later published as *Voyage of the Paper Canoe*, that includes entries about visiting Bodie Island. Bishop wrote,

In this circa 1950s photograph, the Bodie Island Lighthouse and keepers' quarters sit in the midst of vast coastal land protected within the Cape Hatteras National Seashore. Heeding two previous lessons about building too close to potentially erosion-prone areas, builders constructed this tower about one mile north of Oregon Inlet. The light station remains effectively untouched by twenty-first-century intrusions.

Nag's Head Beach is a most desolate locality, with its high sand-hills, composed of fine sand, the forms of which are constantly changing with the action of the dry, hard, varying winds. A few fishermen have their homes on this dreary beach, but the village, with its one store, is a forlorn place. The bright flashes of Body Island Light, ten miles distant, on the north side of Oregon Inlet, showed me my next abiding-place. Captain William F. Hatsel, a loyal North Carolinian, is the principal keeper, and a most efficient one he is.

Bishop went on to explain that he was shivering with cold when he beached his canoe and approached the lighthouse. The keeper and his wife warmly welcomed him and offered him fine hospitality, as was expected of keepers when anyone was in need.

People who visit Bodie Island Lighthouse today often question the location, as it appears to be set back far from the ocean. Some of them even think that it has been moved. In reality, the first two towers stood on opposite sides of the location of Oregon Inlet at the time, and both sites are now underwater, swallowed by the southerly migration of the inlet—this change in the coastal geography taught the members of the Lighthouse Board a harsh lesson about the dynamic nature of barrier islands. They wisely chose to erect the third tower away from the eroding inlet, halfway between the ocean and sound, and it continues to serve mariners on both.

History shows that there had been no greater proponent for a third Bodie Island light than fifth district engineer W. J. Newman. He wrote the board several times during 1861–67 with urgent emphasis in his annual report that the light must be replaced. As a result, lighthouse engineer J. H. Simpson wrote the chairman of the Lighthouse Board the following during October and November 1870:

> In regard to the site of the old Light House at Bodys Island, I have to report that as the island is rapidly wearing away to the west and northwest of the site, and the shore having already encroached to within 1200 to 1500 feet, I consider the site unsafe for the location of the new light house. A much better location is on Nags Island on the north side of the inlet, about two miles in a north 36 [degrees] west location from the old site, and about a mile in the same direction from said inlet. As the Nags Head Island is making at its southern extremity, and the proposed site would be removed from the Atlantic shore about three quarters of a mile, I consider this the safest spot for the light house, and accordingly recommend that I be ordered to purchase say ten acres for the purpose.

The Lighthouse Board had considered building the third Bodie Island Lighthouse at Paul Gamiel's Hill (now called Gamiels Hill) near Kitty Hawk, about fifteen miles to the north. However, since the board had already planned to build a light at Currituck Beach, they chose to adhere to their goal of building lighthouses approximately forty miles apart. Correspondence to the board and members of Congress about the number of lives and amount of cargo lost in this area supported the decision to build the lighthouse on Bodie Island. Keepers' children remembered their fathers

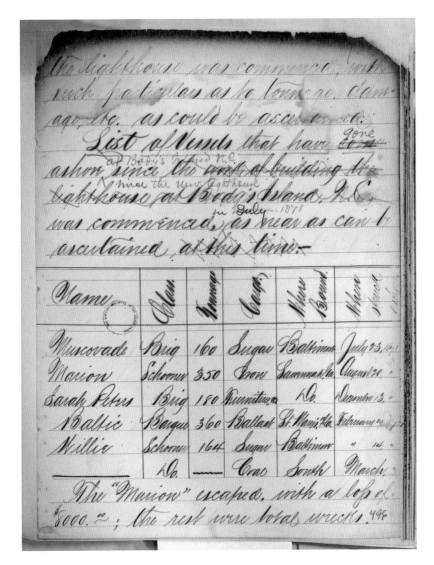

The lighthouse was commenced, with such particulars as to tonnage, damage, &c. as could be ascertained:

List of Vessels that have gone to ashore since the work of building the lighthouse at Body's Island, N.C. since the new lighthouse was commenced, in July 1871, as near as can be ascertained, at this time.—

Name	Class	Tonnage	Cargo	Where Bound	Where from
Muscovade	Brig	160	Sugar	Baltimore	July 23,
Marion	Schooner	350	Iron	Savannah, Ga.	August 20
Sarah Peters	Brig	180	Furniture	Do.	December 13
Baltic	Barque	360	Ballast	St. Marys, Fla.	February
Willie	Schooner	164	Sugar	Baltimore	" 14 "
Do.	—	Crao	South	March

The "Marion" escaped, with a loss of $5000.—; the rest were total wrecks.

In an effort to convince Congress to fund a third lighthouse at Bodie Island, a letter was written to document a "List of Vessels that have gone ashore at Body's Island, N.C. since the new lighthouse was commenced in July 1871, as near as can be ascertained at this time." The value of these lost ships and their cargoes and passengers more than outweighed construction expense. *From the author's collection.*

telling them about five ships that wrecked during the fifteen months it took to build the lighthouse, and the Lighthouse Service *1872 Annual Report* listed six ships lost here: the *Muscavado, Marion, Sarah Peters, Baltic, Willie,* and a sixth unidentified vessel. Board officials made the point that, for the value of cargo lost, estimated at $133,000, the expense of the lighthouse construction, about $140,000, would "pay for itself."

The surviving third Bodie Island Lighthouse serves as a distinct example of the fine workmanship that went into building a standard, tall

Bodie Island Lighthouse

LOCATION 4 miles north of Oregon Inlet

NEAREST TOWN Nags Head, N.C.

COMPLETED 1872

TOWER HEIGHT By laser measure
in 2004, overall height from
ground plane to top of the lighting
rod is 167 feet, 8.05 inches, but
generally stated as 167 feet

ELEVATION OF FOCAL PLANE
ABOVE SEA LEVEL 150 feet

STEPS TO LANTERN ROOM 214

BUILDING MATERIALS
Double-wall brick construction, cast-
iron stairs and lantern, granite plinths,
marble interior entryway floors

DESIGN/PAINT SCHEME Two black
and three white horizontal bands

OPTIC First-order Fresnel lens; range
of visibility, 19 nautical miles

FLASH CHARACTERISTIC 2.5 seconds on,
2.5 seconds off, 2.5 seconds on, 22.5
seconds eclipse for 2 cycles per minute

STATUS Active aid to navigation

ACCESS Open to the public seasonally

OWNER/MANAGER Beacon operated by
U.S. Coast Guard; National Park Service
owns property and the Fresnel lens

FOR MORE INFORMATION
Cape Hatteras National Seashore
1401 National Park Drive
Manteo, N.C. 27954
(252) 475-9000
www.nps.gov/caha
/planyourvisit/index.htm

coastal lighthouse, which featured a timber and granite substructure, dressed granite accents, marble floors, brick walls, and ornate ironwork. The key people involved in designing and constructing this enduring tower included Maj. George Elliot, Lighthouse Board engineering secretary and architect, and Peter C. Hains, West Point Army Corps of Engineers captain, who became the fifth district lighthouse engineer, with duties ranging from site selection to use of artesian well pipes for sinking foundation supports; and Superintendent of Construction Dexter Stetson, who had successfully completed Cape Hatteras Lighthouse a short time before.

The serene beauty of this historic lighthouse belies the tremendous efforts expended in its creation. Just getting the materials to the remote site was a struggle. In keeping with the Lighthouse Board's desire to use recycled and repurposed materials, Stetson broke down the workhouses at Cape Hatteras in June 1871 and moved these and leftover bricks to an area that became known as Stetson's Channel on the sound side of Bodie Island near the lighthouse site. New construction materials had to be delivered by way of Roanoke Sound, as no landing access existed on the ocean side of the site. The route was also too rough to chance losing materials, which had happened when the Cape Hatteras Lighthouse was being built. A good portion of the deliveries were made by the lighthouse tender *Tulip*.

Initially, Lighthouse Board officials specified that only cut stone be used for the foundation, but after weeks of delay they reluctantly accepted rubble stone to partially fill it. Heavily laden schooners sailing out of Baltimore could not negotiate the shallows in Roanoke Sound, delaying construction another six months. While he waited for the schooners, Stetson used recycled materials from

the Cape Hatteras Lighthouse construction site to build a 12-foot-by-12-foot pier for offloading materials. McClenahan & Brothers, who held a contract for the foundation granite, provided a derrick. Nicholas M. Smith and Andrews & Johnson of Baltimore held contracts for brick and dressed granite, respectively. Paulding, Kemble & Company, of West Point Foundry in New York, supplied the ironwork. Phoenix Iron Company in Philadelphia produced the iron beams that secure the iron landings to the brick tower and shipped them to Baltimore, for which the board paid cash. Moving this voluminous amount of materials on land required building a tram for horse-pulled cars and hiring laborers to haul stone, bricks, and pieces of iron from the tram to the building site. The constant threat of mosquito-borne illnesses dogged Stetson and the building crew, causing further delays.

Stetson constructed the Bodie Island Lighthouse foundation the same way he had successfully constructed the one for the Cape Hatteras Lighthouse. In *A History of the Bodie Island Light Station*, NPS historian F. Ross Holland Jr. detailed how Stetson built the tower's underpinning:

> The construction crew dug a pit seven feet deep, and during
> construction they kept it pumped dry of water. At the bottom of
> the pit they placed a wood grillage of six-inch by twelve-inch timber
> laid in two courses, one at right angles to the other. Decay posed

Nature improved an existing masterpiece at the Bodie Island Light Station with a soft dusting of snow during an exceptional Outer Banks winter storm.

These cast-iron stairs were built and installed in sections as they corkscrewed up the Bodie Island Lighthouse's inner wall. Keepers climbed these stairs each day to carry out their maintenance work and stand watch at the top of the tower.

The Lighthouse Board included architectural details that gave lighthouses a striking appearance. The Stick-style architecture during the late nineteenth century was seen often in lighthouses and lifesaving stations. "1871" over the entryway documents the year of the site's establishment.

no problem since the wood was to rest in at least four feet of [fresh] water. The builders then laid large granite blocks, eighteen inches thick, on the grillage. On top of that they laid courses of rubble block weighing one to five tons, so as to raise the foundation an additional five feet. Each course of stone was grouted with hydraulic Portland cement. On this foundation the builders placed the base of the tower

The first-order
Fresnel lens at
Bodie Island is a
splendid bee-hive-
shaped masterpiece
of crown glass
by Barbier and
Fenestre of Paris,
France. It was
installed in 1872,
and its wick lamp
was lighted on
October 1, 1872.
Public outcry kept
this lens from being
removed in the
name of economy,
and it was officially
transferred from
the USCG to the
National Park
Service in 2005.

Up to three keepers
had to share living
quarters in what
was designed as
accommodations
for two, which
made family visits
rare until the 1920s,
when the second
assistant keeper's
position was ended.
Keepers' children
who lived at this
light station claim
that the "front"
of the house
faces the tower to
allow keepers to
watch the light's
performance from
there if necessary.

which was cut granite on the outside and rubble set [in] cement on the inside.

When the light was finally exhibited on October 1, 1872, North Carolina had added another pearl to its string of classic lighthouses. In 1873, the board ordered that the tower be painted with black and white bands, each one about 22 feet in width, to serve as a clear daymark for mariners.

For unknown reasons, other than a tight economy in 1872, only one keeper's house was built for three keepers, an assistant, and their families. Requests for another house went unanswered for years, because no contractor made a bid to match the $7,500 appropriation due to rising costs of construction. The house had two sides that mirrored each other. Before the NPS took over the property, each half had its own entrance and stairway to the second floor. Downstairs, each side housed a kitchen, as well as an office and sitting area where the principal keeper had a desk and a living room. The upstairs sported two bedrooms and a small area for a bathroom, although it was never used for such while keepers staffed the station, until 1939–40. Each keeper's bedroom faced the lighthouse so he could keep an eye on the light, even while at home.

After more than 145 years of service, the Bodie Island Lighthouse, like hundreds of other American lighthouses, needs continuous restoration. While global satellite positioning has taken over these watchful giants' duties, local, state, and federal entities, as well as nonprofit groups, have become their caretakers. Restoration requires experienced contractors and

Photographer Drew C. Wilson recalled capturing this image: "While driving Highway 12 one evening, I passed that open spot where the Bodie Island Lighthouse can be viewed across the marsh. I saw a doe come out from the wax myrtles. Knowing the behavior of a buck to typically wait for a doe to see if the coast is clear, I figured there might be a buck behind her. I stopped the car and took up a position in the ditch on the opposite side the road, lying there for about fifteen minutes before my hunch proved right. This big buck gradually came out and into view."

Being the tallest in a crowd can be a good thing when it comes to having a great view of sound and sea and showing off a guiding beacon. Then again, height tends to draw the attention of lightning. In this photograph, a dramatic strike over Bodie Island Lighthouse is captured. *Photograph by Mark Riddick of Ice Cube Photo.*

enough funding to cover large expenses, but the rewards are tremendous. The NPS is striving to keep the light in Bodie Island Lighthouse shining and allow visitors to climb the stairs and see the beautiful panoramic view from the top. A two-phase restoration project that renewed both its interior and exterior began during 2009 and was finished in 2013. (For more information on this restoration project, see chapter 11.) The lantern room houses one of the few original, active first-order Fresnel lenses, and the

Originally, this light station's name was spelled "Body's," based on the name of the family that originally owned the land on which it rests. It has been determined that the family's name was "Boddie," which was shortened to "Bodie" by a descendant. The marble plaque, which has survived intact, cites the light station's name, its date of completion, and its latitude/ longitude as measured in 1872.

duplex keepers' quarters feature a bookstore on the south side and an exhibit area on the north.

In 2009, the NPS moved the 1878 Bodie Island Life-Saving Station, originally called "Tommy's Hummock," the 1916 boathouse, and the 1925 Bodie Island Coast Guard Station from the edge of the ocean to the entrance of the light station. These three historic buildings, along with the lighthouse, keepers' quarters, and outlying buildings, make up a picturesque light station, surrounded by wildlife hidden amidst the trees, marsh, and pond grasses.

The Third Bodie Island Lighthouse

Bodie Island and the Wright Brothers Memorial

The exact length of Bodie Island has long been argued. Technically, Bodie Island runs from Oregon Inlet on the south all the way to Virginia to the north, currently with no body of water breaking the contiguous land. Therefore, it includes the Wright Brothers Memorial at Kill Devil Hills, as well as the Currituck Beach Light Station.

Built in 1932 as a tribute to Wilbur and Orville Wright, the pioneers of powered flight, the Wright Brothers Memorial features a soaring sixty-foot-tall granite monument topped with a beacon that serves as a lighthouse for airplanes as well as vessels on the Atlantic Ocean and in Albemarle Sound. The Bureau of Lighthouses Airways Division originally controlled the beacon. This little-known division of the Department of Commerce's Aeronautics Branch began in 1927, when more than 200 aids to navigation were discontinued due to the advent of radio navigation. Proportionately, the number of new aids to aviation tripled, all under the jurisdiction of the same civilian-staffed Bureau of Lighthouses.

After the Bureau of Lighthouses extinguished the guiding flashes of light from lighthouses, pilots lost several of the landmarks they had used for years to navigate. During the early days of airmail between 1919 and 1926, thirty-one of forty pilots died not only because airplanes were not very dependable but also because pilots had only a few inland markers to follow. Many used telephone lines because nothing else existed.

Eventually, Fresnel lenses removed from lighthouses were repurposed as airway beacons, some in the shape of searchlights made from bull's-eye panels, and others cut in half lengthwise and laid flat on top of a light to shine a focused, vertical shaft of light, creating a connect-the-dot pathway. Mechanisms on these beacons flashed Morse code to identify each light, just as timed revolutions or fixed lights established the identity of lighthouses. Such place-names as Topeka (Kansas), Salt Lake City (Utah), and Cheyenne (Wyoming) soon appeared in Lighthouse Service annual reports along with the usual names of familiar light stations.

A 1988 restoration of both the interior and exterior of the Wright Brothers Memorial allowed the light to be reactivated, so it shines once again. The light's panels, which are definitely of Fresnel design, conceivably may be surplus Fresnel panels.

Sightseers may walk the grounds at any time and take the easy trek along the Bodie Island Dike trail, adjacent to the lighthouse property, or the walkway to an observation deck over a marshland area. Four granite stones mark the original boundary of the fifteen-acre site—it is a rarity at any light station for all four to be extant and in situ. Some of the estuarine area, once managed by the Bodie Island Hunt Club, was dammed and now forms a freshwater pond, a pristine area that supports a diverse abundance of animals and birds. Sunrise and sunset create chameleon-like skies as the sun casts brilliant firelight hues on the clouds, trees, and water at Bodie Island.

But there are times when being the tallest thing for miles can cause problems. Clouds rushing overhead create static, and a tall tower like Bodie Island Lighthouse is a convenient contact point. In 1877, lightning struck the lighthouse and caused vertical cracks to form along the interior, which are still visible. Not a great deal was known about ways to divert the electrical shock, and one of the keepers was on the stairs and took a jolt that temporarily numbed the lower half of his body.

Memories of Bodie Island Lighthouse
Keepers' Families

By the turn of the twentieth century, only two keepers were on duty at the Bodie Island Lighthouse, but it still made for crowded conditions when both keepers and their families were in residence. John Gaskill, son of Keeper Vernon Gaskill Sr., recalled, "We shared the quarters with no arguments. As much as possible, one keeper and his family stood duty while the other family returned home for a while after a generator was used to charge banks of batteries that powered the light. And when we were at the lighthouse, we could use the other side of the house for visiting family or whatever. We got along just fine."

"When I think of Bodie Island, I think of home and a safe feeling," reminisced Marilyn Austin Meads, daughter of Keeper Julian Austin Sr. "I had to learn to cook from the time I could reach the iron stove because Momma was in the hospital for years. I remember Daddy carrying a big bucket of coal for the warming stove and a five-gallon brass can of kerosene up those stairs with him nearly every night he was on duty. I was happy as long as I was with him." Marilyn's older brother, Julian Jr., had to keep the wood box next to the cook stove well stocked and made sure little sister was cared for while their father tended the light. During the time that their mother, Katherine Austin, was hospitalized, Grandma Dobbs took care of the youngest child, Verna.

It was a happy day in 1937 when their mother and Verna returned to be with the family at the lighthouse permanently. "To

Lighthouse keepers were expected to greet visitors warmly and allow them to view the light station. Keeper Julian Austin Sr. was fortunate to have an enthusiastic tour guide in his daughter, Marilyn, who was always eager to earn a quarter for a rare trip to a movie in Manteo. *Photograph courtesy of Marilyn (Austin) Meads, circa 1937.*

celebrate the occasion, Mr. Gaskill provided us with a pheasant for our Christmas dinner," Marilyn said softly. "Julian and I still talk and laugh about things we did together as kids. We loved to go down to the beach and watch the fishermen haul in their long nets. Daddy helped out some, and they gave him all the fish he wanted. Sometimes he put them in a big wooden barrel with salt. When we wanted to eat some, we'd soak the fish, and then fry them."

A keeper's family ran a marathon to keep up with maintenance at a lighthouse. Every bit of rust, tarnish, peeled paint, and broken parts of the light station had to be repaired or replaced, and the children had to pitch in to help. Both of the Bodie Island keepers' boys helped with the incandescent oil-vapor lamp by extinguishing it just after sunrise and drawing the curtains to protect the Fresnel lens from the harsh sunlight. John and Julian Jr. both stated that, in addition to lighthouse duty and other chores, their fathers expected them to keep the grass cut around the tower and the keepers' quarters. Touring the light station one summer's day at age ninety, John gestured with a wide sweep of his arm and emphasized, "It was one of those push mowers, and that was a *lot* of grass out there."

A rare circa 1911 artifact, Bodie Island lighthouse keeper Christopher Columbus "Lum" Midgett's hat displays the U.S. Lighthouse Service logo. A keeper's first uniform was supplied by the government; afterward, it became the keeper's responsibility. *Keeper's hat courtesy of the personal collection of Marion Midgett.*

Living at Bodie Island even in the 1920s and 1930s was a pioneer's way of life. Water provided the only route to travel among the islands, and the first automobile did not appear until the late 1920s. A bridge finally linked Bodie Island to Roanoke Island in 1928, making it possible for the Austin and Gaskill children to attend school in Manteo. Until that time, only a few fishing shanties and the Bodie Island Life-Saving Station stood on the beach side of the island. Cisterns held rainwater, the only source

The Third Bodie Island Lighthouse

U.S. Lighthouse Board engineer Herbert Bamber captured an 1893 view of the entire Bodie Island Light Station. At far left is a shed that once housed ingredients to mix paint and related equipment; at center are the double keepers' quarters and lighthouse; at right are the same type of ancillary buildings that once were integral parts of the light station. *Photograph from the personal collection of John Havel.*

of freshwater, and families used an outside hand pump as well as one at the kitchen sink to draw water for cooking, baths, and washing dishes and clothes. Outside "privies" served as bathrooms, but the keepers and their families kept hoping to get indoor plumbing. During the 1930s, Keeper Gaskill thought he had finally gotten his wish when the Lighthouse Service installed a bathtub and plumbing to pump water. Keeper Austin's children, upstairs on the other side of the house, remember the first day Keeper Gaskill prepared to lounge in his beloved bath—they heard him let out a loud yelp. There was no way to pipe hot water upstairs—or anywhere else in the house—and the chilly water doused the hope of soothing baths. From then on, Gaskill's daughter, Erline, used the bathroom as a playroom, while on the other side of the house, Austin's son, Julian Jr., slept peacefully in their bathtub for several years.

7   North Carolina Lighthouses, 1861–1865

While peacefully walking along the edge of the Atlantic Ocean and listening to nature's rhythms in endless waves embracing the shore, it can be difficult to imagine that soldiers once walked these same sandy paths and that the sounds of rifle fire and cannon shot once echoed across the dunes of Ocracoke, Hatteras, Bodie, and Roanoke Islands and beyond to the banks along the Cape Fear River. War has walked these beaches, and fear has stalked these sandbanks.

Yet by the time leaders of the southern states held a constitutional convention in February 1861 to form the Confederate States of America (CSA), the general consensus among the southern states threatening "disunion" at that time was that the secession would be peaceful—that the North would not defend the Union—similar to gentlemen agreeing to disagree. Further, the sentiment of succession had already been in the air since roughly 1850—many felt that these were states' rights issues that certainly could be worked out by level-headed representatives through compromise, and the South believed that the federal government would not threaten the South's agrarian economy by abolishing slavery. By the time Confederate forces bombarded and captured Fort Sumter in South Carolina on April 12 and 13, 1861, it was becoming clear that what was coming would be a major event in American history.

The Confederate victory at Fort Sumter was akin to a cataclysmic earthquake that split the country in half. The tsunami of deaths that followed surprised both sides, neither of which had believed that hostilities would endure. In the turmoil of the Civil War, lighthouses and their Fresnel lenses counted among the first victims. The same lighthouses that people of North Carolina had begged their authorities to build, even before being granted statehood, were destroyed or damaged during the war. No other event has had more effect on southern lights than this manmade conflict.

While the North had extensive railroad systems, the South had elaborate, interconnecting waterways, and the Confederates needed to keep

goods, especially cotton, moving so the southern economy would not be disrupted. Many southern leaders believed that continuing to export cotton to Great Britain and other countries would be the salvation of the Confederacy—these countries depended on cotton for their lucrative textile businesses, and if Union forces blockaded southern ports and cut off the supply, they would be willing to intervene to aid the Confederates. To help defend and protect coastal, sound, and river lights in the South, Confederate President Jefferson Davis formed a Confederate States Lighthouse Bureau within the CSA Treasury Department in March 1861, and Secretary of the Treasury Christopher Memminger directed projects related to southern lights and lighthouses. In the coming months, Confederate forces seized lighthouses, forts, and other federal properties, setting the stage for a fierce struggle to control the lights across the South.

Assuming that southern mariners knew the coastlines well and would have less difficulty than Union mariners sailing in unfamiliar waters, Confederate leaders made a concerted effort to darken all major lights from Virginia to Texas and obstruct inland waterways. The goal was to block the Union navy's efforts to control southern ports every way possible. To effect and expedite this goal, the Confederate States Lighthouse Bureau, run by Raphael Semmes, who had been the former secretary of the Lighthouse Board, and North Carolina Governor John W. Ellis ordered all of the state's coastal lights to be extinguished and remain unlit for the duration of the war; they were following South Carolina's lead.

Confederate leaders also feared these Union troops would seize and destroy valuable Fresnel lenses from Cape Hatteras, Bodie Island, and other lighthouses, as well as lenses from river and sound lights if they

On April 30, 1862, CSA treasury secretary Christopher Memminger, acting on the advice of acting chief of the CSA Lighthouse Bureau, Thomas E. Martin, directed Martin to tell the collectors of customs in each lighthouse district to remove property belonging to the "Light House establishment" to safety. This led to removal of Fresnel lenses by Confederate soldiers across the South, with North Carolina a top priority. In actuality, Confederates had assumed authority and had removed several lenses months earlier. *From the author's collection.*

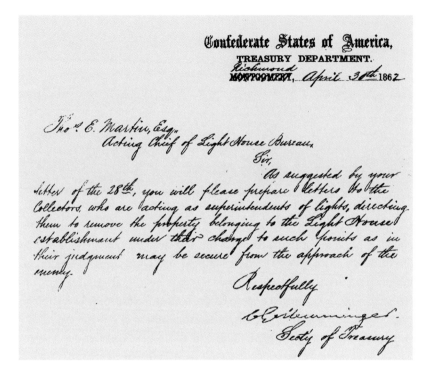

lost control of these areas. As a result, Confederate lighthouse authorities struck first and ordered that the lenses be removed during the first half of 1861 and stored in safe houses. U.S. lighthouse inspectors and engineers had spent decades urging Congress to appropriate funds to buy and install Fresnel lenses in all of America's lights, only to have many of them hidden or damaged.

Confederates had surreptitious plans to destroy the Bodie Island, Cape Hatteras, and Cape Lookout lighthouses to ensure the Union could not take advantage of these coastal lights. However, the CSA wanted to make sure the Fresnel lenses would be safe and made payments to those destroying the lighthouses to ensure the removal and safekeeping of the lenses. Each lighthouse has its own story about the war years.

Dominance of North Carolina's coastal areas was a priority for both the Confederate and the Union governments. Union officials realized that executing a stranglehold on shipping early in the war could be the key to ending hostilities. Initial Union attacks targeted the areas from Cape Hatteras to Cape Fear.

The Hatteras Beacon Light was activated in 1855 to help local fishermen negotiate a shortcut through Diamond Shoals to enter Pamlico Sound. A third assistant keeper living at the Cape Hatteras Light Station tended the light. Situated on the tip of Cape Point, it was vulnerable to storms, causing it to be moved several times. It was discontinued by November 1905. *1893 photo by Herbert Bamber from the author's collection.*

CAPE HATTERAS LIGHTHOUSE

As war came to the Outer Banks in 1861, Confederate leaders recognized that the light at Cape Hatteras was the most needed guide along the coast; however, its light and tower could give Union naval and land forces a strategic advantage. By June 1861 and by order of the governor, Confederates removed the tower's prized first-order Fresnel lens under the skilled supervision of Cape Hatteras keeper Benjamin Fulcher. They carefully packed the crown glass prisms and twelve bull's-eye panels in cotton in forty-four boxes and sequestered the apparatus from Union forces in a town north of Raleigh.

Confederate forces had an opportunity to destroy the tower when Union forces initially were moving northward from Forts Hatteras and Clark to take control of the Outer Banks, but they ultimately let the lighthouse stand. Union troops planned to attack the Confederates on the island and continue their expanded control of the inlets, sounds, and the Cape Hatteras Lighthouse and to drive all southern forces from the island.

HATTERAS BEACON LIGHT

Established in 1855 on Cape Point about one and a half miles south of the Cape Hatteras Light Station, the 25-foot-tall Hatteras Beacon Light marked the turning point from the Atlantic Ocean into Pamlico Sound for local vessels. Confederate forces darkened the tower in 1861, but Union troops near the Cape Hatteras Lighthouse afforded this beacon protection as well. The Lighthouse Board reestablished the light after the war and moved it several times due to ocean overwash. It continued to shine until it was discontinued in late November 1905.

THE INVASION OF HATTERAS ISLAND

Union troops under the command of Maj. Gen. Benjamin Butler first came ashore at Hatteras Inlet on August 28, 1861, to take control of Forts Hatteras and Clark and unload armed troops, turning the Outer Banks into a war zone. Union naval gunboats—part of the Gen. Ambrose Burnside expedition—complemented by troops on the beach under the supervision of Butler swiftly took command of Hatteras Inlet, as well as Ocracoke Inlet and the fortification there.

Maj. Gen. Butler landed troops and fired from gunboats on Forts Hatteras and Clark; it took only until August 30 to ensure the forts' surrender, leaving no Confederates on the island. Both forts were at or near Hatteras Inlet, the only deep-water inlet on the coast at the time, that led to the "great inland sea" of the Pamlico-Albemarle Sounds to ports at New Bern and beyond. Butler wanted and won approval to hold onto these strategically placed fortifications. He left Col. Rush C. Hawkins in charge at Fort Hatteras with authority over the soldiers.

Confederates fled, but some officers who had escaped Fort Hatteras

teamed up with Third Georgia Regiment reinforcement troops already on the way to Hatteras Inlet. They changed course, planted their flag on Roanoke Island, and proceeded to build entrenchments. Fort Ocracoke (aka Fort Morgan or possibly Fort Morris after its designer, Col. Ellwood Morris), the fortification on Beacon Island overlooking Ocracoke Inlet, surrendered. Union forces then controlled all inlets that punctured this part of the coast: Ocracoke, Hatteras, and Oregon Inlets.

Union colonel Hawkins at Fort Hatteras was convinced that the Confederates were fortifying forces and entrenchments on Roanoke Island. In late September, he sent Col. W. L. Brown's Twentieth Indiana Volunteers, about 600 strong, to the northern end of the island by boat. This move would come back to haunt Hawkins. They encamped near Chicamacomico after reaching the island, and soon a complex and often confusing series of skirmishes broke out. The struggle to control the island became known as the Chicamacomico Races. Among retellings of this event, two that clarify an otherwise confusing tangle of details are by Thomas Lee Oxford in *The Civil War on Hatteras: The Chicamacomico Affair and the Capture of the Gunboat Fanny* and John G. Barrett in *The Civil War in North Carolina*. The mix-ups were mainly caused by military rumors from both Union and Confederate sides that made each fear that they were about to be attacked by the other. Union and Confederate maneuvers were also no doubt influenced by the notion that each commander was under the impression that his troops were outnumbered by the enemy at least two to one.

Meanwhile, on Roanoke Island and given similar, though wrong, information that Union troops were up to mischief, Col. A. R. Wright heard that a Union gunboat was patrolling Chicamacomico. He decided to capture it and find out just what the enemy was planning and vowed to take the Hatteras Lighthouse "if nothing else." Confederates were hell-bent on destroying the nation's premier lighthouse, while Union soldiers were unreservedly committed to protecting it.

Due to the confusion and rumors, both defenses were about to gather at Chicamacomico, neither side aware of exactly what the other was doing or why. The Confederates were ill-prepared for a fight, with only a few vessels in its defensive Mosquito Fleet, made up of young, inexperienced soldiers who had not been aboard a ship, fired a cannon, or seen a shell explode. Commodore W. F. Lynch drilled them for just three days. Then, they went forward into battle.

Confederates did capture the Union tug gunboat *Fanny* off Chicamacomico's soundside, full of valuable provisions surrendered by Col. W. L. Brown; however, to add to the confusion, Union prisoners told them that Federal troops were already encamped there. Alarmed by this information and the insinuation that the Union intended to rout the Confederate's garrison on Roanoke Island, Colonel Wright ordered a preemptive attack on the Federals.

Commodore Lynch ordered the Mosquito Fleet to transfer all troops obtainable and head for Chicamacomico. These troops were to squeeze the Federals from the north while a Confederate gunboat was to attack and cut off retreating soldiers from the south. On October 5, a very long day for both sides, the gunboat grounded. Confederates took charge and slipped off their gunboats to execute an attack, but they would have to wade a long distance ashore, making themselves easy pickings for Federal sharpshooters. Confederates had to turn back to their boats. Although they gained an advantage, wary Union soldiers could hear and see the Mosquito Fleet in the background encircling them in a trap; as a result, they hastened back toward Fort Hatteras.

Aware of the Federal retreat, Georgia troops were in hot pursuit, bolstered by small backup groups in boats. It was a grueling trip for these

The biggest winner of the Chicamacomico Races in early October 1861 was the Cape Hatteras Lighthouse. After skirmishes between the opposing sides, troops from the Twentieth Indiana Infantry bivouacked around the prized tower. *Illustration from the personal collection of John Havel.*

men—the sun was bearing down on them, with many dropping to the searing sand with exhaustion and thirst. Federal troops used the ocean's roar and the muffling effect of sand dunes to make their way past enemy posts to reach Cape Hatteras Lighthouse. They were famished and thirsty, and here they found relief.

The Confederates had continued pursuit of the Union soldiers, dragging at least two heavy howitzers with them despite the deep, sluggish sand. But when the Confederates learned that the North Carolina troops never did achieve a landing, which left them without reinforcements—and remember, they thought they were already far outnumbered—the Georgians started a retreat back to Chicamacomico.

At about the same time, the Ninth New York Regiment had come up from Fort Hatteras to help their comrades. Falling in with the Twentieth Indiana Regiment at the lighthouse, they reversed the chase and took off after the Confederates. Seemingly out of nowhere appeared the *Monticello*, a Union steamer, which opened fire on the retreating Confederates. Rough waters and falling darkness were the only factors that saved the southern forces from total ruin that day. They reached their gunboats to return to their original base on Roanoke Island, but not before creating destructive mischief at the Bodie Island Light Station.

The New York and Indiana regiments left their encampment at Chica-macomico and slogged their way back to Fort Hatteras. Each side claimed victory, but the real winner was the Cape Hatteras Lighthouse. It escaped total destruction because Union soldiers camped there, but the near-disastrous episode prompted U.S. Treasury Secretary Salmon Chase to press the War Department "for better protection for the lighthouse if they were going to entrust Hatteras with a new lens."

The Confederates' worst nightmare became reality February 8, 1862, when they lost the Battle of Roanoke Island, yielding control of Roanoke and Pamlico Sounds. For the next two years, Union troops slowly expanded their control of the Outer Banks, including northeastern North Carolina and other coastal areas. The Lighthouse Board sent inspectors on light-house tenders to replace lenses as soon as it was safe, turning the hos-tilities into a duel between Confederate forces determined to darken the coast and Union forces determined to keep the lights burning. During the last week of June 1863, Jeremy P. Smith, acting lighthouse engineer and inspector, wrote Admiral Shubrick of the Lighthouse Board that he had fitted and lighted a replacement first-order Fresnel lens in the Cape Hat-teras Lighthouse "last night." This encouraging accomplishment sent a beam sweeping over the Graveyard of the Atlantic, seemingly a good omen for the Union. For another two years, however, the hostilities continued to rage in North Carolina over the lights on the Pamlico and Albemarle Sounds, with the majority of the action taking place along the Cape Fear River for control of Wilmington, one of the South's key ports.

BODIE ISLAND LIGHTHOUSE

The Civil War struck down the new Bodie tower, built in 1859, before its time, like a young soldier. Early in 1861, while anticipating that Union forces would try to take control of the lighthouse once they reached North Carolina's coast, Confederate forces removed the Fresnel lens from the lantern room and stored it, along with its lamps, in the state's capitol build-ing in Raleigh. Later that year, while retreating during the Chicamacomico Races, Confederate forces blew up the tower. No doubt they were upset at their failure to overcome Union troops and retake control of the Cape Hat-teras Lighthouse and Forts Hatteras and Clark, as well as angered at the mere presence of Union soldiers on the island. Confederates also feared that Union forces could use the tower as a lookout point for their antici-

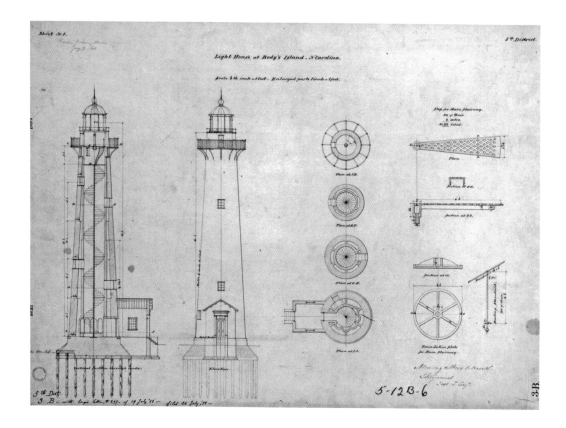

pated attack on Roanoke Island. Ultimately, Confederate explosives leveled the tower, destroying the Lighthouse Board's large investment.

CAPE LOOKOUT LIGHTHOUSES

Both the abandoned 1812 tower and the new 163-foot-tall tower, lighted only two years before the outbreak of hostilities, stood on Cape Lookout at the onset of the war. In November 1861 Josiah Bell, who was in charge of lighthouses in the Beaufort district of the Confederate States Lighthouse Bureau, reported that the new lighthouse was dark and the first-order Fresnel lens had been removed for safekeeping. After the fall of Fort Macon in 1862, Union troops occupied Beaufort and Cape Lookout, and the Lighthouse Board installed a third-order Fresnel lens in the lighthouse and relighted it to aid Union ships. Union commanders expected Raphael Semmes, Confederate rear admiral, to attack both towers with his sea raider, the css *Alabama*, and they alerted nearby warships to protect them, but Union troops did not camp on the island to guard the towers.

The relatively unguarded, Union-controlled lighthouses made tempting targets for destruction for Confederate forces. Fort Macon ranger and historian Paul Branch writes that a small band of Confederates "intended to destroy the lighthouses with a secret land expedition":

> So just how could this be accomplished when the lighthouses lay miles behind enemy lines? The answer involved a carefully planned operation between a military detachment and Confederate secret agents in Carteret County. The manpower for the operation would come from the 67th North Carolina Regiment, commanded by Colonel John N. Whitford. The lighthouse operation was to consist of a handful of picked men, led by L. C. Harland . . . and [to] meet Confederate agents who would conduct them across Core Sound to the Cape where they would blow up the lighthouses.
>
> It was probably in March 1864, when Mary Francis Chadwick first received word of the impending lighthouse operation to carry back to Confederate agents in Carteret County. This 22-year-old woman was an agent whose job was transporting messages between Carteret County and New Bern. She usually carried these in special pockets sewn inside her skirt.

According to Branch, Chadwick was charged to get the messages back to Josiah Bell, who was to orchestrate moving Confederate agents over the Banks, as well as provide safe passage for Chadwick. On April 3, in boats full of explosives that Bell had arranged, the soldiers carefully navigated the Straits, using muffled oars to silence their journey over the open water of the Core Banks and the Cape. Branch writes, "While [Acting Keeper] Royal was working, Confederate soldiers appeared out of the darkness from nowhere. Harland's men told him what was about to transpire and took him over to the keepers' house. Everyone there was instructed to stay inside and make no alarm. Offshore in the bay were the two Union gunboats which must not be alerted." Royal and his family were told to get behind protective dunes away from the impending explosion.

However, something was wrong with the powder; it was low quality, and Harland's men could not get it to ignite. Eventually, using live coals from the keeper's fireplace, they managed to set the powder ablaze, igniting the explosives. According to Branch, "By the time anyone tried to or-

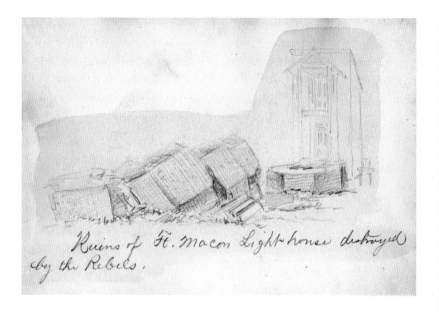

Ruins of Ft. Macon Light-house destroyed by the Rebels.

ganize a search party for the Confederate raiders, they were already well across the sound, making a successful escape back to the Crow Hill house" and back to Confederate lines.

Though the lighthouse was damaged, much to the angst of the two keepers who witnessed the entire ordeal, it was certainly still standing when Harland's men made their escape. The attack had left the walls "cracked and bulged"; the iron spiral stairs were damaged, and the lantern oil was a complete loss. As iron was hard to come by during the Civil War, the Lighthouse Board replaced the lower sections of damaged stairs temporarily with wooden ones and refitted the tower with a third-order Fresnel lens, putting the lighthouse back into service but with a reduced range; the original first-order Fresnel lens was installed in 1867.

Today, over 160 years later, this lighthouse continues to stand tall and serves as the focal point of the southern area of Cape Lookout National Seashore.

BOGUE BANKS RANGE LIGHTS

Mariners approaching Beaufort Inlet used the 1855 Bogue Banks Range Lights to determine a safe channel by lining up the taller rear light over the shorter front light. A 50-foot-tall brick tower, located 200 yards northwest of Fort Macon and fitted with a fourth-order Fresnel lens, served as the rear range light. A 30-foot-tall wooden tower holding a sixth-order Fresnel lens served as the front range light, also known as the Bogue Banks Beacon. In 1861, Confederate forces took Fort Macon and moved the two Fresnel lenses to safety. In March 1862, they felled both towers in preparation to defend the fort. Union forces won the battle, but the Lighthouse Board did not rebuild the destroyed range lights.

THE BATTLE TO CONTROL THE CAPE FEAR RIVER

The lengthy battle to control the Cape Fear River was a four-year investment for the Union government. In 1861, Union lieutenant general Winfield Scott devised the Anaconda Plan, a proposal to enact a blockade of all southern ports along the Atlantic and Gulf coasts, starving the Confederate economy. During the last two years of the American Civil War, Wilmington remained the only major southern port with rail connections (the Wilmington & Weldon Railroad) that Confederate blockade-runners could use to send supplies to Petersburg and Richmond. North Carolina had Gen. Robert E. Lee's back, so to speak, by keeping this main artery open for a flow of supplies, and protecting the port became one of the Lee's priorities. Wilmington's location far up the Cape Fear River rendered it safe from Union assault as long as Confederate forces held Forts Holmes, Caswell, Campbell, and Fisher at entrances to the river. Beginning in 1862, the Union navy's North Atlantic Blockading Squadron struggled to block the mouth of the Cape Fear River and close the way to Wilmington, but nature had provided the Confederates even more advantage, with a choice of two inlets for outsmarting attempts to choke the South's import and export of goods.

Ten-mile-long Bald Head (Smith's) Island sits in the center of the mouth of the Cape Fear River and separates two marked, navigable channels: Old Inlet, also known as the Western Bar, at the southern entrance from the Atlantic into the river, and New Inlet at the northern entrance at Fort Fisher. The distance between the two inlets is only six miles, but the deadly Frying Pan Shoals lie submerged outward into the Atlantic for at least eighteen menacing miles. Dozens of Union blockaders tried to catch the Confederate blockade-runners, but each blockader had to cover a fifty-mile arc while keeping out of range of Confederate shore batteries, which provided a perfect escape scenario for experienced blockade-runners oper-

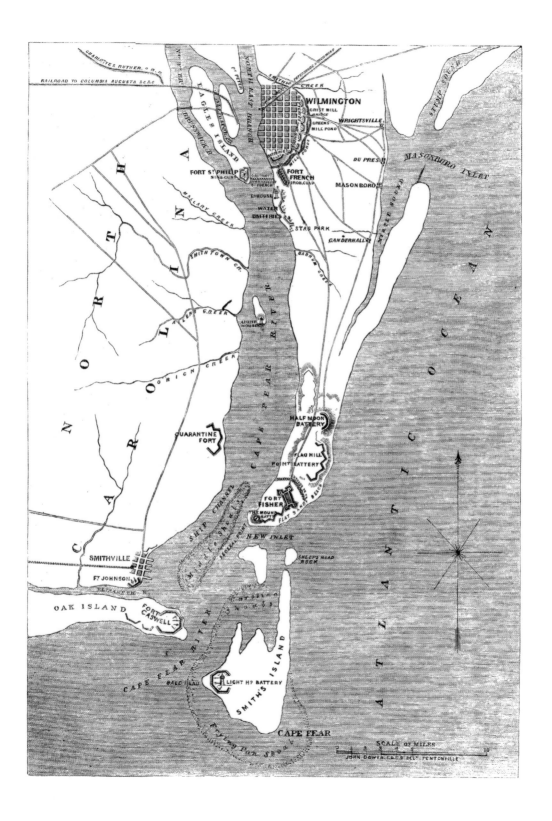

ating steam-powered seagoing vessels, the majority of which were built in Great Britain and designed for quick, quiet speed.

Blockade-runners preferred to use New Inlet, so Confederate forces gave it the heaviest protection. During spring 1863, Confederate major general W. H. C. Whiting used his West Point engineering skills to design Fort Fisher and build it from sand and logs on Federal Point, stretching it out along the beach and boldly calling it "Confederate Point." At the pinnacle of Fort Fisher stood Mound Battery, which appeared on every blockade-runner's map, proving its formidable significance. The two cannons on Mound Battery kept Union blockaders at a respectable distance, while soldiers used a light beacon device to guide incoming blockade-runners. When the Confederate forces garrisoned at Fort Fisher received the designated "friendly vessel" coded light signal from a blockade-runner, they ignited the beacon. The ship's captain used this beacon, set on the beach as a front range light, to line up with the Mound Battery beacon, which served as a rear range light.

The Mound Battery Light became an important light of the Confederacy. It lighted the way for blockade-runners to slip shipments of cotton and other staples out of the Cape Fear River so they could take their cargo to Cuba or Nassau in the Bahamas and have it transshipped by neutral countries to Great Britain in exchange for clothing, armaments, munitions, and other provisions for Lee's Army of Northern Virginia—and it lighted the way for them to slip back into the Cape Fear River so they could return to Wilmington with supplies. During the last months of the war, more than half of all Lee's supplies came through this port.

In spite of the danger, Confederate captains such as Henry Swan, whose son Charlie Swan later became a longtime keeper of the 1903 Cape Fear Lighthouse, risked their lives to continue blockade-running, even after being taken prisoner and surreptitiously regaining their freedom. Though bold in their supply runs for the Confederacy, blockade-runners may not have been absolute in their support of the Confederacy: they could make a fortune transporting valuable cargoes. Range light keepers, however, steadfastly tended their beacons as long as possible—perhaps more out of loyalty to keeping the light shining than political allegiance.

The Mound Battery Light was kept active until a replacement lighthouse for Federal Point was built.

FEDERAL POINT LIGHTHOUSE

Built at New Inlet, which became a shortcut for reaching Wilmington, this lighthouse had been renovated between 1843 and 1847. During wartime it was where Fort Fisher and the Mound Battery were built; however, since it provided great target practice for blockading gunboats, the lighthouse was ordered taken down.

As tragic as war can be, the seemingly safe task of razing a small lighthouse turned deadly for Pvt. Alfred Campain (also recorded as Campen). Chris E. Fonvielle Jr. tells the story in *Faces of Fort Fisher: 1861–1864*. Col. William Lamb, Fort Fisher's commander, kept the keeper's house as his headquarters but wanted the tower gone, and he ordered several men assigned to the fort to do the job. Campain was on a scaffold trying to break bricks away from the lighthouse while others dug under the foundation; a wall broke away, and the young soldier fell ahead of it, crushed by the enormous weight of the wall. One of his fellow company members wrote his sister to describe what happened, explaining that her brother had died quickly, even before he could be extricated from under the fallen wall.

Unremitting Union forces attacked and took Fort Fisher on January 15, 1865, delivering a devastating defeat for the Confederacy, hastening the war's end a few months later. Union navy admiral David D. Porter ordered the Mound Battery Light to be used until a new Federal Point Lighthouse was completed in 1866.

OAK ISLAND RANGE LIGHTS

The first set of 27- and 37-foot-tall range lights established on Oak Island in 1849 were two brick towers that helped mariners cross the Oak Island sandbar at the main entrance (called Old Inlet) to the Cape Fear River (before a storm opened New Inlet). By late 1861, Confederate forces darkened and removed the Fresnel lenses from these two towers. According to U.S. Lighthouse Board Light Lists, the towers were rebuilt as wooden structures and reinstated in 1866. The rear range light tower was built on skids to allow it to be moved to align with the front range light as the channel moved, with ongoing erosion in one area causing buildup of sand in another.

CAPE FEAR RIVER LIGHTS

Although Governor John Ellis ordered all "lenses & fixtures and appurtenances" of the lighthouses in the Wilmington district to be taken to a place of safety in April 1861, Confederate military authorities objected—they wanted to keep the lights burning to help blockade-runners. As keepers exhausted their supplies of oil to fuel the lamps, however, the lights gradually went dark, including Price's Creek, Orton's Point, Campbell's Island, and Upper Jetty Range Lights, which were established between 1849 and 1855. Only the ruins of the Price's Creek front range light remain today.

OLD BALDY, A SURVIVING SOLDIER

In 1863, Confederate major general Whiting ordered the Bald Head Island Lighthouse to be destroyed, for two reasons: he didn't think he had sufficient troops to occupy Bald Head Island, and he feared that Union soldiers would use the lighthouse as a lookout tower. He reconsidered his decision, however, when he remembered that Federal troops had occupied Morris Island in South Carolina, which helped them successfully blockade Charleston, and he realized that Confederate forces needed to control Bald Head Island to successfully continue blockade-running in and out of the Cape Fear River. Instead of taking down the tower, Whiting established Fort Holmes, a series of five fortifications guarding the river's inlets surrounding the lighthouse site, which remained in Confederate hands until the fall of Fort Fisher. Presumably, it served as a lookout tower for Confederate signal officers, afforded a front-row seat to observe the ongoing blockade, and was relighted for brief periods during 1864 to benefit blockade-runners. In all probability, this is why the lighthouse survived and was not destroyed by either side during the war.

Mystery surrounds the relighting of the lighthouse in March 1864. A letter from the Confederate States Superintendent of Lights dated November 21, 1861, reported that the lighting apparatuses from the Federal Point, Oak Island, and Cape Fear Lighthouses (later known as Old Baldy) had been removed and taken to the former U.S. Customs House in Wilmington for safe storage. After the Confederates built Fort Holmes in 1863 and occupied Bald Head Island, famous and daring blockade-runner Capt. John Wilkinson was ordered to relight the previously darkened lighthouse. In his book *Narrative of a Blockade-Runner*, Wilkinson noted:

It was deemed expedient, at this period, to reëstablish the light on Smith's Island, which had been discontinued ever since the commencement of hostilities. . . . At the beginning of the war, nearly all of the lights along the Southern coast had been discontinued; the apparatus being removed to places of safety. Under special instructions, I was charged with the duties of relighting the approaches to the Cape Fear River, and of detailing pilots and signal officers to the blockade-runners. To provide the means of light, every blockade-runner was required to bring in a barrel of sperm oil. In addition to these aids to navigation, the signal stations were extended farther along the coast, and compulsory service was required of the pilots.

Either Wilkinson himself or someone he tasked with the job recovered a lighting apparatus and used it in the lighthouse for this purpose.

Meanwhile, U.S. acting lighthouse engineer and inspector Jeremy P. Smith had carried out light inspections of coastal and Cape Fear lights with all the solemn dedication of any soldier, even though traveling the sounds of North Carolina was risky at best during the war. Smith even tried to keep the Orton's Point keeper supplied with food in fear that the old gentleman would starve. For all of his loyalty to the Lighthouse Board and concern for the safety and physical welfare of the keepers he visited, Smith became alarmed when he returned to Fifth Lighthouse District headquarters in Norfolk, Virginia, to learn that he had been drafted. He urgently wrote the board and pleaded that he be excused. Evidently Smith escaped military duty since Union navy rear admiral William Branford Shubrick, who was then the chairman of the board, dispatched him to Wilmington to inventory recovered Fresnel lenses, have them repaired, and reinstall them in their respective lighthouses. Shubrick recognized that Smith's experience with Fresnel lenses was indispensable in restoring the lighthouses to some normalcy so they could once again help Union captains safely navigate the North Carolina coastal, sound, and river waters and get back to business.

PRICE'S CREEK RANGE LIGHTS

Established 1849, the range lights at Price's Creek near Southport helped mariners navigate the mouth of the Cape Fear River. They had originally been outfitted with a series of eight lamps focused with 14-inch reflectors.

War damage reached the Price's Creek Rear Range Light that also served as the keeper's quarters. The lights were targets since they served as signal stations to blockade-runners. *Photograph courtesy of the State Archives of North Carolina.*

Samuel C. Mason was first assigned keeper, but it appears he never accepted the position. John Bell would become Price's Creek's first keeper.

At the start of the war in 1861, the old lighting systems had been updated in the range lights along the river to a sixth-order Fresnel lens housed in a brick tower that served as the front range light, and a second sixth-order Fresnel lens on the second level of the keeper's quarters that served as the rear range light.

During the war, blockade-runners scurrying out of the Cape Fear River and rushing into nests of Union blockaders watched for signals being relayed to Price's Creek from the Fort Fisher Mound Battery Light about blockade action at New Inlet and from Fort Caswell about blockade action at Old Inlet. Blockade-runners could then choose the best inlet to use for their escape.

On March 23, 1865, Acting Lighthouse Inspector Edward Cordell of the Fifth Lighthouse District was aboard the Lighthouse Schooner *Lenox* in Wilmington and wrote to Union navy rear admiral William Branford Shubrick, chairman of the Lighthouse Board in Washington, D.C. He gave the board one of the few reports that it had received about the condition of lights on the Cape Fear River since the war began. Cordell explained

Before war damage, the Price's Creek Rear Range Light was an attractive structure. This is an artist's version of what the brick keeper's quarters and range light looked like prior to its being shelled and abandoned. *Pen and ink drawing by Brent Westwood.*

that Keeper Hanson K. Ruark saved the lights from destruction by staying with them during the hostilities. Ruark wanted the board to rehire him as the keeper, but one sentence in Cordell's letter possibly prevented that—staying with the lights meant that Ruark had kept the lights burning after the war started, which technically meant that he was working for and aiding the Confederate government, tainting his service record. Anyone who worked for the Confederates would face great scrutiny before being able to vote again or gain a federal job. The least that was required was taking an Oath of Allegiance to the United States to become a citizen again.

Although the tower suffered war damage and has gaping holes in its brick walls, it remains standing on what is now restricted commercial property. The corporate owner of the property stabilized the tower but has done nothing resembling a restoration. The keeper's quarters disappeared long ago, leaving but a single clue to its existence in what experts think is the ruins of its foundation.

Lighthouses knew no bias, but they were nonetheless ravaged during the Civil War on American soil from 1861 until 1865. The Price's Creek Front Range Light, shown here, was left to ruins in spite of its historical significance. In general, however, postwar Reconstruction included repair and quality construction of coastal lighthouses, including at Cape Hatteras (1870), Bodie Island (1872), and Currituck Beach (1875). *Photograph courtesy of the State Archives of North Carolina.*

INNER BARRIER ISLAND AREA LIGHTS

The defense of inland waters and the lights that guided shipping in these inner barrier island areas was also important. Despite Confederate efforts to block Union access to major rivers and sounds, Union soldiers and sailors were better prepared and armed. But this is not to say that Confederates didn't wield a great deal of damage before the federal government resumed control.

The Croatan Light Station, also known as Mashoes Creek, saw war action when its keeper was taken prisoner and the station demolished by Confederates in efforts to block the channel between Albemarle and Croatan Sounds. It was rebuilt the year after the war ended because its presence was important for travel between the sounds to ports of business. *Photograph courtesy of the David Stick Collection, Outer Banks History Center.*

Croatan Lighthouse

At the outbreak of the conflict, Confederate forces darkened the first Croatan Lighthouse, also known as Croatan Shoals or Mashoes Creek, established in 1860 to mark the northwest end of the passage through Croatan Sound. The Croatan Lighthouse was a screwpile-style structure, meaning it stood on long piles screwed into the soft mud underneath the waters of the sound. After Union forces reached and occupied nearby Roanoke Island, they relighted the lighthouse.

According to one Confederate account, a raiding party from the formidable Confederate ironclad ram css *Albemarle,* moored in Plymouth for repairs with its restless crewmembers, destroyed the light sometime between September and October 1864, also capturing Assistant Keeper Tillet and his wife in the process. The Confederates released the keeper's wife but took the keeper to their prison in Salisbury. All that remains of this event is a 4-inch-square piece of gold-flecked blue stationery with a handwritten message from Tillet pleading with the Confederates to orchestrate a prisoner exchange for his freedom. In late October, the css *Albemarle* met its demise at the hands of Lt. William Cushing during a demoralizing moment when the South lost its glimmer of hope to regain control of the inner barrier islands.

The Lighthouse Board rebuilt the Croatan Lighthouse in 1866.

Wade's Point Lighthouse
(aka Wade Point or Pasquotank River Light)

The first Wade's Point Lighthouse, a screwpile structure built in Albemarle Sound in 1855, marked the mouth of the Pasquotank River, which leads to the port of Elizabeth City. Early in the war, Union forces removed the Fresnel lens and burned the structure to take it out of service. The Lighthouse Board rebuilt the structure, restored the Fresnel lens, and returned the lighthouse to service in 1866.

Roanoke River Light Vessel

In 1835, the straw-colored Roanoke River Light Vessel was anchored in Albemarle Sound to mark the mouth of the Roanoke River. The lightship was originally a wooden-hull, three-masted ship that had been redesigned as a lightship. It marked the river's entrance until the start of the Civil War when Confederate forces seized the ship and purposely sank it upriver. Scuttling a light vessel and turning it into an obstacle to Union boats was a common strategy used by Confederates. In 1866–67, the Lighthouse Board replaced the lost vessel with the screwpile Roanoke River Lighthouse. Later, after fire destroyed the building, the board ordered the reconstruction of the light in 1887, and today it is located on the Edenton waterfront as the sole survivor of the river lights. A reproduction of the 1866 Roanoke River Lighthouse is also on display at the Plymouth waterfront.

Roanoke Marshes Lighthouse

In 1861, Confederate forces darkened the second Roanoke Marshes Lighthouse, a light dating back to 1857. Roanoke Marshes was built to mark the south entrance to Croatan Sound and the channel connecting Pamlico and Albemarle Sounds. The Confederate States Lighthouse Bureau in Richmond received a report that CSA officials had taken the lens and other equipment to Elizabeth City for safekeeping. In 1863, after the Union captured Roanoke Island, the Lighthouse Board reestablished the light with

The first Roanoke River Lighthouse replaced a destroyed 1835 light vessel that marked the entrance to the Roanoke River leading to the Port of Plymouth between 1866 and 1867 (see chapter 11). The light station was reconstructed in 1885 after destruction by fire and then again in 1887 after ice floes destroyed its foundation. It survived two relocations and is now on the Edenton waterfront. Note the fog bell at the second-story level and the protective linen cover on the fourth-order lens above. *1893 photograph courtesy of the H. Bamber Collection, Outer Banks History Center.*

a replacement lens. In 1864, a raiding party of ten sailors and an officer from the Confederate ironclad ram css *Albemarle* based in Plymouth, the same group that allegedly destroyed the Croatan Light, set out to destroy the lighthouse. However, Union guards reached it in time, and the Confederates returned to Plymouth.

Royal Shoal Light Vessel

During the war, Confederate forces seized the lead-colored Royal Shoal Light Vessel, which was established in 1825 to mark a dangerous shoal in Pamlico Sound and exhibited a light in 1826. In 1867, the Lighthouse Board replaced it with a screwpile lighthouse named Southwest Point Royal Shoal Lighthouse, which stood in 7 feet of water in Pamlico Sound nine miles northwest of Ocracoke Light. Most screwpile lighthouses were about 1,000-square-foot wooden rectangular structures supported by iron pilings "screwed" into the muddy bottoms of the sounds. They had an iron lantern with a fourth- or fifth-order Fresnel lens and a mechanically struck fog bell.

Long Shoal Light Vessel

The straw-colored Long Shoal Light Vessel, which was established in 1825 and refitted in 1854, marked a dangerous sandbar that ran east-west across the northern end of Pamlico Sound. The vessel met its demise at the hands of Confederates early in the war and was replaced by the Union to continue service from 1864 to 1867; the Lighthouse Board replaced it with the screwpile Long Shoal Lighthouse in 1867.

Pamlico Point Lighthouse

The 1863 Lighthouse Board's Light List reported that the 1828 Pamlico Point Lighthouse was operating. By 1865, however, Confederate forces had darkened the tower, which held a fifth-order Fresnel lens. The board rebuilt the lighthouse in 1867, and it helped mariners safely navigate Pamlico Sound for many years.

Northwest Point Royal Shoal Light

The hexagonal screwpile Northwest Point Royal Shoal Lighthouse was established in 1857 and stood in 7 feet of water (or slightly less) in Pamlico Sound approximately 9 miles from Ocracoke Lighthouse. It warned of dangerously shallow water in the area and marked a safe channel. Confederate forces removed its fourth-order Fresnel lens in 1861. By 1863, Union forces had taken control of the area, and the Lighthouse Board restored the light since it was considered one of the most important guides in the North Carolina sounds. The USCG continues to mark the shoal area with a warning sign.

Harbor Island Light Vessel

Established in 1836, Harbor Island Light Vessel helped guide mariners from Pamlico Sound into Core Sound toward Cape Lookout to the south. Confederate forces seized the ship during the war, and the Lighthouse Board replaced it with the screwpile Harbor Island Lighthouse in 1867.

As an exception, the Neuse River Lighthouse, a screwpile, was built in 1862 during the Civil War. Begun prior to the war, it was completed by Union forces once North Carolina's inland waters were under their control. *Photograph courtesy of the State Archives of North Carolina.*

Neuse River Lighthouse

The screwpile Neuse River Lighthouse, an anomaly among American lights, was built by Union forces in 1862 to replace a lightship that Confederate forces had seized earlier in the war. It stood in 5 feet of water on pilings, which were painted red, and it marked the entrance of the Neuse River leading to New Bern, an important port occupied by Union forces during the war.

HIDDEN FRESNEL LENSES RECOVERED AND A MYSTERY SOLVED

Union general William Tecumseh Sherman's troops eventually found many of the Fresnel lenses from North Carolina lights hidden in the state capitol building in Raleigh. They were either immediately returned or sent to France for restoration and later reset in their original lantern rooms. What had happened to one of the most famous of lenses, that of Cape Hatteras, became a mystery. For over a century, clues eluded those researching the subject. A letter from David T. Tayloe, preserved in the National

Archives in Washington, D.C., documents the removal of the Cape Hatteras Lighthouse first-order Fresnel lens, composed of over one thousand "crown glass" prisms. Tayloe, a doctor from Washington, North Carolina, was entrusted with removing the lens and explained that, although the precious glass was carefully handled and packed with cotton to prevent breakage, it had encountered damage but was restorable.

For many years, the only clue researchers had about what happened to the Cape Hatteras Lighthouse lens was in another letter in the National Archives, dated September 13, 1865. Lighthouse Board secretary, Maj. O. M. Poe, wrote to Brevet Maj. Gen. Thomas H. Ruger, the commanding major general at the Union army's Department of North Carolina at Raleigh:

> Certain portions of the illuminating apparatus formerly in use at Cape Hatteras Lt House NC have been recovered at Henderson NC but other parts of the same lens are withheld by parties in that vicinity—probably in the hope that a reward will be offered for their restitution. Mr. Simon W. Kitrell of Henderson reports that H. Harris refused to deliver up certain parts of this lens now in his possession. The Board would be obliged if you will give such orders in the case as will insure the prompt restitution of this property to the U.S. Lt. H. Establishment.

But the exact whereabouts of the Cape Hatteras lens went unsolved for decades until historian Kevin Duffus looked through records at the National Archives about the Staten Island Lighthouse Depot, where all lenses were received or shipped abroad for repair. The "new" lens shipped to Cape Hatteras to be illuminated in the second (1870) tower was in reality the original 1854 lens that had been removed from the first tower. Union forces had recovered the lens and sent it to Staten Island, whereupon it was shipped to France for restoration, and it was returned to the new Cape Hatteras Lighthouse built in 1870, as described in the next chapter.

The Second Cape Hatteras Lighthouse

THE MOVE OF THE CENTURY

Cape Hatteras boldly juts out into the turbulent waters concealing the treacherous Diamond Shoals—the heart of the Graveyard of the Atlantic—and it has served as a warning of danger for mariners ever since it first appeared on nautical charts in 1585. A century ago, onlookers could see sailing ships waiting offshore for a breeze or trade wind to quicken and push them around the cape and shoals, out of harm's way. Lacking the ability to foretell approaching bad weather, however, captains all too often learned the hard way that breezes can "freshen" and winds turn into raging storms. Twelve to fifteen miles offshore, the agitated waves that break in the shallows surrounding the shoals can reduce mighty vessels to mere sticks of wood, drown crews and passengers, and send valuable cargoes, including sugar, molasses, and lumber, to the unforgiving deep.

The first Cape Hatteras tower was planned and built during the end of the eighteenth century. These were during the early years of the USLHE, when the civilian accountants and lighthouse officials were still learning about the most appropriate sites, designs, materials, and equipment. It was an old Federal-style, octagonal sandstone tower on a sandy hill—one that was slowly eroding away—and outfitted with inexpensive and often ineffective Argand lamps that burned a great deal of oil and frequently became covered with smoke and soot. The lamps required constant cleaning—a tough job for the lighthouse keeper to accomplish in a small lantern room while trying to handle poker-hot glass chimneys and the metal of each lamp's oil reservoir.

The fifth auditor of the U.S. Treasury, Stephen Pleasonton, exhibited his lack of experience in constructing and equipping lighthouses when, perhaps as his swan song, he suggested *lowering* the light at Cape Hatteras in 1851. He mistakenly decided this would make it easier for mariners to see the lantern at the top of the tower in foggy weather—but lowering the light would reduce its reach by two and a half miles, decreasing the chance of light reaching beyond Diamond Shoals, exactly where it was needed.

In 1854, the Lighthouse Board responded to mariners' complaints that the 90-foot-tall Cape Hatteras Light was too short to warn of Diamond Shoals, which was to be avoided at all costs. It was heightened 60 feet, raising the new first-order Fresnel lens to an elevation where it could warn mariners of the shoals at least 15 miles out to sea. *Sketch by assistant engineer George Nicholson from the personal collection of John Havel.*

Criticism of the Cape Hatteras Lighthouse and other lights reached a crescendo with a report that verified I. W. P. Lewis's 1843 report on the deplorable condition of the lighthouses due to poor administration. U.S. Navy lieutenant David D. Porter, who was sent to inspect East Coast lights, including Cape Hatteras, wrote a report to the Senate during the first session of Congress in 1851: "The first nine trips I made I never saw Hatteras light at all, though frequently passing in sight of the breakers; and when I did see it, I could not tell it from a steamer's light, excepting that the steamer's lights are much brighter—it is still a wretched light." His epistle continued, "I will proceed to speak of Hatteras light, the most important on our coast, and, without doubt, the *worst* light in the world."

The report of Lieutenant Porter, a highly respected naval officer, was no doubt the final blow to Pleasonton, and orders came down to form a new administration. The Lighthouse Board took Porter's diatribe seriously and

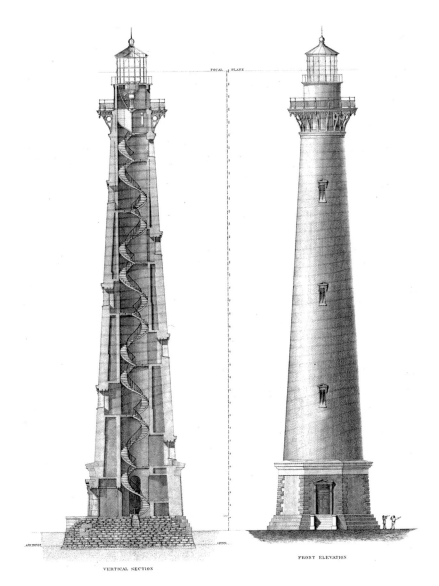

FOCAL PLANE

LOW WATER
LEVEL

VERTICAL SECTION

FRONT ELEVATION

In 1868 the Army
Corps of Engineers
designed the new
Cape Hatteras
Lighthouse, which
was 50 feet taller
than the average
American coastal
light. It was com-
posed of the finest
materials available
and a valuable first-
order Fresnel lens.
It withstood hurri-
canes, earthquakes,
and a relocation.
Note the low-water
level indicating the
freshwater table,
where a grillage
of timber was laid
to support the
foundation—130
years later, it
would become its
Achilles heel.
*From the author's
collection.*

rapidly moved to improve Cape Hatteras Lighthouse. Porter would later serve with distinction in the American Civil War and as superintendent of the U.S. Naval Academy; he eventually achieved the rank of full admiral.

In 1853, after federal reorganization created the professionally staffed Lighthouse Board, Congress authorized $15,000 to raise the old Cape Hatteras tower to 150 feet, install a first-order Fresnel lens, and erect a new keeper's house. According to the official Light List, by 1854 the lighthouse

A late afternoon view of the 1870 Cape Hatteras Lighthouse from the west shows the tower in its new location.

Keepers had to negotiate 269 steps to reach their work space at the top of the tallest lighthouse on the East Coast. The cast-iron stairs hug the inner wall instead of spiraling around a central newel post. Occasionally these stairs need bracing to accommodate the weight and vibration from hundreds of climbers during peak season.

Cape Hatteras Lighthouse Keeper's
Family's Recollections

Keeper Unaka Jennette began serving at Cape Hatteras Lighthouse in 1919 and faithfully fulfilled his duties there for the next twenty years, making him the longest-serving keeper at the light station. He expected his oldest son, Rany, to help him with the light housekeeping chores, including climbing the tower each day to polish the brass fixtures. Rany loved to watch his father feed kerosene from the five-gallon brass can—which had been carried up the 269 stairs to the lantern room—into the mantle lamp, trim its wick, clean the slender chimney glass, and then begin cleaning the hundreds of prisms of the first-order Fresnel lens, all before lighting the lamp at the center of the lens every day one-half hour before sunset.

Rany, who was an industrious boy, strove to be the perfect keeper's son, but sometimes boredom at the light station lured him into mischief. A vat of tar sat beside the granite steps leading to the entrance of the lighthouse, and during the summer it was quite thin—the consistency of paint. Finding a paintbrush or two was no problem, and Rany and one of his friends decided that the base of the tower needed a little sprucing up. When Keeper Jennette saw the tar-stained base, he demanded to know who was responsible for the deed, and Rany proudly accepted credit. Rany knew that his father was angry about the well-intentioned deed, but he would have to wait three days to find out what his father was going to do about the situation because Keeper Jennette had to pick up District Inspector "Captain" King in Norfolk, a long trip back then. After the inspection, Rany's father approached him with a leather razor strap, and Rany knew his father did not intend to shave—his face, that is.

Rany loved to swim in the ocean, hunt for things that washed up after a storm, and ride his favorite pony, Wildfire, one of the wild horses that once grazed and roamed freely on Hatteras Island. "We didn't miss electricity or plumbing," Rany said. "As long as the Hatteras Light worked, that's what mattered. It flashed one and one-half seconds on and six seconds eclipse. I saw that flash every night through my bedroom window. It put me to sleep."

The Jennett(e) family can be called the alpha and omega of this light station. (Generations of Jennett family members spelled their name without an "e." It appears that the spelling changed with Keeper John B. Jennette [1871–1951] when he added an "e" to the end of his surname.) The original land for the 1803 Cape Hatteras Lighthouse was purchased from Christian Jennett, widow of Joseph, who sold the original four acres of land used for the first lighthouse to the government in 1798. She sold the land for fifty dollars on behalf of her four young children. These children began a long line of lighthouse keepers that ended with Unaka Jennette. When Keeper Jennette started his career at Cape Hatteras, he had already served duty on lighthouse tenders, also known as buoy tenders, for fifteen years. He had also worked on the U.S. Lighthouse tender *Maple* and the Diamond Shoals Lightship as quartermaster and later captain. He weathered the final two hurricanes in 1933 and the resulting erosion damage that prompted the Bureau of Lighthouses to decommission the Cape Hatteras Lighthouse. Jennette sold to the government land one mile inland in Buxton Woods on which it built the steel skeleton tower that would be a stand-in until the Cape Hatteras Lighthouse was later reactivated by the USCG. He tended that light until 1939, when he transferred to finish his career at Roanoke Marshes Light and retired as a civilian keeper in 1943.

had a new look: the bottom 20-foot section of the taller tower was to stand out from the green foliage behind it: the upper section top was painted red, giving it an easily identified daymark against the sky. Its new 1854 first-order Fresnel lens sent out a strong warning signal with this flash pattern: 6-second white flash followed by a 9-second eclipse (dark) each 15 seconds for 4 flashes each minute. While these changes made it easier for mariners to see the tower and its light, erosion undermined the future of the lighthouse.

When the tower's interior wooden stairs needed to be replaced in the late 1860s, fifth district lighthouse engineer W. J. Newman convinced the board that building a new tower would be a better economic investment than spending $20,000 for repairs to the existing light.

The board chose Dexter Stetson, an experienced builder from New England, to serve as the construction supervisor of the new Cape Hatteras Lighthouse. The building plans, approved by Brevet Brig. Gen. James Hervey Simpson, raised the focal plane to 180 feet, placing the tower's

National Geographic photographer Clifton Adams captured Keeper Unaka Jennette, known locally as "Cap'n 'Naka," cleaning the first-order Fresnel lens a short time before two hurricanes in 1933 flooded the compound and caused damage. The lighthouse closed and the keeper darkened the beacon on May 13, 1936. Another light was immediately established nearby. *Photograph courtesy of the National Park Service.*

height at nearly 200 feet. Double-wall brick construction allowed its record height. The inner brick wall was a cylinder, and the outside brick wall tapered like the frustum of a cone, with interstitial walls connecting the two. The double-wall construction also provided natural venting of ambient moisture, as well as insulation against thermal temperature changes. In addition, the design afforded flexibility and a low center of gravity, which would become a major factor in its successful relocation nearly 130 years later.

The Second Cape Hatteras Lighthouse

The Cape Hatteras Lighthouse has a massive cast-iron lantern that rests on its brick column. The weight is supported by sixteen Italianate cast-iron brackets that are decorative but also have an important job. The entire lighthouse weighs a colossal 4,830 tons.

Unique architectural details in the Cape Hatteras Lighthouse include the exquisitely cut granite quoins on either side of the entrance, its front door pediment, and the precision-cut steps. According to the historian John Havel, the superior granite from the "Golden Pink Quarry," belonging to Beattie, Dawson, and Company in Connecticut, had to be mined, cut, finished, shipped by schooner, landed, and offloaded. This marble was highly prized for monuments rather than for bases of structures, proving that the materials ordered for this lighthouse by the Lighthouse Board were carefully chosen. *Photograph by John Havel.*

The Cape Hatteras first-order Fresnel lens, which is 9 feet, 5 inches tall, consists of 1,008 prisms. They produced a continuous, 360-degree arc of light with flashes produced by twenty-four bull's-eye panels. This photograph was taken in May 1945 by photographer John Hemmer, who documented many sites for the North Carolina Department of Conservation and Development. *Photograph from the personal collection of John Havel.*

Originally, plans called for 601 wood pilings to be driven 16 feet deep into the sandy soil for the tower's foundation. According to National Archives records, however, as written in Stetson's personal notes, he had available only a primitive steam-powered pile driver, and his construction crew could drive the pilings no more than 10 feet deep. Drawing on his shipbuilding knowledge, Stetson had the crew dig a hole 7 feet deep, reroute the freshwater that flowed only a few feet below the surface of the sand, and lay a two-layer grid of southern yellow pine in a 48-square-foot area. The top layer of 6-inch-square timbers ran north-south while the bottom layer lay east-west. This timber mat provided a stable surface to hold the load of the structure, and the wood would be continuously bathed in freshwater, keeping it durable.

The crew placed a layer of granite rubble on top of the pine timber mat and then built an octagonal base of Vermont granite, comprised of five layers called plinths, one of which was underground, and a tower using 1,250,000 bricks crafted from the banks of the James River, surmounted by an iron lantern room. Bartlett, Robbins and Company of Baltimore manufactured the ironwork, including the graceful spiral stairs workers assembled section by section within the tower. A blacksmith shop was set

The Second Cape Hatteras Lighthouse 153

This photograph was taken from an elevation afforded by the ruins of the 1803 Cape Hatteras tower. Researcher and historian John Havel commented, "As a climber ascends, there is an eight/sixteen/twenty-four symmetry: The eight-sided brick and granite base, as was the original iron fence; sixteen cast-iron brackets supporting the gallery deck; twenty-four ornate iron railing posts; and twenty-four windows that mirrored the twenty-four-sided, first-order Fresnel lens." *1893 photograph courtesy of the H. Bamber Collection, Outer Banks History Center.*

up on-site to make each section fit the inner wall, as well as any needed adjustments to the upper decks.

On September 3, 1870, Newman wrote in his annual report to the board that "materials and work of the most excellent quality necessitated some changes in the ironwork. This with other things caused much delay in getting it ready. It was not until the 10th of Sept that the tender *Tulip* was despatched [*sic*] with men to work at the site in preparing for the ironwork."

By the time the new Cape Hatteras Lighthouse was completed, the construction price had inflated to more than $150,000, but the tower overshadowed anything on the East Coast and housed its repaired original, post-Civil War first-order Fresnel lens. A letter from Peter C. Hains, captain of engineers, dated January 12, 1871, to Rear Adm. W. B. Shubrick, chairman of the Lighthouse Board, announced in his progress report that the lamp was lighted on December 16, 1870. The twenty-four-panel Fresnel lens turned on chariot wheels to increase the number and speed of flashes compared to the old tower. According to the 1870 Light List, the lens turned at one-quarter revolution per minute, four minutes per revolution, and exhibited six white flashes 3.3 seconds on followed by 6.7 seconds off.

The completed, lighted tower must have been a source of pride for everyone involved in creating her. Stetson wrote a personal letter to Gen.

The lower portion of the Cape Hatteras Lighthouse is pictured here showing the golden pink granite quoins that connect the stepped granite foundation and the brick tower. In the background are the double keepers' quarters (left) and the principal keeper's quarters (right). In 1853, the Lighthouse Board began building its own beacons under the supervision of its chosen foreman, also called "superintendent of construction," hiring day labor and ordering only approved materials.

J. H. Simpson giving him credit for his "work of topographical [engineer] genius." Stetson's letter also reported that he had demolished the old tower on February 16, 1871.

Documents in the National Archives show that in 1862 the Lighthouse Board created a standard set of plans for engineers to use for building lighthouses. An engineer could use any of the plans that were appropriate for the site and met the required distance for the light to be seen at sea. For more than two decades, historian and graphic artist John Havel has studied the architectural plans used for the Cape Hatteras Lighthouse: "It is the one lighthouse that is architecturally unique—not designed off any standard pattern. Observe the massive twenty-foot-high octagonal brick-and-granite base, or the sixteen cast-iron railing posts and Italianate gallery brackets and their elaborate sculptural design, as well as the cast-iron pediments or windowheads—removed in 1963—that once graced the six tower windows. You will find no other lighthouse with these architectural features and details."

The next great improvement for the 1870 Cape Hatteras Lighthouse came when an incandescent oil-vapor lamp was installed in 1913. The lamp produced an intense light by converting oil into vapor under pressure and mixing it with air to burn in a mantle made of silk infused with crushed zirconia. Akin to today's Coleman lantern, the incandescent oil-vapor lamp generated thousands of candlepower for about a quart of oil every two hours. Placing the lamp in the center of a Fresnel lens further inten-

In 1913 Cape Hatteras received its first incandescent oil-vapor lamp, which sat at the center of the nearly ten-foot-tall first-order Fresnel lens. According to Fresnel lens expert Thomas A. Tag, a trained lampist had to instruct keepers on how to light the complicated design. Stepping inside the lens, the keeper prepared to light the lamp each evening. First, he pressurized kerosene to a main oil chamber below the lamp. Next, he lighted a brass "spirit lamp" (at left) by its own wick and moved it to a position to preheat the main oil chamber. While slowly opening a valve to allow pressurized kerosene flow to the silk mantle (white, center), the keeper carefully lighted it with a long candle. The flame burned the silk, leaving ash of the infused zirconia still shaped in the form of the original mantle. It was this ash on which the fuel incandesced. After being extinguished, the ash cooled and

sified and focused the individual light rays, producing a brilliance visible for quite a distance.

Unfortunately, beach erosion persistently plagues Cape Hatteras, steadily bringing the ocean closer to the lighthouse. The lighthouse originally stood about 1,600 feet from the edge of the Atlantic Ocean, but waves came as close as touching the tower after two severe storms in the 1930s.

The Second Cape Hatteras Lighthouse

could be restarted many times, but if touched it would disintegrate. Keepers had many spare mantles, usually several dozen. A mantle could last for up to one month before it fell apart on its own and had to be replaced. *Photograph courtesy of Thomas A. Tag, technical adviser for the U.S. Lighthouse Society.*

The Second Cape Hatteras Lighthouse

LOCATION Hatteras Island
NEAREST TOWN Buxton, N.C.
COMPLETED 1870
TOWER HEIGHT 198.5 feet
ELEVATION OF FOCAL PLANE ABOVE SEA LEVEL
   189 feet (National Park Service stated
   192.2 feet mean sea level to light)
STEPS TO LANTERN ROOM 269
BUILDING MATERIALS Brick, granite
   foundation, cast-iron stairs and lantern
DESIGN/PAINT SCHEME Black and white spirals
OPTIC Two searchlight beacons with 1,000-watt
   bulbs; range of visibility, 19 miles
STATUS Active aid to navigation
ACCESS Seasonally open for climbing the third
   Friday in April through Columbus Day
OWNER/MANAGER U.S. Coast Guard maintains
   beacon; National Park Service owns property
FOR MORE INFORMATION
• Cape Hatteras National Seashore
   1401 National Park Drive, Manteo, N.C. 27954
   (919) 473-2111
   www.nps.gov/caha
• Graveyard of the Atlantic Museum
   59200 Museum Drive, Hatteras, N.C. 27943
   (252) 986-2995
   graveyardoftheatlantic.com
FOR INFORMATION ON HATTERAS ISLAND
   FAMILIES AND AREA HISTORY
• Outer Banks History Center
   1 Festival Park, Manteo, N.C. 27954
   (252) 473-2655
   archives.ncdcr.gov/researchers
   /outer-banks-history-center
• Hatteras Island Genealogical Preservation Society
   hatgensoc.weebly.com

The dual aero beacon was a product of the Crouse Hinds Company and provided an electrified light when the lighthouse was relighted in January 1950 by the USCG. These lights were replaced in 1972 by two Carlisle and Finch beacons, positioned back-to-back and facing opposite directions. The site of the 1803 tower can be seen at ground level, in a large sandy patch where a boardwalk meets a sandy road.

Beginning sometime in 1934, an electric light sat in the center of the Fresnel lens for several months. Diesel engines housed in the oil house nearby charged banks of batteries and provided electricity to the light. The incandescent oil-vapor lamp's housing remained intact at that time, but an electric bulb sat inside where wicks once burned and provided a guiding light.

Then, in 1936, the erosion problem became so severe that the Lighthouse Service decommissioned and closed Cape Hatteras Lighthouse. A steel skeleton tower in Buxton Woods equipped with a modern optic served as a substitute lighthouse under the supervision of the USCG; the old tower flashed for a final time May 13, 1936. Since the 1930s, the federal government, as well as the NPS, the U.S. Navy, and other organizations, has tried several methods to stop the erosion, including beach nourishment to reinforce the soil and groins (low-profile steel walls placed perpendicular to the shoreline) to trap sand.

On July 31, 1936, under provisions of the Historic Sites Act, the lighthouse and forty-four acres were transferred to the NPS for potential historic site designation—but to create the historic site, land would need to be donated. Next, on August 17, 1937, the NPS authorized America's first national seashore—the Cape Hatteras National Seashore, which included the spiral-striped Cape Hatteras Lighthouse and Diamond Shoals. With the advent of the Cape Hatteras National Seashore, the NPS had officially

Erosion erased over 1,000 feet of protective beach and dunes in front of the Cape Hatteras Lighthouse over a span of 150 years. Groins, or steel walls running perpendicular to the shoreline, were meant to catch downdrift sand and abate the loss of beach. They only increased erosion to the southwest, taking away what tentative hold the tower had remaining and created a situation that proved unstoppable.

Cape Hatteras Lighthouse:
Navigation Point for German U-Boats

It may come as a surprise, but Axis powers sank more ships off the North Carolina coast in 1942 than at Pearl Harbor in 1941—dozens of ships were sunk during this time by German submarines, better known as U-boats, or by mines laid by them. Critically needed oil for the war effort traveled the mandatory route from Texas and Aruba past the panhandle of Florida and northward along the Atlantic coast on the Gulf Stream. "Torpedo Junction," the place where the ships either continued north to American ports or eastward toward Europe, became the choke point where the crews of German U-boats, under the supervision of German Naval Commander Karl Dönitz, took advantage of spotting ships silhouetted against the Cape Hatteras Lighthouse or other island lights to gain easy targets.

The crews of other U-boats played out this same scenario with ships illuminated by lighthouses up and down the southeastern seaboard. Given strict orders to ruthlessly sink as many Allied vessels as possible, Kapitän-leutnant Reinhard Hardegen and other U-boat captains who were prowling these waters proved deadly to Allied shipping and the entire Allied war effort. Dependency on oil shipped along the eastern coast of the United States nearly became the tipping point in Germany's favor when Allied forces did not receive the petroleum they needed to run ground and air attacks in Europe. At one point, England's reserves reached a four-day supply, and British Prime Minister Winston Churchill pleaded with President Franklin Delano Roosevelt to do something. The president ordered U.S. Navy admiral Ernest J. King to increase Allied convoy protection and step up air surveillance.

In response, defense of the East Coast became a priority. U.S. Coast Guardsmen outfitted yachts and other vessels claimed for the war effort as U-boat hunters. Additionally, Army Air Corps pilots joined the action and helped make East Coast cargo transport safe again by mid-1942. But until Allies sank the last German submarine in July 1942 near Cape Hatteras, the outcome of the war had been tentative. Although Germany lost the war after three more grueling years of conflict overseas, it considered its assault against Allied shipping along Cape Hatteras and Cape Lookout a success.

gone into the business of owning sand and preserving maritime history. As part of a make-work project during the Depression, Civil Conservation Corps workers helped staff the skeleton tower and implemented a land improvement plan by building protective sand dunes and planting sea grass to anchor the wind-whipped and ever-shifting sands. They would also help restore the tower with repaired ironwork, doors, and interior and exterior painting.

While the skeleton tower was operating, the Cape Hatteras Lighthouse was frequently left unguarded and open to anyone who ventured by. During the USCG's watch, vandals damaged the prized first-order Fresnel lens. Park officials reluctantly agreed to its removal in 1949 when it was deemed that no other lens could be found as a replacement. On a brighter note, at the time the efforts to stem the beach erosion were succeeding, allowing the grand old lighthouse to receive a facelift consisting of repairs and fresh coats of paint. The USCG asked to renew the light in the striped tower, and its light came back to life on January 23, 1950, in the form of duel beacons, one surmounted by the second, made by the Crouse Hinds Company.

On January 12, 1953, the NPS, having made enough land acquisitions, established the Cape Hatteras National Seashore, with the Cape Hatteras Lighthouse as its focal point. The sweeping DCB 224-1 electric lights that we have known since they were installed in 1972 are duplex back-to-back beacons emitting a white flash every 7.5 seconds. There are two custom-made 24-inch-wide directional code beacons, hence DCB 224, with the

War came again to the Outer Banks of North Carolina in 1942. The busy Allied shipping lanes off Cape Hatteras were vulnerable to prowling German U-boats. The fuel-oil-laden *Dixie Arrow* fell victim to a torpedo attack by the *U-71* on March 26, 1942. Captain Johansen, dressed in full uniform, went down in a blaze with his ship. Altogether, eleven brave souls died in the tragic event. *Photograph courtesy of the Ocracoke Preservation Society.*

Congressional funding for the relocation of the Cape Hatteras Light Station was awarded in October 1998. The following January, preparations were begun to brace and support the two keepers' quarters. They and the brick oil house were the first parts of the light station to be moved to the new site.

"1" signifying that the beacons were created just for Cape Hatteras with a slight design change.

Although the lighthouse had begun a new era of active service, beach erosion became a leitmotif, and it took another half-century to find a solution; "move it or lose it" became the rallying cry of lighthouse preservationists around the country.

MOVING A LANDMARK: IT WAS ABOUT TIME

Whoever wins the battle of ideas over what to do with the Cape Hatteras Light will . . . set the tone for our response on a national scale to the problem of retreating shores. —WASHINGTON POST, January 11, 1987

Given time and enough scientific merit of a cause, science will win out. The futility in holding back the sea is reason enough for supporting relocation of this historic lighthouse. —STAN RIGGS, Coastal geologist

Between June 17 and July 9, 1999, the brawny 4,830-ton, 198.5-foot Cape Hatteras Lighthouse rolled inland 2,900 feet in a race against time to move it back from the ocean. In addition to beach erosion threatening to claim it, summer hurricanes were heading for the Outer Banks, and it was

This unified hydraulic jacking system was designed and built specifically for this lighthouse relocation project. The device accomplished the heavy work required to lift, support, and lower the massive Cape Hatteras Lighthouse.

As mining the foundation stones opened up a two-foot-square area beneath the lighthouse, shoring towers were installed with cross bracing for added strength. The cross bracing was eventually removed, and then support and travel beams were slipped in.

not farfetched to believe that a storm could topple the lighthouse perched on the edge of the Atlantic.

For a long time, North Carolina's Outer Banks have been slowly migrating westward toward the mainland through overwash, a natural process involving oceanside erosion and soundside accretion. In spite of all the available erosion control methods that were used—at a cost of approxi-

Oak cribbing temporarily supported the lighthouse as shoring towers were removed and "move steel" was put in place. The "move steel system" in the photograph consists of three layers. From top to bottom are strong-backs, cross steel, and main beams (also called travel beams). Three-foot-high yellow strongback beams provide rigidity to the lower portion of the lighthouse. Below them are fourteen cross-steel beams that run perpendicular to the seven duplex, wide-flange beams, also with yellow sides, with 100 hydraulic jacks built in. The main beams are laid in the direction of the move.

mately $17 million between the 1930s and the 1990s—in 1987 the Cape Hatteras Lighthouse, which had been built at least 1,600 feet from the shore, stood only 120 feet from the ocean. Lighthouse officials and preservationists favored relocating the lighthouse over further hardening the coast with groins, jetties, or sandbags, which often prove more harmful than effective.

In both 1988 and 1997, the National Academy of Sciences urged relocation as the best long-term protection plan. Due to saltwater intrusion of the wooden platform on which the tower's granite foundation rests, wood-boring marine organisms threatened the "floating foundation," the tower's Achilles' heel, which would have eventually failed, ensuring the tower's collapse.

After a decade of debate over "to move or not to move," by October 1998 North Carolina senator Duncan McLauchlin "Lauch" Faircloth had sought and received $11.8 million in funding. This allowed the NPS, the stewards of the light station, to plan and begin the relocation process, which included transporting all of the parts of the light station—the brick oil house, keepers' houses, cisterns, and lighthouse—and relocating them in their original relative position to one another at the new site.

The NPS selected International Chimney Corporation, Inc., of Buffalo, New York, as the moving contractor to head a team of skilled engineers, conservation architects, and environmental scientists. Expert House

On June 17, 1999, the lighthouse was ready to roll, very slowly—the movement was indiscernible to onlookers.

Movers, a national structural elevation and moving company based in Virginia Beach, Virginia, funded and operated the updated unified hydraulic jacking system, which was designed by Pete Friesen, a gifted, self-taught, expert structural engineer. This hydraulic system lifted, supported, and lowered the lighthouse during the move.

Workers cleared, graded, proof rolled, and compacted the move cor-

Hydraulic clamps on the push jacks at the back of each main beam significantly reduced the time necessary to unclamp and reset the jacks. It took only eleven days for the lighthouse to reach the halfway point in its journey to a site out of harm's way.

ridor, the path the lighthouse and two keepers' houses traveled to reach new foundations. One hundred hydraulic jacks, each with 50-ton capacity, cushioned the lighthouse. The jacks were rigged in common pressure on three zones, and compensation of pressures between the hydraulic zones kept the support system and structure level.

The Second Cape Hatteras Lighthouse

Before the move, the tower's entry stairway was removed and stored, and the exterior granite plinths at the base of the lighthouse were braced to keep them stable. The movers rigged a scaling ladder on the outside of the lighthouse in case it had to be accessed.

Since freshwater ran just 4 feet below ground level, the moving crew used pumps to dewater the lighthouse foundation area before they removed the soil and sand from the tower's perimeter to a depth of about 6 feet, to reach the underlying pine timber mat. After excavating exposed the granite foundation, workers used a wire saw fitted with a ³/₈-inch diamond-cutting cable to separate the lighthouse from its foundation. These professionals were disassembling the foundation in reverse of exactly what Dexter Stetson had done in 1869–70. While they labored, the world watched.

Simultaneously, workers completed coring, mining, and shoring up the rock foundation. For several weeks, workers used hydraulic equipment to cut two feet at a time. They mined one section of rock at a time and then put temporary shoring in its place. As space opened up, workers laid steel beams to form a solid, supportive steel beam mat over the pine timber mat and welded them together to cover the wood, which had become waterlogged over the last 130 years. The steel beam mat afforded a solid layer to evenly spread the load of the transport system and lighthouse tower.

Shoring towers and 9,000 pieces of six-inch-square oak cribbing pro-

The Cape Hatteras Lighthouse glows from half an hour before sunset until half an hour after sunrise. A fiery sunset at dusk in this case provides a stunning backdrop for the lighthouse just as it goes to work.

Thirty-four face stones were cut from the first granite plinth and engraved with the names of keepers of both the 1803 and 1870 towers. The Outer Banks Lighthouse Society researched keepers' names and dates of service and sponsored the stones' engraving. Eventually, erosion also forced the relocation of these stones to form a small amphitheater near the lighthouse. The lightest stone weighs 2,322 pounds, and the heaviest weighs 5,711 pounds. *Photograph by John Havel.*

vided the main sources of temporary support. The shoring towers consisted of four individual steel posts bolted laterally together with built-in jacks to tension against the steel beam mat. The moving crew repeated the steps of coring, mining, and shoring until the lighthouse rested on oak cribbing and shoring towers. An additional final layer of shoring beams completed the temporary support system.

After the moving crew removed the lateral bracing, they threaded steel main beams between the shoring towers. The steel main beam assembly consisted of double-wide flange steel beams welded together with built-in, heavy-duty hydraulic jacks and base plates that sat directly on the steel beam mat. The main beam assembly, laid in the move's southwest direction, replaced the shoring towers as support for the lighthouse. Cross steel beams, placed over and perpendicular to the main steel support system and clamped to the main beams, completed the temporary support system.

With all of the pieces fitted tightly together, the moment had come to put it to work lifting the lighthouse out of the excavation area and up to ground level, at which point the travel beams would be slipped underneath so it could roll to the new site. The moving crew engaged each of the hydraulic jacks, which were hooked to hydraulic hoses that ran to the unified jacking machine, where a central panel measured the pressure on each jack. When each jack reached the desired pressure, the workers closed its shutoff valve. When all of the jacks reached the correct pressure and all of the valves were closed, the machine operator opened the main unifying valve.

The first step was to raise the lighthouse 1.5 inches. Then the lighthouse was lifted about a foot at a time; once the machine operator locked off the hydraulic jacks, the moving crew set safety blocks before they added cribbing to the height of the lift, and the operator repressurized the newly cribbed jacks to lift the lighthouse another foot. This slow, steady process was repeated until the lighthouse had been lifted about 6 feet.

Workers had prepared the move corridor by carpeting the first several hundred feet with a mat of steel beams to support the combined weight of the lighthouse and move system. While all of the other main beams were supported with oak cribbing and shoring posts for temporary support, the operator retracted the jacks in one main beam, and the moving crew installed a roll beam under the main beam assembly. With the roll beam in place, the workers installed roller dollies (like putting skates on the lighthouse) under the hydraulic jacks within the main beams. Then the operator slowly pressurized and locked off the jacks.

The moving crew added support to the next main beam, the operator retracted the jacks, and workers installed a roll beam and roller dollies. This sequence was repeated for each main beam until the load of the lighthouse had been transferred to the cribbed transportation system—the main beams and jacks on roller dollies supported by the roll beams. When the main beams and the cribbed roll beams met at the same level, Cape Hatteras Lighthouse was ready to roll.

On June 17, 1999, long-armed hydraulic push jacks positioned behind the lighthouse pushed the main beams to make the entire move assembly and lighthouse roll. The machinery operator reset the hydraulic jacks within the main beams for three-zone, common pressure and then activated the push jacks in unified hydraulics to push in a uniform movement. The tower rolled almost indiscernibly on the roller dollies along the travel beam at the rate of 5 feet per push. After each push, the moving crew retracted the jacks, added shoring, and moved the roll beams from behind the tower and placed them in front, thus recycling the pushing system.

Once the lighthouse reached the new site, the moving crew reversed the process of transferring the load onto the new foundation to lower the tower to its new base, which is composed of a steel-reinforced mat surmounted by a brick foundation. The new site stands about 3 feet higher above sea level than the original site. On July 9, the lighthouse was home.

Cape Hatteras Lights: Timeline

1802 Adam Gaskins appointed keeper of Cape Hatteras by President Thomas Jefferson.

1803 Tower completed and activated; whale-oil lamps produce its light.

1813–14 Twenty-one Argand lamps with bowl-shaped mirror reflectors hung on an iron chandelier in three tiers.

1824 Lightship for Cape Hatteras stationed thirteen miles east-southeast of the lighthouse to mark Diamond Shoals.

1825–27 Lightship blown off station about two dozen times in strong storms; removed 1827.

1853–54 Cape Hatteras heightened from 90 feet to 150 feet tall; first-order Fresnel lens installed in 1854.

1855 Hatteras Beacon Light placed at Cape Point to help boaters using Hatteras Inlet.

1861 Confederates remove first-order Fresnel lens from Cape Hatteras.

1862 Union soldiers reclaim the lighthouse; temporary, second-order Fresnel lens installed.

1863 In June, replacement first-order Fresnel lens restored to tower.

1867 Funds allocated for a new, taller tower; construction begins 1868.

1870 December 1, new tower illuminated with its restored first-order Fresnel lens.

1871 February 16, old tower demolished.

1873 Black-and-white spiral daymark applied to tower.

1892 Keepers' quarters expanded for third keeper, who tends the Hatteras Beacon Light; oil removed from tower and stored in brick oil house nearby.

1897 *LV-69* placed on Diamond Shoals, first lightship placed there in seventy years.

1905 November 15, Hatteras Beacon Light discontinued; Cape Hatteras Light Station third assistant keeper position abolished.

1913 Illuminant changed from kerosene to incandescent oil-vapor lamp to intensify light.

1930 Nine hundred feet of groins installed to protect adjacent U.S. Navy installation; as a result, erosion worsens southwest of lighthouse.

1933 Back-to-back late summer hurricanes force abandonment of keepers' quarters.

1934 Light electrified by two diesel engines that charge a bank of batteries housed in the oil house adjacent to the lighthouse.

1935 Land purchased for new tower site from Keeper Unaka Jennette; erosion forces plans to abandon 1870 tower.

1936 May 13, erosion threatens the lighthouse; light extinguished and replaced by a light exhibited from a steel tower one mile west of lighthouse in Buxton Woods.

1937 November 9, tower transferred from USCG to NPS.

1939 President Franklin Delano Roosevelt gives lighthouse responsibilities to USCG.

1942 By lease, U.S. Navy takes control of lighthouse in wartime; lighthouse used to watch German U-boat activity until 1945.

1950 In January, USCG and NPS together reactivate the lighthouse after successful erosion-control methods by Civilian Conservation Corps; the tower had been left unattended for years and first-order Fresnel lens vandalized.

1953 Cape Hatteras National Seashore officially established.

1966 USCG erects Texas-oil-rig-style Diamond Shoals tower.

1972 New directionally coded beacons, or DCB lights, made by Carlisle and Finch Company, installed.

1977 Texas tower automated.

1980 Storm causes severe erosion and severe dune damage around lighthouse and destroys ruins of 1803 tower.

1998 August 5, Cape Hatteras Lighthouse awarded National Historic Landmark status by the secretary of the interior.

1999 Lighthouse relocated 2,900 feet southwest, after various erosion control techniques since 1980 have failed.

2000 Lighthouse reopened for climbing; visitation reaches more than 250,000 annually.

2001 Texas tower deactivated; Outer Banks Lighthouse Society holds reunion for more than 1,100 Cape Hatteras keepers' descendants. In June, tower closed for repair of stairs.

2003 Celebration of 200 years of light held; tower reopened for climbing.

2006 Pedestal and clockwork removed from tower, now exhibited at the Graveyard of the Atlantic Museum in Hatteras Village; known existing lens prisms put in frame on display at the museum.

2012 Diamond Shoal Tower privately purchased, sight unseen, for $20,000.

2018 Plans for Diamond Shoal Tower restoration as research center continues; Cape Hatteras Lighthouse repainted; plans for cast-iron restoration ongoing.

More than 20,000 visitors viewed the progress of the move each day during the twenty-three days of the relocation process. The last brick was laid at 3:33 P.M. on Tuesday, September 14, 1999, and the mortar had barely dried before Hurricanes Dennis and Floyd rolled up the East Coast, causing damage of historic proportions to eastern North Carolina. Fortunately, damage to the lighthouse was limited to smashed windows in the tower because it was a safer distance from the brunt of the severe weather at the edge of the ocean.

Structural engineers predict that the new setting and steel-reinforced brick foundation will ensure the light's continued survival for a hundred years. On November 13, 1999, the NPS hosted a relighting ceremony, including tributes in words and music in celebration of the successful move. The lighthouse opened to the public in 2000, closed in June 2001 for repairing the stairs, and then reopened for climbing on Good Friday, April 18, 2003.

In what some have called an event "larger than life, where all the right people with all the right skills all came together at the right time," the Cape Hatteras Lighthouse expanded its fame by earning a Guinness World Record for a lighthouse moved the farthest. As with all great events, however, not all went smoothly during the pre-move years, when arguments raged over whether to even move the structure. Now that the tower, keepers' quarters, and other historic light station structures have been successfully relocated, everyone can judge the worthiness and value of the relocation. A new chapter in history has begun for this cherished National Historic Landmark.

Light Vessels and a New Type of Offshore Tower

WORKING OFF THE GRID

Duty on a lightship consisted of hours of monotony that often turned to moments of sheer terror, especially when approached by larger vessels that strayed too close. Crewmen practiced escape techniques every day and could evacuate spaces such as the engine room in less than fifteen seconds on a lifeboat kept at the ready. —DOUG BINGHAM, founding member of the U.S. Coast Guard Lightship Sailors Association

In many ways, lightships have not received their due respect in history. Perhaps it is because no one knows about the conditions crews endured. It's hard to imagine being onboard a ship like the *Flying Dutchman* in a hurricane packing winds reaching 120 miles per and hurling unbelievable walls of seawater. Only seasickness, storms, near-misses by passing ships, and cleaning duties interrupted the daily boredom, so it is not surprising that these ships had a high personnel turnover.

A general description of early lightships would include schooner-type vessels under sail power, with a lantern high on a mast consisting of several oil-burning lamps with reflectors, and a five- or six-hundred-pound mushroom anchor with heavy chains deep into the ocean bed to keep it in place. These vessels were updated over a span of decades with continuing improvement in engine power, heavier anchors and chains, and Fresnel lenses.

Journalist and author C. H. Claudy received permission from the U.S. Lighthouse Board's naval secretary to visit the Diamond Shoals Lightship in August 1906. Claudy hailed from Washington, D.C., and his life as a writer must have seemed a world away from a crewman's life aboard the lightship anchored off the Outer Banks of North Carolina. In the November 1907 issue of *Yachting* magazine, he shared his observations of the ship and crew:

The lightship *LV-105/WAL-527* sat in deep, dark waters on Diamond Shoals as a chained guardian to warn approaching ships of the shallows caused by mountainous sand just beneath the surface. At the masts are two brilliant lights that were lighted each evening and kept burning until dawn. *Circa 1940 photograph by North Carolina Department of Conservation Development, courtesy of the State Archives of North Carolina.*

Paint, paint, paint. Scrub, scrub, scrub. Eat, sleep, stand watch, get wildly excited over a sail miles away. Paint, scrub, work! Such is the life of the officers and crew of the lightships. Nothing to do but stay there—nothing to see but water and passing ships, nothing to eat but seventeen cents worth of food a day (fifty cents a day for officers) and this, three months at a time! It is the other end of the pleasures of the sea—the small, hard end of the stick that someone has to hold on to that the rest can ride in safety. Captain, first mate, chief engineer, assistant engineer, two boys from the Navy running the wireless station, and a crew of ten men besides [that] man these vessels which are among the largest in the service. And how big a lightship, do you ask, is supposed to ride in safety and at anchor through the worst storm which can blow? Four hundred and fifty gross tons is the largest lightship in the service, and Number 71, built in 1898, two years before Number 72, is but 412 gross tons. Built of steel and wood, 112 feet long, and 28.5 feet beam, these vessels riding high in the water and built to roll and let the seas pass under, are regarded as the most substantial lightships in the world.

Lightships, lighted ships used where lighthouses could not be built, were a mandatory service for safe passage around shoals and other offshore

Light Vessels and a New Type of Offshore Tower

On August 6, 1918, submarine *U-140* shelled the Diamond Shoals Lightship *LV-71* with deck guns while hunting prey among the Allied tanker convoys. The crew abandoned ship and reached shore safely. *Photograph by International Film Service, courtesy of the State Archives of North Carolina.*

obstacles. Losing a lightship, which was the most expensive navigational aid to build and keep repaired, did not go unnoticed. On August 6, 1918, German submarine *U-140* destroyed Diamond Shoals Lightship *LV-71* by shelling it with deck guns, giving it the luckless distinction of being the only American light vessel destroyed during World War I. Fortunately, all twelve crewmembers survived.

Not only did the U.S. Bureau of Lighthouses, as it was then known, lose a light vessel valued at nearly $80,000, but also the captains of merchant ships lost a critical warning light. Since this lightship marked such a deadly part of the Graveyard of the Atlantic, the bureau replaced it after the war with *LV-72* and a parade of other light vessels for another four decades.

Light vessels also served inland waters. In 1824 Congress appropriated $10,000 for the first floating lighthouse, a light vessel for Pamlico Sound. Congress authorized one light vessel after the other, many serving as replacements for earlier floating buoys at strategic points in North Carolina's sounds and rivers. In his 1980 book *North Carolina Lighthouses*, David Stick noted that nine lightboats then in service varied from the 145-ton lightboat at Long Shoal to the 70-ton lightboat at Nine Feet Shoal. All of them exhibited lights about 40 feet above the water, and each light vessel typically carried a captain, a mate, and two to four crew. There were also a few "lightboats" in sounds and rivers during the early 1800s that were unmanned and tended by someone living elsewhere.

A lightship took up station where no lighthouse could be built. The name and number on its hull identified it during daytime, and two warning lights atop each mast signaled its identity at night. Instead of a spiral stairway, ship's ladders led to the lanterns for maintenance. As identified by lens expert Thomas A. Tag, the major producer of Fresnel lenses in America was Macbeth-Evans from 1912 until 1930, predominantly for lightships. Called simply "glass lenses," they were usually 375 mm in size, equivalent to a third-and-one-half-order Fresnel lens. *Photograph courtesy of the State Archives of North Carolina.*

Regarding their varying name references, lightships, also referred to as light vessels, kept their original Lighthouse Service numbers until 1947, when the USCG began naming some of them "WAL" and assigned each a new identification number. Later, starting in 1965, all lightships were re-assigned "WLV" and a number.

Hurricane of 1933: David versus Goliath

Lightship duty demanded a high level of resolve, courage, and endurance—the faint-hearted simply disappeared the first time they touched land again. Lighthouse Commissioner George Putnam's 1937 book, *Sentinel of the Coasts: The Log of a Lighthouse Engineer,* retells Master Claudius Cecil Austin's personal account of extraordinary courage when he rode out a 1933 hurricane on his light vessel stationed at Diamond Shoals:

> On the morning of [September] 15th the weather showed indication of a hurricane. At 8 A.M. wind forty and forty-five miles per hour, increasing, barometer falling. . . . Seas getting rough and washing ship badly.
>
> At about 2 P.M. station buoy sighted for the last time as the weather was thick with rain and spray. I judge the ship began to drag anchor at about 4 P.M. From 8 P.M. to midnight, wind east-northeast, between seventy and eighty-five miles per hour, barometer falling. Seas were getting mountainous high and washing the ship terribly.
>
> September 16, between midnight and 1 A.M. ship went into breakers on southwest point of Outer Diamond Shoal (having dragged the fifty-five-hundred-pound anchor and twenty-four thousand pounds of chain five miles from her station). Wind about one hundred and twenty miles per hour. The first breaker which came aboard broke an air port in the pilot house which struck me (master) in the face and around the neck and on arm, cutting face and neck badly. This same breaker carried away one ventilator close to the pilot house. Mate S. F. Dowdy tried to get a stopper in the hole in the deck and was washed against a davit and broke some ribs. He was almost washed overboard. From 4 to 5 A.M. wind decreasing to about fifty miles per hour, barometer falling to 28.19 (lowest point).
>
> We laid in the breakers from 12 midnight until 6:30 A.M., breakers coming aboard, breaking up everything on upper deck, washing boats, ventilators, awning stretchers away, bending awning stanchions inboard. At 5:30 A.M. day began to break, so I could see the conditions outside. I could see an opening about south-southwest from the ship that looked like a chance to get away.

Breakers coming over at intervals and I decided that it was the only chance out . . . for when the wind comes from the west it would carry her into the breakers and finish her up. I slipped the mooring at 6:30 A.M. and got the ship outside the breakers, at about 7:15 A.M. being in the center of the hurricane. I had just got the breakers behind me when the wind struck from the west at about ninety miles per hour. I ran the ship southeast until I was sure I was all clear and then ran northeast thinking the hurricane would pass. I ran this course for a while and it did not get any better. I considered it was moving very slow so I changed my course to south and ran this course until I ran out of the hurricane.

Austin's family recalled that he returned home with cuts all over his face and multiple bruises from being tossed around and hit by flying objects onboard. Fellow lightship member Clyde Farrow told his family that they were dragged across Diamond Shoals after the winds shifted and that the sand was rolling around in the water like it was boiling. The winds and the waves were the strongest he had ever seen. The wind bent the lightship's railings all the way down to the deck, and the ship was keeled over so far that he walked on the walls.

Austin framed his letter of commendation from President Franklin Delano Roosevelt and placed it aboard the lightship.

DIAMOND SHOALS

During the 1820s, the USLHE anchored large lightships offshore, and many keepers, new to the job and on an initial probationary period, had to prove their pluck by first serving on lighthouse tenders and lightships. Coastal shipwreck hot spots lay off Capes Fear, Hatteras, and Lookout, with conditions off Cape Hatteras considered the greatest challenge. In 1823, lighthouse officials used a congressional appropriation of $25,000 to make the aggressive move to "bell the cat" on Diamond Shoals with a 300-ton lightship, which went into service the following year.

Things did not go well for the Diamond Shoals Lightship and her crew. After staying on station for only eight months, a ferocious storm forced her

In 1897, seventy years after the last lightship had been blown off station multiple times, the Lighthouse Board again marked Diamond Shoals. *LV-72* was steam powered, displayed electrified lights, and boasted a steel hull. She took up station when *LV-69* or *LV-71* was taken in for repairs, about every three months, until 1966. *Colorized digital version originally in Scientific American, from the author's collection.*

onto the beach, and her crew sailed her to Norfolk for $12,000 worth of repairs. In May 1826, only five months after the ship and her crew returned to station, a severe storm broke the anchor cables, forcing the captain to put to sea and return to Norfolk to be repaired again. Fifth Auditor of the Treasury Stephen Pleasonton, who was serving as the general superintendent of lights, demanded that Captain Life Holden return to the site and search for the lost property (anchor and chains) and later offered a $500 reward (equivalent to about $12,000 today), but all of the recovery efforts were in vain. After the repairs, the lightship and her crew kept their lonely vigil until another storm caused them to be blown off station. In August 1827, the lightship broke loose in yet another ferocious storm and washed up on the beach at Ocracoke—this time she was a total loss. She was the last lightship and crew to mark that part of the Graveyard of the Atlantic for seventy years.

During the USLHE's early history, its officials slowed construction of new lightships, delayed repairs due to expense, generally did not support keeping spare parts on board for faster maintenance, and allowed only enough funds for one relief lightship. It took decades for lightships to

Although a lightship rarely moved from its anchored station at sea, its wheelroom was manned round the clock by a crew member. The only instances when a lightship was meant to travel were when it was going to or from its duty station, heading for repairs, or revving its engines to maneuver its head into storm winds to avoid being broadsided and sunk by a big wave. *Photograph courtesy of the State Archives of North Carolina.*

evolve into highly efficient light stations where crewmembers could immediately detect and correct faulty equipment. When coal-steam power replaced sail power, lightship masters gained more control over their vessels and could maneuver more quickly in stormy weather. In 1906, lightships *LV-71* and *LV-72* carried 150 tons of large anthracite "egg coal," and refueling cost $825 each time they were serviced. The 1940s brought diesel-electric power, which further improved control and self-propulsion, although at the time seven to ten knots was considered warp speed.

FRYING PAN SHOALS

Lightships anchored on Frying Pan Shoals off Bald Head Island fared better than those on Diamond Shoals. From 1854 until 1964, ten lightships were on station there, and records show that lightships served there for an impressive 112 years, with only a four-year interruption during the Civil War.

On December 30, 1861, Union troops burned the original Frying Pan Shoals Lightship, which had been moved into the Cape Fear River. The Lighthouse Board replaced the lightship, but Confederate forces seized and sank it to make a navigational obstruction to block advancing Union

ships. Fortunately, there is a happy ending to this story: after the war, the lightship was raised and towed to a shipyard for repairs.

In 1865 the Lighthouse Board placed *LV-39*, with "Frying Pan Shoals" emblazoned on her yellow hull, back on Frying Pan Shoals. The lower masts of the schooner-rigged, two-masted lightship were painted yellow, while the upper masts were white, with two black daymarks on each mast. Her colorful appearance helped attract the attention of mariners who might wander too close to her—passing ships inadvertently hit lightships, a threat second only to hurricanes.

As technology advanced in the 1850s, lighthouse officials began replacing smaller light vessels with screwpile lighthouses. These lights looked like small cottages on pilings screwed deep into the mud of sounds, many at the mouths of rivers to mark entrances to ports. Screwpile lighthouses played a key role in the growth of North Carolina's commerce by helping guide mariners on inland waterways and providing protection for boaters. The keepers at these "water stations," as they were commonly called, regularly received commendations for assisting travelers on Core, Pamlico, Albemarle, Roanoke, Croatan, and Currituck Sounds as well as the Cape Fear River.

ATTEMPTING TO BUILD A LIGHTHOUSE
ON DIAMOND SHOALS

The U.S. Lighthouse Board and Congress refused to give up on building a lighthouse on Diamond Shoals. In 1889, they earmarked nearly $500,000

to build an iron-plated, brick-lined lighthouse similar to the famous French icon La Jument. Like a lighted monument, the tower would illuminate the dark, dangerous waters of Outer Diamond Shoals that caused the demise of many ships and the tragically destined souls onboard. After previously successful construction in other challenging locations, including the titan lights of the Florida reefs and the second Minots Ledge tower off the rocky Massachusetts coast, the board expected an encore.

In 1888, the Lighthouse Board announced in its annual report that it had created canvas/muslin pennants that were to be flown "whenever a member of the Light-House Establishment or a member of the Light-House Board is afloat in a vessel of the Light-House Establishment." *Drawing courtesy of Jim Claflin, Kenrick A. Claflin & Son Nautical Antiques.*

In 1890, the board judged Anderson & Barr, experienced marine contractors from New Jersey, to be the best of the five firms that had bid on the project. The Lighthouse Board reported in its *1890 Annual Report* that the contractors agreed to build a tower "to be an enclosed structure, solid and massive to withstand the waves at its base; the site all around the structure is to be protected by a riprap packing of granite blocks weighing not less than two tons each." Reports of the day exclaimed zeal for the project, and the *Engineering News and American Railway Journal* followed the event for years.

According to coastal charts, a barrier shoal on "outer-Outer Diamond Shoals" had up to 12-foot-deep water at its seaward edge. John F. Anderson, who served as the captain of the firm's boat, as well as supervisor of marine construction on the project, wrote that he had "secured a set of charts bearing the dates 1862, 1885, 1887, and 1890 marked 'Corrected up to date for navigation,' with none indicating any significant change in position of the shoals." He and his partner believed that a suitable caisson could be floated out and sunk firmly into place during the summer season. His hope was dashed when he visited the area, because nearby Hatteras Inlet was not suitable to support the operations needed for building and loading the caisson, an integral part of the structure's foundation. Norfolk was the closest port meeting the contractors' needs, and unbeknownst to the contractors, they were working with charts that contained twenty-year-old information.

The July 30, 1894, issue of *Engineering News* reported:

After a failed attempt to build a lighthouse on Diamond Shoals in 1890, two other plans were initiated by the Lighthouse Board, but efforts went no further than the drafting board. These are the plans that were published in *Scientific American* on March 24, 1906. Conditions were too rough on the shoals to build on them with a conventional foundation design. *Engraving from the author's collection.*

The light-house which Anderson & Barr proposed to erect on the shoals was to have a foundation carried down by dredging to hard material, or in case only sand was found, it was to be sunk 100 feet below the bed of the shoal. It was to be built of cast-iron plates with a steel bottom. The latter as designed was to be a cylinder 54 feet in diameter and 50 feet high. On top of this was bolted a cast-iron conical section 20 feet high, 54 feet in diameter at the lower base and 45 feet at the upper base, which diameter was continued up for the remainder of the foundation.

To get an idea of this tower's planned, gigantic size, consider that the base of Cape Hatteras Lighthouse is 37.5 feet wide.

The caisson's height of 50 feet allowed it to be towed to the construction site without overturning and afforded enough height to rise above the waterline at Diamond Shoals. As the caisson was sunk with ballast of water and concrete, workers would continue adding 6-foot-tall iron plates to complete its 150-foot height above the water. The contractors dispatched a seagoing tug to do borings to determine the amount of materials needed, based on the depth to reach hardened sand and the bedrock at Diamond Shoals. A persistent storm greeted the tug not far out of port at Norfolk, but the tug's pilot fought the way to Cape Hatteras and waited out the storm in the lee of Hatteras Inlet. The pilot attempted to reach the construction site on Diamond Shoals again, but he could not make it.

The board then sent the *Blake* and a coast survey team in an attempt to take soundings, locate a buoy placed earlier to mark the outer edge of Outer Diamond Shoals, and add a buoy to mark the exact spot where the lighthouse would stand. Anderson and his work crew set out at the same time on the *Jupiter*. On arriving off Hatteras, the captain of the *Blake* sent two of his officers and a quartermaster to board the *Jupiter* with instructions to search the area for that illusive original buoy. The survey team could not find it, nor could they locate an area of shoals in only 8–10 feet of water—all they found were shoals in 22 and 25 feet of water. Anderson commented that he could assure the men that the first buoy marking the shoals had not been seen on government charts for years, meaning that months of work and planning had been wasted searching for a missing buoy and phantom shoals.

Another factor working against the builders was that "there was shown no barrier shoal to break up the waves and protect the working party from the heavy seas." Anderson went straight to New Jersey to talk with his partner about this additional challenge, and Barr convinced his colleague that since they already had invested $100,000 in the project, they should go ahead and put the caisson in place. Before Anderson returned to Norfolk, however, he stopped off in Washington, D.C., and made his way to the offices of the Lighthouse Board to visit Maj. James F. Gregory, the engineering secretary. Anderson knew Gregory had the power to stop the project until the contractors' concerns could be addressed, but Anderson learned Gregory had left his position, and no one else was of help.

Soldiering on, Anderson's work crew left Norfolk with three ocean-going tugs towing the floating caisson, followed by eight working vessels. On the morning of July 1, 1891, they were in position on Diamond Shoals and started filling the caisson with seawater to sink it. Immediately, it settled 3 feet out of vertical, and Anderson ordered his crew to dredge on the high side. By dusk, they had leveled the caisson—but morning's light revealed that scouring action by underwater currents had caused the caisson to lean 9 feet. Anderson finally understood the critical need for a light on Diamond Shoals—the shoals continuously moved, and mariners could never count on them being in a specified place on a chart. It was the *area* that critically needed marking.

Anderson's crew struggled for three days in a futile effort to settle the caisson into a level position so they could add height to raise it above the water; regrettably, their efforts could not overcome the quicksand effect of scouring. While the rest of the country paused to celebrate the Fourth of July, Anderson and his workers toiled—the weather had turned stormy, and the chances of keeping the caisson level and above water disappeared into churning waves. An unnamed tropical cyclone that was spinning off the Cuban coast across the southern North Atlantic finished off what the scouring and sinking action had started, creating a chaotic scene filled with tossing boats, frantic workers, and the listing caisson. Like an unseen stagehand, the storm drew a curtain on the act, and Anderson gave the order to stop work. He and the other captains turned their vessels windward, and everyone returned safely to Norfolk.

The board's annual report for 1892 succinctly states, "Since the destruction of the caisson on July 8, 1891, reported in the Board's last annual report, no further attempt was made to erect this light-house." The office of Messrs. Anderson & Barr issued the following statement: "LOST. On Diamond Shore [*sic*], off Cape Hatteras, July 8, during a severe storm, one

The Bureau of Lighthouses used technological advances to design the offshore Frying Pan Shoals Light Station. Looking like an oil-rig-style structure, it was constructed in stages. In this photograph, the living quarters and light tower are being delivered by barge to be lifted onto the platform by crane. *Photograph courtesy of the David Stick Collection, Outer Banks History Center.*

caisson. A liberal reward will be paid to any one [*sic*] finding and returning the same in *good order* to the undersigned."

In 1894, the board planned a second attempt to erect a lighthouse on Diamond Shoals, to be built by the respected West Point–trained engineer, lighthouse designer, and Civil War hero Gen. George Gordon Meade. The plans never made it off the drawing board. Congress redirected $79,000 of the appropriation for the failed Diamond Shoals Lighthouse to build the sturdy lightship *LV-69*. For the first time in seventy years, since the last lightship had broken loose in a storm in 1827, Diamond Shoals would be marked. Later lightship *LV-71* would also take up duty on the shoals until it met its fate in World War I.

In 1904, the board made yet a third endeavor to mark Diamond Shoals with a permanent structure by offering $590,000 to anyone who would build a lighthouse and operate it, at the builder's expense, for a year, with an increase to $750,000 if the lighthouse remained standing for at least four years. Reportedly, the offer tempted Capt. Albert F. Eells, but there are no records that he ever did any work on the project.

When Commissioner George Putnam took the helm of the reorganized Bureau of Lighthouses in 1910, he called for a 5,500-pound mushroom anchor mooring and 24,000 pounds of chains for lightships, parts

Light Vessels and a New Type of Offshore Tower

The lightship historian Douglas M. Bingham explained that the retiring lightship *WAL-537* circled the Frying Pan Shoals Light Station on November 24, 1964, gave three farewell whistle blasts, and continued on to Morehead City. She later took up duty as a relief vessel. The USCG changed the procedure for naming lightships. "W" stands for a Coast Guard–commissioned vessel, and "AL" stands for "anchored light." *Photograph from a U.S. military release.*

that were critical because a wandering lightship was more dangerous to passing ships than no warning light at all. In time, these weights would grow even larger to increase the stability of lightships with the capability to mark deadly shallows like that of Diamond Shoals.

A LIGHTSHIP FOR CAPE LOOKOUT SHOALS

About 1903, the board stationed an old lightship on Cape Lookout Shoals to warn approaching ships of danger—specifically, the piled-up sand that

Note that the bow of the lightship *WLV-189* is almost in the water as she maintains her station in rough waters. She soon left station for a final time as the new tower took over duty. *Photograph courtesy of the USCG Historian's Office.*

created shallow water where captains expected deep water. Like other lightships braving raw conditions and tough storms along the coast of the Outer Banks, this lightship was blown off station several times. In December 1904, a new $90,000 lightship, *LV-80*, took up vigil eight miles south-southeast of the outer end of the shoals, which placed the two-masted schooner approximately eighteen miles from Cape Lookout Lighthouse. The light vessel, held in place by a 3.5-ton mushroom anchor, made a colorful addition to the shoals. It had a red hull from the bow to the pilot house and from the mainmast aft, a bright-yellow midship section with "Cape Lookout Shoals" in bold letters on each side, and "#80" painted on each bow, plus one white and one red mast. Her foul weather equipment included a steam chime whistle and a fog bell that could be struck by hand, which probably made the crew feel a little safer knowing that approaching ships could at least hear them when fog made the lightship invisible. To add to the misery of serving on a lightship, these noisy protections must have been deafening. *LV-80* and *LV-107/WAL-529* dependably stood watch here until 1933, when the Lighthouse Service pulled the last Cape Lookout Shoals Lightship from service and replaced it with a buoy bell.

Light Vessels and a New Type of Offshore Tower

A "TEXAS OIL RIG" PLATFORM LIGHT STATION

Innovations in construction and technology meant lightships had a limited life span. This was proven in 1964 when a light station, whose design was similar to that of a Gulf Coast oil-drilling platform being planned, known as a Texas tower, was built in Louisiana and brought in sections by barge to Frying Pan Shoals. The new light station replaced the *LV-115/WAL-537*, the last lightship to serve watch over Frying Pan Shoals at the southernmost point of the Graveyard of the Atlantic, and continued a warning signal to passing ships. The tower's massive steel legs are 60 feet apart and driven an incredible 293 feet into the ocean bottom to account for the dynamic movement of the shifting shoals that cause an average shallow 50-foot-deep water depth far at sea. The living quarters are 75 feet above sea level, and the lantern room is 130 feet above sea level. The light station, positioned approximately thirty-two miles off the state's southeastern coast, required an average twelve to fifteen men on board, with an additional three to five men ashore as a relief crew. In 1966 the USCG would repeat this successful design with the Diamond Shoals tower, located off Cape Hatteras. As technology improved with the advancement of global satellite positioning, the USCG automated the Frying Pan Shoals Light Station in 1979 and removed its crew. Replaced by a buoy that transmits weather data in 2003, the massive structure had been completely abandoned by 2004.

After the successful construction of a light station on Frying Pan Shoals (1964), Diamond Shoals was next in line. The USCG erected the Texas-oil-rig-style light station in 1966, complete with helipad for transfer of crew and supplies.

Both of these light stations were on the brink of being demolished by the USCG as exposure to the elements continued to reduce them to scrap. The schedule for demolition by 2004, at an estimated cost of $1 million each, was delayed, however, and these towers came under the standards of the 2000 National Historic Lighthouse Preservation Act, when a number of American light stations were declared surplus property and made available to county, state, nonprofit, and, as a last resort, private entities.

Several institutions investigated the possibility of practical usage of the two towers, but the responsibility and cost of restoration, maintenance, accessibility, and liability overwhelmed the enthusiasm to save and use them. Fortunately, two men stepped up and submitted bids for these stations, sight unseen (preinspections were not allowed).

Since the purchase of the Frying Pan Shoals tower in 2010, restoration efforts have turned the station into a working bed-and-breakfast, welcoming visitors for overnight stays. The current owner of the Diamond Light Station, who purchased it in 2012, has plans to transform it into a research facility as a "benefit corporation" and an on-ocean technology center for the betterment of society and the environment. These orphaned towers are not perfect yet, but they have promising futures.

WORLD WAR I: DESTRUCTION OF *LV-71*

On the afternoon of August 6, 1918, First Mate Walter Lambeth Barnett found himself in an incredible situation. Roaming German submarine raiders had arrived in American waters, the first enemy believed to do so since the War of 1812. Barnett had recently transferred to *LV-71* as first mate, and his captain was on shore leave. He felt secure in the lightship because he believed that if U-boats ventured into the Cape Hatteras area, they would need the navigational aid to negotiate Diamond Shoals as much as the merchant ships that were their prey.

The Germans were proving that a new class of submarines could travel long distances, lay mines, cut antisubmarine steel nets installed at entrances of major harbors, and interrupt allied shipments. The busy shipping lanes off the North Carolina coast, especially those at Cape Hatteras, gave them perfect hunting grounds.

When Barnett heard shots north of his vessel, he climbed the mast to investigate from the gallery surrounding the lightship's light and spotted the *Merak* under attack. The coal-laden merchant ship had successfully eluded the German subs until she grounded on Diamond Shoals. Unknown to either the lightship or the sub captain, a convoy of twenty-eight Allied ships was heading north toward Cape Hatteras, and they made perfect targets. Barnett ordered an alert broadcast, and wireless operator Rozzell Finley sent it at breakneck speed.

The *U-140*, captained by Fregattenkapitan Waldemar Kophamel, overheard the alert message; in response, he ordered his men to fire on the lightship, taking out the wireless antennae with its first shot. The German captain ordered, "Abandon ship or be killed!" Barnett knew the lightship had no chance of outrunning the sub—it would take about five hours to get the awkward, heavy ship under way, and even then, she could never outmaneuver the submarine. Everyone scrambled to lower the lifeboat, a

Life Aboard a Light Vessel

Mike Shepherd served on Diamond Shoals Lightship WAL-390 in the 1960s during an era in which the USCG supervised all activities concerning lighthouses and light vessels. Robust lightships were designed to ride out any storm, and as with buoys, position was everything. A 3.5-ton mushroom anchor held her in position, but sailors reported one storm had "tied" overhand knots in the anchor's chains—just imagine the force required to lift, turn over, and drop an underwater anchor of this scale.

The crew had duties similar to those at a light station. They always maintained a watch to make sure that the light, fog signal, and radio beacon operated exactly on schedule. In addition, they performed the normal tasks that must be accomplished on any ship at anchor, including auxiliary watches in the engine room and the ceaseless battle against corrosion on deck—and there was always "if it doesn't move, paint it."

On the lightship WAL-390, each man spent four weeks at sea with two weeks off, if he was lucky. If bad weather set in or the lighthouse tender assigned to pick the men up got involved in continuous search-and-rescue assignments, the relief crew might not arrive for several days, even weeks, until finally the men onboard the lightship were taken ashore. If the lighthouse tender was delayed for four days, the men were allowed only ten days' leave. If most of a man's leave was lost, or its entirety, the USCG made individual arrangements for leave.

Shepherd served as a fireman/engineman on the WAL-390, one of the most important jobs onboard since fire was a deadly enemy on a ship anchored in place with miles of ocean between its men and safety. His duties included standing four-hour engine watches to make sure that the generators were running properly, with one of the four diesel engines running at all times. The foghorn sounded fifteen-second blasts every sixty seconds, sometimes for days—the crew learned to talk in forty-five-second intervals.

In November 1963, Shepherd and his crew returned from leave to the WAL-390 after being on a tender all night. After the tired crew turned in, Shepherd listened to the radio and heard the announcement that President John F. Kennedy had been shot. Shepherd ran up to the bridge and alerted the deck watchman, and together they woke up the chief, who ordered the flag lowered to half-mast. For the next five days the isolated, lonely crewmen were glued to the television. As if out of respect for the president and the crewmen both, the sometimes fickle television reception remained steady throughout one of history's most defining moments—the *WAL-390* lost television reception the day after President Kennedy was buried.

"whaleboat," and escape. Meanwhile, from their homes on Hatteras Island, the family of crewman Guy Chestwood Quidley recalled being very concerned about him and his mates. They and other crew members' families listened to the shots of the German U-boat and anxiously awaited word.

According to a letter Finley wrote to his family, the crew of *LV-71* continued their seven-hour row to shore as they watched their lightship become another statistic. The members of the crew expressed their great angst as they witnessed a third explosion that cut the lightship in half and sent it sinking into the Graveyard of the Atlantic. After they reached the beach, they walked five miles to a lifesaving station.

Finley's warning broadcast sent the Allied convoy heading for the safety of Cape Lookout Bight forty miles south and the harbor at Beaufort. More than thirty ships picked up the alert, saving invaluable lives and ships.

Today, the *LV-71* rests 200 feet below Diamond Shoals and is part of the *Monitor* National Marine Sanctuary, administered by the National Ocean Service of the National Oceanic and Atmospheric Administration. A sonar image of the ill-fated LV71 lying at rest on the ocean bottom can be seen at https://monitor.noaa.shipwrecks/lv-71.html.

For a complete list of lightships, including those that have been restored and are serving as floating museums or restaurants, see the USCG Lightship Sailors Association International, Inc., website, http://www.USCGlightshipsailors.org; or the U.S. Lighthouse Society website, https://www.uslhs.org.

Currituck Beach Light Station

LIGHTING THE WAY TO LIVING HISTORY

Historic Currituck Beach, on the northern Outer Banks, is brimming with history. Considered one of the loneliest U.S. lighthouse outposts during its first century of existence, the 1875 Currituck Beach Light Station is no longer alone—now it is a vital part of an authentic living-history district. Outer Banks Conservationists, Inc. (OBC), the nonprofit steward of the light station, has guaranteed the historic site a promising future with one of the most successful restorations in America. Exhibits and tours here offer visitors insights into the American cultural identity.

To provide visitors a better representation of what the area looked like when the tower and the other historic structures were built, OBC is purchasing the properties leading from the beach to the light station. Even though modern coastal development surrounds the light station, just seeing the old brick lighthouse and the superior ironwork on the lantern room takes visitors a step back into the past. Climbing the completely restored tower, seeing the rare first-order Fresnel lens—one of the few original lenses still operating in an American lighthouse—and admiring the restored keepers' quarters and other buildings takes people back to when the residents of this small fishing village at Currituck Beach lived in tune with nature, where tides were the only clocks, and every activity was in sync with the weather and sea.

The Lighthouse Board had its eye on this area as early as 1854. A letter from Henri Lepaute, a maker of Fresnel lenses in Paris, France, dated February 1855 documents an order for an illuminating apparatus for "Currituck" Lighthouse. A letter from Lepaute dated September 12, 1855, states that a "2nd order [Fresnel lens is] to be shipped per *Mountaineer*," and he sent an invoice for the lens the same day. On April 4, 1856, Inspector Case at the Stanton Island Lighthouse Depot in New York recorded that the depot would send the lens intended for "Currituck" to Key West, Florida.

About this same time, the Lighthouse Board decided to delay building the Currituck Beach Lighthouse until a replacement tower had been

The Currituck Beach Lighthouse, built in 1875–76, was the final brick coastal lighthouse built by the Lighthouse Board on North Carolina's coast. It wears a natural brick color for mariners to distinguish it from the state's other lighthouses, which are painted in black-and-white daymarks.

erected on Bodie Island. Even though the board intended to go ahead with the new lighthouse at Currituck Beach, the American North–South conflict placed those building plans on hold for another thirteen years.

By 1870, Congress had made an appropriation for a lighthouse to be built on Paul Gamiel's Hill near Kitty Hawk, only about twenty miles north of the Bodie Island Lighthouse. The board reconsidered the site when they realized that lighthouses proved to be the most helpful for mariners when

No roads or bridges connected the Currituck Beach Light Station to the mainland until the mid-1980s, lending an isolated feel to the site. Until then, visitors arrived by boat or traveled many miles on the beach at low tide. Three keepers and their families filled the keepers' quarters until a smaller house was added to the light station to alleviate overcrowding. The small brick structure at the base of the tower is the oil house entryway. *1893 photograph courtesy of the H. Bamber Collection, Outer Banks History Center.*

they were approximately forty miles apart. The board dropped the hill site in favor of a site farther north, where shipping was continuing to increase, making it mandatory that a lighthouse mark North Carolina's northern coastline.

An excerpt from the June 1872 annual report of the Lighthouse Board states:

> The distance from Body's Island to Cape Henry is eighty miles, of which there is an unlighted space of forty miles. The land along the coast in this vicinity is low and in many places without trees, so that even in day-time there is danger of vessels getting into unsafe proximity to the coast before becoming aware of it. This danger is enhanced by the fact that vessels bound around Cape Hatteras from the northern and eastern ports keep well to the westward, in order to avoid the strong current of the Gulf Stream, and for the additional reason that they have a favorable current of about a mile an hour, nearly as far as Hatteras, and a smoother sea in bad weather; but in the absence of powerful sea-coast lights sufficiently near each other to give warning of approach to danger, many vessels laden with

valuable lives and cargoes are in danger of being lost between these points. . . . An appropriation therefore of $50,000 is accordingly submitted to commence the work. It is estimated that the total cost of a first-order light-house at this place will be $90,000.

By 1873, the numerous wrecks reported on the shoals off Currituck Banks, now known as Corolla, pushed Congress to build the Currituck Beach Lighthouse. However, in an urgent move to finally erect a tower to light the dark and dangerous forty-mile stretch between Bodie Island and Cape Hatteras, it appears that some confusion was afoot. In March and April 1873, Maj. Peter C. Hains, the Lighthouse Board's fifth district engineer, wrote two letters requesting permission to advertise and complete proposals for the ironwork for the Currituck Beach Lighthouse, but the U.S. district attorney's office was still investigating land titles for the proposed site—evidently Hains was not waiting around for a clear deed before getting construction bids and materials lined up. He had already completed boring soil samples in the area to enable Superintendent of Construction Dexter Stetson to understand what kind of foundation was needed. On January 9, 1873, Stetson drove pilings about 3 feet apart approximately 24 feet deep into the soft earth. On top, he laid sturdy timbers and nailed them to the pilings. A second layer of timber was laid perpendicular and nailed to the first to create a strong foundation. Granite was placed on top of this wooden grillage to form an octagonal base for the tower. Brickwork of the conical tower started from there. When one of the two tracts of land in consideration was approved on July 30, 1873, Hains was already moving ahead to get this tower reaching skyward and shining seaward.

Building the Currituck Beach Lighthouse caused a flurry of activity that awakened the quiet Outer Banks fishing village. Carpenters hammered together temporary quarters for the construction crew plus a carpenter's shop, blacksmith's shop, and cement shed. The construction workers also built a pier at Church Island, approximately 5.5 miles westsouthwest of the mainland, for landing materials, as well as a tramway to the site. Stetson knew this successful setup well from his experience at the Cape Hatteras and Bodie Island Lighthouses.

Approximately one million bricks shipped from Norfolk arrived at Long Point Beacon Light (no. 8) depot building. The little-known beacon at this depot was on the east end of the boat house, as noted in Herbert

Lighthouse Board engineer Herbert Bamber photographed the Currituck Beach Light Station from different survey stations, which he referred to numerically in his documentation. This photograph is of the rear of the keepers' quarters, with the lighthouse in the background. Traditionally keepers in uniform and their families were included in Bamber's photographs. *1893 photograph by Herbert Bamber from the personal collection of John Havel.*

Bamber's June 1893 topographical survey on Church Island across Currituck Sound. It was here that workers transferred the massive shipment of bricks to a shallow-draft, side-wheel steamer for the journey to the construction site.

At Currituck Beach Light Station, as with other tall coastal lights, vertical windows spaced along the spiral staircase not only provided natural light during an era before electricity but also gave the keepers a bird's-eye view of approaching ships at sea or in Currituck Sound as well as added ventilation when needed. During the late 1800s, keepers also watched for ships in distress and relayed the information to the nearby Currituck Beach Life-Saving Station.

The dignified red-brick lighthouse, which poses on the east side of the light station, has two anterooms, one on each side of the entryway. Both anterooms had fireplaces and heavy wooden doors, which could be closed for warmth. One room served as an office and general work area, providing a comfortable working environment on the ground level of the tower, and the other served as a spacious oil room, with a larger entrance and counters containing semicircular cutouts that held oil barrels until 1890, when lighthouse officials ordered that, for safety reasons, the oil barrels must be stored outside the tower. The two anterooms opened into a central hallway leading to the graceful, cast-iron, spiral stairs.

Five windows, staggered at different landings on opposite sides of the Currituck Beach Lighthouse, provided natural light and panoramic views. A keeper was isolated at over 160 feet in the air; therefore, visual contact with all parts of the station, ocean, and sound were important. Keepers were expected to signal anyone watching, ideally a nearby lifesaving station crewmember, if they saw a ship in distress.

Outside, brick sidewalks with elliptical paths connect all of the structures, including the beautiful two-and-a-half-story double keepers' quarters. Construction workers assembled the Victorian Stick-style duplex from precut labeled materials, which arrived by barge in 1876. The two sides of the house mirror each other, and each contains two large rooms with fireplaces downstairs plus an attached front porch. Two outside cisterns collected rainwater, the only source of freshwater on the light station. Double walkways connect the duplex to the tower, and a fence once separated the two yards.

Currituck Beach Light Station

Among the distinct characteristics of this light station are separated elliptical sidewalks that are interconnected. Each side of the keepers' quarters had its own brick path to create a feeling of ownership.

The dwelling was designed to house two keepers and their families, but for many years the principal keeper and his family lived in one side of the house while his two assistants and their families shared the other. In 1920, lighthouse officials alleviated the cramped living quarters by moving the circa 1860s one-and-a-half-story Long Point Beacon Light (no. 8) depot building across Currituck Sound to the north side of the light station as quarters for an assistant keeper and his family. The small house's Victorian Stick style fits in like a member of the family, and it affectionately became known as the Little Keeper's House.

The light station property also includes two provisions buildings and two outbuildings, which were probably used to store firewood. The keepers and their families used the provisions buildings to store supplies or as a detached kitchen to keep living quarters cooler in summer—and perhaps at times they were "privies," as private outside bathrooms were called then.

During the summer of 1874, Franklin Harwood, fifth district engineer, took over lighthouse construction project responsibilities from Hains. Letters regarding the construction of this lighthouse by various engineers, inspectors, and administrators often have not survived in their entirety. In several instances, fires destroyed the original letters, and brief summaries, located in the National Archives, are all that remain. These summaries reveal details about this light station's completion. According to the indexed letters on Currituck Beach Light Station, Harwood ordered the first-order Fresnel lens, made by Sautter, Lemonnier and Company in France, on August 21, 1875, and just four days later, the lens was on its way from the Lighthouse Depot in Tompkinsville, New York. On August 25, I. C. Woodruff, Lighthouse Depot engineer, wrote that after a damaged prism had been repaired, the lens was shipped to Harwood.

On October 1, Harwood named a man to serve as head keeper, and a week later the board announced the assistant keepers and their salaries. The starring roles of the light station were played by the first-order Fresnel lens and its wick-burning lamp. The giant lens rested on a pedestal, while three ruby glass panels, created in France by pouring gold into molten glass, were placed over three bull's-eye panels. These red flash panels revolved on bronze chariot (round) wheels around the clear, fixed glass prisms of the lens, pulled by an iron weight, approximately 275 pounds, that was connected to a steel rope that ended above the first landing of stairs. The rope coiled around the barrel of a clockwork mechanism, similar to the weight movement in a grandfather clock, on the level below the lens. As the weight slowly descended through metal guides down the center of the tower, its steel rope pulled the red flash panels steadily around the fixed lens. The design caused a flash characteristic of a 85-second fixed white light varied by a 5-second red flash during each 90-second cycle, a unique flash pattern that alerted mariners to steer clear of the coast. The

The Currituck Beach Lighthouse's first-order Fresnel lens is one of only a handful of American lenses in its original lantern room and still active. The USCG maintains the light, but the Outer Banks Conservationists, Inc., owns the tower and maintains all other parts of the expertly restored historic light station.

flash panels made a full revolution every 4.5 seconds. The weight's descent was kept smooth and steady by means of a "governor." Every two and a half hours from dusk to dawn, the heavy weight was carefully rewound by a keeper.

On October 18, fifth district inspector Francis H. Baker requested coal and wood for the keepers. Harwood also ordered supplies for the keepers to maintain every part of the lighthouse in top condition, including an emergency, or extra, oil-burning wick "Funck" lamp, as well as stoves for the keepers. By 1875, lard oil had become the preferred illuminant, and the lamp consumed up to three gallons each night. The light station was coming to life and becoming home for the keepers on duty.

Finally, on December 1, 1875, the Currituck Beach Lighthouse, the only tower erected on the site and the last tall coastal brick light built by the U.S. Lighthouse Board on North Carolina's shoreline, shed light on the remaining dark stretch of the featureless coast between Cape Henry and Bodie Island for the first time in history. In mid-December, curtain rollers were added to hold the lantern room curtains, which, when drawn closed during the day, shielded the Fresnel lens from damaging heat and sunlight and provided a cooler working area for the keepers.

A wreath of netting installed around the outside of the lantern room area collected waterfowl that were blinded by the light. Sometimes entire flocks dropped into the net as they followed the lead goose. According to

oral histories, they provided welcome dinners for keepers, their families, and villagers.

Looking at the Currituck Beach Lighthouse and its accompanying keepers' quarters, it is obvious that architects and builders were interested in more than just using bricks and mortar to build the structures. The architectural drawings for this tower are the same as those used for the St. Augustine, Florida, and Bodie Island Lighthouses, but the Currituck Beach Lighthouse features flairs in its ironwork and other details not found in other North Carolina lights.

The lighthouses south of Currituck Beach were painted with distinguishing daymarks, which allowed the natural red-brick color of the Currituck Beach Lighthouse to serve as its daytime identity. The completion of this light station gave North Carolina the best lighted coast, with the finest, tall towers and a series of first-order lenses showing the way from Cape Lookout to Currituck Beach.

On August 31, 1886, an earthquake shook the entire East Coast, testing the durability of the Currituck Beach Lighthouse. Centered in Charleston, South Carolina, the earthquake registered an estimated magnitude of 6.9–7.3, making it one of the strongest to hit the area, and trembled southeastern lighthouses. Fortunately, lighthouses are built of unreinforced masonry, such as brick, and held together by mortar. These structures are dynamic and can withstand extreme wind or accommodate moderate shaking by being flexible to the point of not breaking apart or crumbling under stress.

Fortunately, the Currituck Beach tower sustained only minor cracks down the interior wall. Principal Keeper Amasa J. Simpson, First Assistant Keeper Fabius E. Simpson, and Second Assistant Keeper Charles E. Ansell all reported feeling the quake. A keeper's wife reportedly was in the tower when the earthquake rippled the ground beneath the structure just before 10 P.M., causing the lighthouse to shiver and roust about so much that, holding her baby in her arms, she had to bump down each of the 220 steps.

During the early 1900s, the Bureau of Lighthouses ordered that three keepers man the lighthouse around the clock so they could stand watch for ships in distress, especially during World War I, when German submarines were sinking Allied ships off the North Carolina coast. The three keepers split the twenty-four-hour duty by each taking an eight-hour watch on that long stretch of low-lying barrier island from Cape Henry to Bodie Island for ships fallen victim to shoals, weather, or enemy ships.

OPPOSITE
Aycock Brown was the one-man Dare County tourist bureau beginning in 1951; he publicized the Outer Banks for its recreational and scenic opportunities. In 1948 he photographed the Currituck Beach Lighthouse surrounded only by sand. The netting around the lantern room prevented wildfowl, blinded by the light, from flying into it and damaging the Fresnel lens. *Photograph courtesy of the State Archives of North Carolina.*

The 1881 handbook, which was given each keeper and his assistants, lists 204 individual rules, and failing to follow any one of those rules meant potential dismissal. This helps explain why most principal keepers ran a tight ship and often were referred to as "Captain" or "Cap'n."

MAKING CURRITUCK BEACH LIGHT STATION A LIVING-HISTORY SUCCESS

The restoration of Currituck Beach Light Station is a best-case scenario in lighthouse restoration and preservation. After the USCG automated and abandoned the light station in 1939, the stately keepers' house fell victim to time and the elements. By the late 1970s, the house looked as if it had been used as a bombing target. The building had no doors or windows, and vandals had wrecked the interior. The sight of this forgotten and neglected light station was nothing short of depressing, and it appeared to be the end for this once vital light station.

When John Wilson, an architect and the great-grandson of Keeper Homer Treadwell Austin, visited Currituck Beach Light Station and saw his great grandfather's forsaken and windowless home and the corroding lighthouse, he dreamed of rehabilitating them. He, along with William "Bill" Parker and their friends, formed Outer Banks Conservationists, Inc., for the purpose of restoring and preserving the light station. The group initiated what would become a fifteen-year project; the result was the long-overdue renovation of a beautiful light station, a task that would become a lifelong endeavor.

In an interview with author Angel Ellis Khoury, Wilson shared stories about his great-grandfather, who served as assistant keeper from 1928 to 1936, and why he wanted to save and restore this light station. "Growing up, you hear stories. How William Riley Austin, one of the assistant keepers, used to give his grandson the job of trimming the grass between the bricks in the walkway with a pocket knife. My mother and her aunt used to share a pair of roller skates between them and skate down that same walk. But when I went there as a boy, after the light station had been abandoned, there weren't any brick walkways. Or at least I didn't think there were."

Wilson's mother used to spend her summers at the "Little Keeper's Quarters" when she was a child, but Wilson himself did not often visit the lighthouse. During his childhood in the 1960s, it was a long way from

Manteo to Corolla, with much of the way accessible only by skirting the ocean tides in a four-wheel-drive vehicle. Although the light station was abandoned by the USCG in 1939 when it took ownership, in Wilson's mind it was a place filled with family birthday celebrations, neighbors visiting on the keepers' porches, biscuits coming out of the oven, the routine of everyday life. "The lighthouse was alive to me," he recalled. "It was where you collected eggs each morning, tended the vegetable garden, shooed the boars and wild horses out of the yard, hung out the washing, and meanwhile, kept the light burning in the tower. At least, that's how I grew up hearing about it from my mother and my grandmother."

In 1979, just out of architecture school and working toward his master's in historic preservation, Wilson, along with some close friends, piled into a Jeep, drove down from where they were living in Washington, D.C., and made the trip along the hard-sand beach at low tide, the only way to reach the lighthouse by vehicle—there was still no paved road to Corolla. Wilson recalled:

> Of course, I knew the light was automated and no one had lived in the keepers' house for forty years. But I guess I was naïve. It was a National Register property. It was a symbol of the nation's lifesaving heritage. Of course it would be tended to. Sure, I knew that the days when a light keeper could occupy his restless grandson with trimming the grass between the bricks were long gone. I surely didn't expect to see a manicured lawn. But I never expected to see such a shambles. The house was a wreck. Holes in the roof. Holes in the plaster. Mantels ripped from the walls. Windows completely gone. It was wide open to the weather, and if something weren't done, and soon, I knew the keepers' house would be gone forever.

Like Rapunzel's tower, the red-brick beacon stood out of reach of the vines and brambles growing rampant at its base. But vines climbing through the gaping rectangles where double-hung windows once kept out the elements had even invaded the rooms where children once played. Wilson continued,

> I was shocked, and we all were dismayed to see this historic property on the verge of ruin. As young architects in our midtwenties, we didn't know where to start or what to do, but we knew we had to do something. We learned that the keepers' house had been transferred

from the federal government to the state. Currituck County officials had asked that the house be demolished as a public nuisance, and state officials said they had no money to stabilize the house, much less restore it. That's when we knew we had to become creative and find another way. So we formed a nonprofit, Outer Banks Conservationists.

In the early years, Wilson and the rest of the group did the restoration work themselves. "You can imagine what it was like to discover under several inches of soil and briar root, the brick walkways where my mother once roller skated. But it was even more of a shock to find another entire house on the property, completely covered in vines."

The OBC has now restored both of the keepers' houses, as well as the light tower itself, which is open to the public for climbing. They have added exhibits to help interpret the light station's history, and docents engage visitors and answer questions about the lighthouse and its restoration. Since its formation in 1980, the nonprofit group has privately raised nearly $6 million for the project.

Looking back over the projects they have accomplished over the past two decades, its founding member and chair Bill Parker offers a perspective that might help others involved in historic preservation: "When you are immersed in the daily work of preservation—scraping paint, salvaging a sill or a joist, rebuilding a cistern—you become caught up in the past, and you don't realize that your own present reality, too, is worth preserving," he says. "I wish we had kept a journal of our work, had taken more pictures, and had recorded our impressions, all of which now are part of the history of the light station."

As the USCG is ending its stewardship of American lighthouses, approximately 300 historic lighthouse properties are involved in transfers to federal, state, and local agencies, nonprofit corporations, educational agencies, or community development organizations for education, park, recreation, cultural, or historic preservation purposes under the National Historic Lighthouse Preservation Act of 2000. The act requires qualifying groups to submit an application, and in a precedent-setting case, OBC was awarded ownership of the Currituck Beach Lighthouse on June 30, 2003, after a lengthy defense of its application against the competing applicant, the County of Currituck Board of Supervisors. The final decision lay with the secretary of the interior, who delegated the final decision to an assistant

There are 220 cast-iron steps that wind their way up to the lantern room at the Currituck Beach Lighthouse. They are nearly identical to those in Bodie Island Lighthouse. Every day, a keeper took five gallons of oil up the stairs with him to tend the light. The lamp burned three gallons each night. The oil weighed approximately thirty-five pounds—no light load, especially for an older keeper. The lighthouse is of double-wall construction, and both the interior and exterior walls keep their natural brick color.

secretary. Following long consideration of the county's appeal of the first decision by the Department of the Interior to award OBC the lighthouse, Judge Craig Manson, assistant secretary for fish and wildlife and parks, upheld his first decision in favor of OBC. Manson found OBC to be the rightful heir to the historic lighthouse when he stated, "Under the [act], the preser-

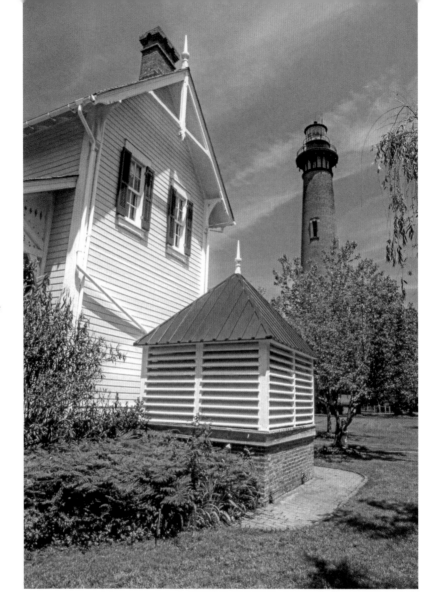

One of the light station's two cisterns is in the foreground of this photograph. They stored rainwater that ran off the roof and was funneled through gutters. The water in the cisterns was the keepers' and their families' only source of freshwater, making the cisterns' care of utmost importance. The Outer Banks Conservationists, Inc., restored them, not only meeting but surpassing preservation standards set by the N.C. State Historic Preservation Office and the U.S. Department of the Interior.

vation of the lighthouse comes first. The standard to be applied is the 'best stewardship' standard; that is, on the record, which applicant appears best able to provide for the preservation of the lighthouse. No other consideration is relevant. That was the sole basis for today's decision."

The rest of the light station is owned by the state of North Carolina and managed by its Department of Natural and Cultural Resources. The immediate grounds outside the light station's fenced perimeter are managed by the North Carolina Department of Wildlife Resources Commission. As part of a restored and growing community, the Currituck Beach Light Station is a member of the Currituck Heritage Park, Historic Corolla, and Historic Albemarle Tour.

The ruling to recognize OBC as a permanent steward for this lighthouse due to the nonprofit's preservation efforts set the bar high for any organization applying for ownership and, in some cases, private individuals wishing to take over a light station. The priorities for ownership include education, the betterment of society, and where possible, making the property available to the public.

Without the efforts of volunteers and dedicated stewards of these awe-inspiring lighthouses and other American treasures, there would be little chance for visitors to learn firsthand about American maritime heritage and revisit a simpler time when man lived much of life helping his fellow traveler. Currituck Beach Light Station represents these plans well by committing to keep the tower and other structures open to the public in perpetuity; currently, more than 150,000 people visit every year. Part of the beauty of this light station is its different seasonal appearances. From snowy dustings to spring blossoms, it offers a friendly feeling as if it were yesterday and the keeper will step out of the tower at any moment.

OBC's successful restoration and preservation of the Currituck Beach Light Station provides a guiding light for future living-history projects. It is a hard act to follow, but great efforts are being made to restore and preserve structures in places from Bodie Island and Edenton to Cape Lookout and the Frying Pan Tower, located about thirty-four miles far out into the deep, blue sea.

COASTAL PARADISE

Before English settlers arrived in the area, Poteskeet Indians came from their village on the mainland to

Currituck Beach Lighthouse

LOCATION Currituck Sound
NEAREST TOWN Corolla, N.C.
COMPLETED 1875
TOWER HEIGHT 162 feet
ELEVATION OF FOCAL PLANE
ABOVE SEA LEVEL 158 feet
STEPS TO LANTERN ROOM 220
BUILDING MATERIALS Brick, granite foundation, cast-iron lantern
DESIGN/PAINT SCHEME
Unpainted red brick
OPTIC First-order Fresnel lens; range of visibility, 19 nautical miles
FLASH CHARACTERISTIC
one white flash every 20 seconds (3 seconds on, 17 seconds off)
STATUS Active aid to navigation
ACCESS Seasonally open for climbing
OWNER/MANAGER
Beacon operated by U.S. Coast Guard; lighthouse property owned by Outer Banks Conservationists
FOR MORE INFORMATION
Outer Banks Conservationists, Inc.
P.O. Box 58
Corolla, N.C. 27929
(252) 453-8152 or the lighthouse
(252) 453-4939 seasonally
www.currituckbeachlight.com
FOR MORE INFORMATION ABOUT
THE WILD HORSES IN COROVA
Corolla Wild Horse Fund,
www.corollawildhorses.com

Isolated no longer, the Currituck Beach Lighthouse offers visitors spacious grounds to walk from light station to sea. Today its brick outer wall is surrounded by an abundance of green foliage and rests amidst the serenity of coastal paradise. It represents the finest lighthouse the U.S. Lighthouse Board could build.

hunt and fish on Currituck Banks. In 1584, English settlers unsuccessfully attempted to make their first settlement in the New World on Roanoke Island, and the first permanent settlers came to the Currituck Beach region in the late seventeenth century. They survived by farming and fishing, using techniques they learned from Native Americans.

Until the early 1800s, at least one inlet cut through Currituck Banks, linking Currituck Sound to the Atlantic Ocean. The sound was once a saltwater niche, and both the Native Americans and settlers found it abundant in shellfish, including oysters, clams, and scallops. Old Currituck Inlet opened to the ocean at what was the historic starting point for Col. William Byrd's 1728 survey to officially determine the North Carolina–Virginia boundary line through the Great Dismal Swamp. In 1786, the Currituck Custom House reported stopovers by "194 schooners, 43 sloops, and 5 brigs at the inlet."

As inlets do, however, the inlet at Currituck Sound began shoaling as early as 1680 and closed completely in 1828. Once saltwater tides stopped entering the sound, the salinity level dropped and promoted lush marsh and estuarine growth, which afforded other opportunities. Waterfowl started coming in droves, and so did hunters and fishermen. The area became the hunting grounds of rich Northerners, and hunt clubs dotted Currituck Sound. The Whale Head Club, restored by Currituck County, provides a reminder of this tradition.

Currituck Beach Light Station

Currituck Beach, which is located within the Atlantic Flyway, attracts a surfeit of birds, including egrets, herons, falcons, ducks, swans, and geese. Previously overhunted, many birds now return to nest here and raise their young, including the indigo bunting and bobwhite. Currituck Sound also contains a rich resource of fish, including largemouth bass, yellow perch, bluegill, and striped bass. The marshland and connecting areas teem with muskrats, gray fox, raccoons, river otters, minks, and even wild hogs.

In more isolated spots to the north, wild horses still graze on available grass. The North Carolina Division of Coastal Management protects approximately 700 acres about one mile north of the Currituck Beach Lighthouse as the Currituck Banks Estuarine Research Reserve, where visitors can meander on the 1,900-foot-long elevated boardwalk and observe birds, deer, otters, and other wildlife along Currituck Sound, just as eighteenth-century settlers did.

SHIPWRECK OF THE *NUOVA OTTAVIA* NEAR THE CURRITUCK BEACH LIGHTHOUSE CHANGES HISTORY

A life-saving surfman is an angel dressed in oilskins. —UNKNOWN

On March 1, 1876, the *Nuova Ottavia*, an Italian bark, stranded about 200 yards offshore near the newly lighted Currituck Beach Light Station, and the principal keeper assisted the crew of the nearby Jones Hill (later renamed Currituck Beach) Life-Saving Service Station.

The *Nuova Ottavia* stranding was a teaser: the ship was close enough for the surfmen to attempt shooting a lifeline from a Lyle gun and haul the victims to shore by breeches buoy, but approaching darkness made it difficult to see and minimized the chances for success. However, the shipwreck victims could not wait another ten hours or more until morning to be rescued—they needed help immediately. The undaunted rescuers launched their surfboat into deadly waves with only a small lantern to help light their way. The Life-Saving Service's history has seen these attempts countless times, and for many surfmen it was their last.

Onlookers, including Currituck Beach Lighthouse keeper N. H. Burrus, saw the surfmen's pitiable lantern go dark after watching it bob up and down along with their boat, which was tossed about in the breakers—only a scream in the dark signaled the surfmen's fates. The keeper and the villagers did everything they could to help, even shooting a lifeline from a

Currituck Beach Lighthouse: Timeline

1875 December 1, Currituck Beach Lighthouse finished and first-order Fresnel lens illuminated.

1876 The Victorian Stick-style double keepers' quarters completed.

1886 Earthquake shakes the lighthouse.

1878 Keepers' quarters host to seventy-six survivors of the *Metropolis* wreck.

1890s One-room schoolhouse built for lighthouse keepers' children.

1920 A circa 1860s dwelling moved from the Long Point Depot to the site as a smaller keeper's residence.

1921 Second assistant keeper's position ended.

1939 Light automated under USCG control.

1980 Consortium of OBC, N.C. Department of Cultural Resources, U.S. government, and N.C. Wildlife Resources Commission successfully applies for a 30.58-acre tract on the National Register of Historic Places.

1990 July 21, lighthouse opened to public climbing.

1995 Light station restoration considered complete.

1999–2000 Structural and safety enhancements project spends an estimated $400,000 on gallery deck, handrails, brackets, belt course system, repairs to roof, lantern exterior, lantern deck, and ventilation system; OBC holds homecoming for keepers' descendants.

2003 February 7, OBC applies for ownership of light station; June 30, U.S. Department of the Interior awards OBC ownership; deed recorded October 17.

2012 Old schoolhouse reopened in the village as North Carolina's smallest charter school.

2017 Continuing repairs include "replenishing" and recoating gallery deck cast-iron brackets, replacing three lantern windows, repointing oil house chimneys, and repointing keepers' house foundation and chimneys.

Lyle gun until all charges were spent, in an attempt to help save the ship's crew and passengers, but all nine perished. That night, the Life-Saving Service lost Jones Hill Life-Saving Station keeper (Capt.) John G. Gale and his mustered crewmen: Spencer Gray, Lemuel Griggs, Lewis White, Malachi Brumsey, Jerry Munden, and George Wilson, who was substituting for the absent surfman John Chappell. On November 21, 1876, the secretary of the treasury noted a commendation for Keeper Burrus for his efforts to help.

These wrecks held great personal meaning for any of the villages that surrounded the lifesaving stations; indeed, these were men at the heart of each small community. Losing one would have been heartrending, but to lose several was even more difficult.

Of the numerous and fatal shipwrecks in the Graveyard of the Atlantic, this and three other wrecks made a major impact on lifesaving measures. First, the 1837 wreck of the *Home* near the Ocracoke Lighthouse stirred the government to legislate requirements for ships to carry a life preserver for each passenger. The USS *Huron* went down near the unmanned Nags Head Life-Saving Station on November 24, 1877, during what was considered a quiet time for shipping between late fall and spring. Only four of sixteen officers were reported to have survived, and 85 of 115 crew members perished at the hands of an angry sea while stranded on a shoal. This one incident alone would have convinced Congress to give more funding to the lifesaving station. But to add insult to injury, just weeks later, the wreck of the *Metropolis* on January 31, 1878, also occurred near the Currituck Beach Lighthouse. The surfmen had to trudge nearly five miles with heavy equipment only to arrive exhausted. And they were too late.

Public outcry moved Congress to complete plans that were in progress to expand the Life-Saving Service along the entire East Coast. For the first time, lifesaving stations were to be professionally staffed around the clock and built about five miles apart to add prompt response with proper equipment to their lifesaving techniques. Further, it became law that each ship had to have a life preserver at the ready for every person aboard.

Facelifts in Old Age

RESTORATION EFFORTS AND CHANGING ROLES
FOR NORTH CAROLINA'S LIGHTS

A visitor to North Carolina's coastal lights will see the results of the hard work put into preservation. Whereas hundreds of these historic structures have been abandoned and linger in dilapidated conditions in other states, things are much better for North Carolina's lighthouses, which sport some of the finest facelifts of any in America, and several of these towers have been opened to the public.

Once the USCG made the decision to declare most American lighthouses surplus property, charging the U.S. General Services Administration with the task of dispersing the properties to new guardians, experts soon determined that a process was needed to determine qualified applicants for ownership. The National Historic Lighthouse Preservation Act of 2000, an update of the 1966 act, created the mandate that only lighthouses that are eligible for listing in the National Register of Historic Places are eligible for transfer to new owners under this program. It isn't a simple process of filling out a form. The USCG and General Services Administration determine eligibility and must follow strict guidelines in cooperation with the secretary of the interior and local state historic preservation offices. But all this red tape has not appeared to discourage those who genuinely desire to own and maintain a lighthouse.

A statement in the 2008 *Historic Structure Report* for Cape Lookout Lighthouse succinctly enters lighthouses' new roles into the history books:

> In June, 2003, the Coast Guard turned over control of the lighthouse
> to the National Park Service while retaining operational control
> of the lights. On the day the lighthouse opened to the public, the
> crowds were unprecedented. More people ascended the tower's
> stairs in a few days than had in the previous one hundred-plus years.
> In addition, the following year a Coast Guard survey of the public
> regarding the quality and usefulness of the light revealed a strong

One of the greatest architectural embellishments at the Currituck Beach Light Station is the ornate 1876 Victorian Stick–style double keepers' quarters. The Outer Banks Conservationists, Inc., formed in 1980 and began restoration plans. *Before- and after-restoration photographs by Bill Parker and Melody Leckie, respectively.*

public appreciation for the lighthouse far beyond its initial purpose. Clearly, the lighthouse has become an important local attraction as well as a navigational aid.

Visitation at the North Carolina lights continues to increase, no matter how difficult it is to reach some of them. In fact, it appears that the challenge to get there is part of the fun and memory. Here are examples

Lens conservators from Lighthouse Lamp Shop disassembled the first-order Fresnel lens and moved it to ground level for cleaning and storing while the Bodie Island Lighthouse underwent two phases of interior and exterior restoration. Further strengthening of the stairs is planned. *Photograph by Kim Fahlen for the Lighthouse Lamp Shop.*

At a dizzying angle from the gallery deck of the Currituck Beach Lighthouse, workers from Lighthouse Industries adjust rigging around the girth of the lighthouse during a project to clean the red brick facade of the historic light tower. The perpetual maintenance is handled by Outer Banks Conservationists. *Photograph by Drew C. Wilson.*

of restoration projects that have happened in North Carolina, including two reproductions that add to the state's intriguing group of lighthouses.

CURRITUCK BEACH LIGHTHOUSE

The USCG worked with the General Services Administration to declare the Currituck Beach Lighthouse surplus property and available for purchase to an eligible owner. For the first time in history, the amended National Historic Lighthouse Preservation Act 2000 placed nonprofits on equal footing with government organizations applying for ownership of lighthouses. The Outer Banks Conservationists, a private nonprofit group, applied for ownership. The NPS Review Committee, following strict standards set by the secretary of the interior, reviewed the OBC's application while comparing it to that of the second applicant, Currituck County, and awarded the

Restoration Efforts and Changing Roles

lighthouse to OBC in March 2003. OBC's refurbishment project raised the bar for standards to restore and preserve a tall coastal light and, more important, to keep the site open to the public. During the summer of 2017, members of the OBC carried out several restorative processes, including corrosive rust removal, newly painted ironwork, repointing, and brick replacement.

The elegant tower retains its working first-order Fresnel lens. Since being electrified in 1933, its flash characteristic has been a fixed white light "on" for three seconds and seventeen seconds "off" during three cycles per minute. Its comforting light continues to flash across sea and sound.

BODIE ISLAND LIGHTHOUSE

Bodie Island appeared as if encased in a giant erector set during a two-phase restoration by the NPS, starting in 2009 and lasting until 2013. Accompanying the twelve-story, 2,000-piece scaffolding was a specially built interior scaffolding for brick repointing and painting. Restorers found the greatest stress at the gallery deck level where the enormous iron lantern and Fresnel lens are supported on the brick tower. Cracks within the upper walls had to be corrected, which extended the restoration time frame. For all the reasons Bodie is special, this is perhaps the most important: it, along with Currituck Beach Lighthouse to the north, is one of only a dozen American tall coastal lights remaining with its still-operational, first-order lens. The Outer Banks Byways has its starting point nearby at Whalebone Junction and meanders 138 miles plus 25 ferry miles south across Pamlico Sound to Harkers Island near the Cape Lookout Lighthouse. Bodie Island now joins a strand of lighthouse gems open to the public for climbing, although from time to time closure is necessary for maintenance and repairs.

CAPE HATTERAS LIGHTHOUSE

Officials closed Cape Hatteras Lighthouse in 1984 when chunks of iron fell off the gallery deck area of the tower from a height of over 150 feet. To make matters worse, by 1987 the ocean had drawn within 129 feet of the tower's base. Officials ordered a study, and as a result, a decision, based on counsel

During fiscal years 2009 and 2010, the federal omnibus budget bill included long-awaited funds to restore ironwork and masonry at the Bodie Island Lighthouse. The supporting cast-iron brackets were removed, melted down, and remolded for greater strength. New ones were also added to support the lantern and its 2,840-pound first-order Fresnel lens.

Scaffolding encased the Bodie Island Lighthouse during its restoration by the National Park Service. Preservation of historically and culturally important architecture offers improved quality of life to all who work and visit the site. Not only is the architecture aesthetically pleasing, but it is also a wellspring of human tradition and achievements. *Aerial photograph by Margaret N. Harker.*

OPPOSITE, LEFT In 2009, the Ocracoke Lighthouse underwent four months of significant restoration work. The fourth-order Fresnel lens was restored, all-new lantern room panes of glass were installed, lightning protection was added, and metalwork received repairs. In the photograph, wood covers the areas in which new panes of glass would be installed. *Photograph courtesy of the National Park Service.*

from the National Academy of Sciences, was made to relocate the tower, a National Historic Landmark. Preparation for relocation started in 1990 with restoration work that was preparation for the move. While the world watched, the lighthouse was successfully relocated in 1999. The relocation project received two civil engineering awards, one of which was the 2000 Outstanding Civil Engineering Achievement by the American Society of Civil Engineers. In keeping with ideals of new ownership of a lighthouse, it opened for climbing following its relocation; however, it was closed again in 2001 to strengthen the stairs. Its reopening in April 18, 2003, for climbing was met with great approval by visitors. The light station hosts hundreds of thousands of visitors annually. Future plans involve more repairs to the stairs to enable them to continue supporting the weight of hundreds of thousands of future climbers.

OCRACOKE LIGHTHOUSE

Ocracoke, the second oldest operating lighthouse in America, was transferred to the NPS in 1999. Thanks to federal grants, the NPS ordered a structural analysis of the tower and its lantern room. Restoration to the brick walls, replacement of windows, and other important repairs to metal-

work, including replacement lantern glass, were completed in the spring of 2010. Though the centered, circular stairs are not safe for frequent climbers, the tower is in excellent condition and the fourth-order Fresnel lens is restored.

CAPE LOOKOUT LIGHTHOUSE

Cape Lookout Lighthouse is located in Cape Lookout National Seashore, one of the few remaining coastal wilderness areas in the world. The NPS restored the lighthouse and opened it to the public in July 2010. Future restoration will take place to strengthen the stairs and the gallery deck level, sites of greatest stress in any lighthouse, especially if it is open to the public for climbing. In May 2017, solar power panels, discreetly hidden from public sight, were installed to provide electricity to the keepers' quarters and lower portion of the lighthouse, as well as provide power for running water at the light station. In late September, the USCG Station Fort Macon changed out the DCB 224 aero beacons for LED lights. The aero beacons took a great deal of amp hours, which relied on a 5-mile underwater

The successful architectural design of Cape Lookout Lighthouse influenced the plans for subsequent North Carolina lighthouses. Since 1859, it has survived the Civil War, a parade of strong storms, and even the ravage of time. After restoration in 2010, it looked like new. Further restoration is planned to keep the tower in good condition. *Photograph by Courtney Whisler.*

The Roanoke River Lighthouse is the only remaining, intact river light in North Carolina. It was privately bought in 1955 and relocated from Albemarle Sound to Edenton. It is now restored and sits on Colonial Park's waterfront as a reminder of the state's prosperous river and sound traffic. *Photograph by Doward Jones.*

power cable that originated on Harkers Island, at an annual cost of nearly $100,000. At the end of its life span, the cable is no longer dependable. Cost prediction for the solar-powered LEDs in the future is $1,200 while operating off the grid.

ROANOKE RIVER LIGHTHOUSE

Roanoke River screwpile, built in 1877, the only one surviving in the state, was purchased from the USCG by Elijah Tate for $10. He floated it on a barge in the mid-1950s from the mouth of the river in Albemarle Sound to his property in Edenton. The Edenton Historical Society then purchased and relocated the light in 2007, but this time the price tag had risen to $225,000. The society had it moved to the town's waterfront, and the state of North Carolina provided $1.2 million for restoration, which included a roof made of materials matching original ones and restoration and replacement of all windows and doors. Its interior is furnished with period furnishings. Its 1887 design has flair: rather than a light centered on a one-story cottage-style screwpile, its light rises out of one corner of the roof of a second story. Thousands visit it each year and learn about river and sound lights that dotted inner waterways. From the early nineteenth century until the mid-nineteenth century, these lights formed the backbone of the state's economy.

BALD HEAD ISLAND LIGHTHOUSE

The state's oldest standing lighthouse on Bald Head Island remains remarkably strong after 200 years due to extensive restoration by the Old Baldy Foundation in 2017. Restoration included the replacement of deteriorated stucco, utilizing a custom mix to match its familiar mottled tones. The foundation funded nearly $300,000 worth of waterproofing that involved replacing the lantern room windows and installing historically correct copper sheeting to protect the cap where the lantern rests on the brick tower. Other renovations included replacing the glass and its glazing with laminated glass; replacing the nonoriginal, mild steel curtain wall glazing bars with bronze; repairing the vent ball to allow for better airflow and to seal leaks; cast-iron replenishment; and a new copper roof. At night, new LED lights at ground level flood the tower upward with warm light.

A drone's camera took a photograph of the new roof and lantern repairs that Old Baldy received during its restoration in 2017. *Photograph by Rob Wright.*

FRYING PAN TOWER

At last, the offshore towers given up by the USCG have been claimed. Diamond Shoals has the potential to become an ocean scientific research station, while Frying Pan Shoals is now an operating bed-and-breakfast inn with eight rooms available. Everyone is invited to have a once-in-a-lifetime experience while enjoying off-the-grid travel. Over the past six decades of its lifetime, the legs and footers under the water

Automated by the USCG in 1974 and abandoned in 2004, the Frying Pan Tower was left to go to ruin. A private buyer, along with donations and a community of volunteers, kicked off continuing stabilization of the tower in 2010. It is now an offshore, off-the-grid bed-and-breakfast more than thirty miles off Bald Head Island. *Photograph by Richard Neal.*

Coastguardsmen occupied the bedrooms of the Frying Pan Tower in an official capacity, but today's guests can simply enjoy the vast expanse of ocean from horizon to horizon. *Photograph by Richard Neal.*

have become natural reefs that draw fish, to the enjoyment of anglers. Of course, if you are strictly a landlubber, try visiting the reproduction 1866 Roanoke River Lighthouse on the peaceful waterfront in Plymouth or the reproduction Roanoke Marshes Light on Manteo's Shallowbag Bay.

A one-half-scale reproduction of the Pamlico Point Lighthouse, built from the original 1891 plans, was completed on the Washington waterfront in 2014. It was made possible through a cooperative effort by the City of Washington, the Boating Infrastructure Grant Program, and the N.C. State Historic Preservation Office. The reproduction functions as the dockmaster's office and a temporary refuge for boaters. Its LED light mimics the original three-second-interval flashes of its ancestor.

For more information on the National Historic Lighthouse Preservation Act of 2000, go to https://www.nps.gov/maritime/nhlpa/intro.htm. For more information on the Outer Banks Scenic Byway, go to http://outer banksbyway.com.

The Town of Manteo built an exterior reconstruction of the Roanoke Marshes Light on its waterfront in 2004. Its fourth-order Fresnel lens guides boats into Shallowbag Bay on the east side of Roanoke Island.

A one-half-scale reproduction of the Pamlico Point Lighthouse, built from original 1891 plans, was completed on the Washington waterfront in 2014. *Photograph by Ray Midgett, USCG, retired.*

HISTORIC SITES THREATENED BY CLIMATE CHANGE

The reality of rising sea levels was revealed in a series of workshops funded by the U.S. Geological Survey, Southeast Climate Science Center to rank coastal cultural resources and NPS property that are at "high risk" from environmental changes. To preserve all vulnerable historic sites is not realistic as the cost of potential, future projects will run into the tens of billions of dollars. The series of meetings addressed the subjects of how will the NPS determine what sites are to be saved based on their historical significance and the feasibility of continuing to protect these structures and sites. Cape Lookout National Seashore is used as the starting point in discovering how to rate each building's historical significance and its need to be protected from possible future flooding. This park's cultural resources include historic Cape Lookout Lighthouse and span from Cape Lookout Village in the southern part of the park to Portsmouth Village, about fifty-six miles to the north. Also being considered for protection are other historic buildings, archeological sites, and the wild horses on Shackleford Banks.

Restoration Efforts and Changing Roles

To date, no such plans exist within the NPS, making these initial efforts in planning for the future meaningful.

Among the project participants were NPS personnel from Cape Lookout National Seashore, the Climate Change Response Program, the Washington Support Office, and Southeast Regional Office, as well as representatives from the N.C. State Historic Preservation Office, regional park partner representatives from Friends of Portsmouth Island and the Core Sound Waterfowl Museum and Heritage Center, and experts in North Carolina coastal dynamics, tourism, and historic preservation. This effort will include North Carolina's lighthouses and has a goal to provide a framework for identifying structures in harm's way and strategies to save them. It is to be hoped that political winds do not blow this project off the table.

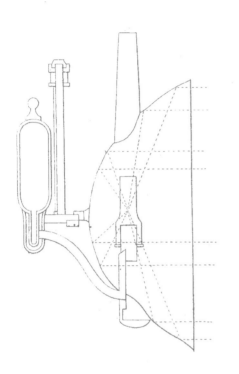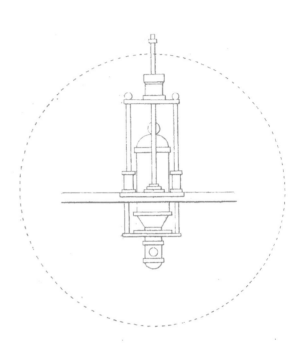

Acknowledgments

The first material for research on North Carolina lighthouses came from David Stick and F. Ross Holland, both of whom were ahead of their time in recognizing the importance of lighthouses as historic sites and future heritage tourism destinations. Their research, conducted largely decades ago, still serves as the standard and has proved invaluable to us.

We acknowledge contributions by Sandra MacLean Clunies, certified genealogist and National Archives researcher, who helped us locate specific documents and drawings among the maze of materials held in Washington, D.C., and Philadelphia over many years. Thanks also to Candace Clifford, researcher, archivist, and historian for the U.S. Lighthouse Society who shared hundreds of National Archives documents that she had copied over two decades. Both of these fellow historians will always be inspirational beacons to us.

Graphic artist, historian, friend, and Outer Banks Lighthouse Society board member John Havel has shared his prodigious research on the Cape Hatteras Lighthouse. His painstaking accuracy provided historical details about this lighthouse that otherwise would have been lost and must certainly one day become a book of his own. He helped with obtaining professional scans of our slides and personally retouched old photos to make them usable, as well as sharing his own photography.

The many people we have worked with at the North Carolina Division of Cultural Resources for three decades are too numerous to name individually. In Raleigh, Audiovisual Materials Archivist Kim Anderson helped us dig through photographs and digital files at the Division of Archives and Records. At state regional archives at the Outer Banks History Center in Manteo, Stuart Parks II and Tama Creef have long helped us mine the historical records and photographs at this library established to hold the David Stick papers.

At Cape Hatteras National Seashore, we thank Cultural Resource Manager Jami Lanier for repeatedly answering our questions and sharing documents. Thanks also go to Bodie Island ranger Jacob Ross, who summarized research on the origin of the name "Bodie."

On Ocracoke Island, we thank Phillip Howard, one of the island's most respected historians, along with (the late) island historian Earl O'Neal. Julie Howard of the Ocracoke Preservation Society also helped us over numerous years.

At Cape Lookout National Seashore, we thank Cape Lookout wildlife biologist Sue Stuska for information about the Shackleford Banks horses. Carolyn Mason created the Foundation for Shackleford Horses and has often rehabilitated injured or sick horses on her farm and returned them to their home on Shackleford Banks. The herd's survival is probably to her credit alone. Park ranger Karen Duggan at Cape Lookout National Seashore shared her research on what happened to the 1812 and 1859 towers during the Civil War. At Fort Macon, park ranger and historian Paul Branch also shared his extensive research on the subject.

In Beaufort at the Carteret County Public Library, David Montgomery found a rare copy of the 1907 C. H. Claudy article about his visit on the *Diamond Shoals Lightship* stored at the Central University of Oklahoma. Claudy's informative and somewhat humorous look at life aboard a floating lighthouse took place during a time when lightships and their crews were respected for their valuable and challenging service at sea.

In Wilmington, Cathy Boettcher and her staff at the Lower Cape Fear Historical Society at the Latimer House Museum offered a gold mine of information about the Cape Fear River. Ray Flowers, historical interpreter at Fort Fisher Historic Site, helped us explore the subject of the mound battery and use of signal lights by Confederate blockade-runners. Chris E. Fonvielle Jr. of the University of North Carolina–Wilmington and author of *The Wilmington Campaign* provided insights and information about the Civil War years and our mutual hero, Major General William Henry Chase Whiting, whose engineering skills were put to use in defending the last port open to blockade-runners. Another source of information was Beverly Tetteron, special collections librarian at the New Hanover County Library, who has written excellent accounts about the Cape Fear area. We also thank Rebecca Taylor and Gayle Keresy of the Federal Point Historic Preservation Society and Federal Point History Center for sharing their research on the lights of Federal Point, historic beacons that were once near Fort Fisher.

On the southwestern side of the Cape Fear River, we thank Mary

Strickland, retired manager and curator of the North Carolina Maritime Museum at Southport, who was most helpful and knowledgeable about lighthouses of the area and all history tied to the river.

At Bald Head Island, Kim Gottshall, Chris Webb, and Susan Grantier, along with the Old Baldy Foundation, deserve thanks for their contributions to preserving and restoring the 1817 Old Baldy Lighthouse and sharing its history.

At Currituck Beach Light Station in Corolla, our appreciation goes to site manager Meghan Agresto and the Outer Banks Conservationists, the nonprofit preservation organization that has brought this famous lighthouse back to life. And we are grateful to Angel Ellis Khoury for sharing her interview with John Wilson, great-grandson of Keeper Homer T. Austin. For artwork, we thank Mike Litwin, a young and talented artist in various media, as well as Brent Westwood and Doward Jones, director of the 1866 Roanoke River reproduction in Plymouth, North Carolina, who ran out and took a picture of whatever we were missing in the book.

Ray Jones, author of this book's foreword and our coauthor for nearly a dozen lighthouse books, has shared our trips and the wonder of discovering America's lighthouses. Rick Polad, auxiliary USCG volunteer, educator, author, and musician who has also been with us for much of the journey, helped with comments on the sea of words in this edition. Norma McKittrick, professional copyeditor and educator, helped stylize the manuscript and offered advice on the text. Lighthouse historian Jim Claflin provided not only information but also, in many cases, the actual documents. Doug Bingham is our go-to expert for information on light vessels. Thomas A. Tag is the expert on Fresnel lenses, having traveled abroad and studied them for decades. He is currently technical adviser for the U.S. Lighthouse Society and patiently answers each time we pepper him with questions.

There are so many others whose assistance we wish to acknowledge; we have gained a great deal of information through oral histories from U.S. Lighthouse Service keepers' descendants, few of whom survive today. We are grateful they allowed us to interview them multiple times and to copy their priceless photographs.

We express our gratitude to University of North Carolina Press acquisitions editor Lucas Church and his assistant, Andrew Winters; acquisition manager Cate Robin Hodorowicz; managing editor Mary Carley Caviness, and copyeditor Trish Watson for all their support and gentle use of expertise for this updated and expanded edition. The value of an editor's sharp eye cannot be overstated.

The fun part of creating a book like this one is meeting old friends and making new ones while looking back at noteworthy moments of history. If we have missed giving anyone due credit, it is unintentional.

To the lights!

Appendix

NORTH CAROLINA LIGHTS TIMELINE

1733   BEACON ISLAND LIGHTS. A pair of beacon lights was placed on Beacon Island to mark the channel through Ocracoke Inlet. The lights were whale-oil lamps, probably mounted on posts. They appeared on Edward Mosley's 1733 map *A New and Correct Map of the Province of North Carolina*, recorded as the first aids to navigation in North Carolina.

1794   FIRST BALD HEAD ISLAND LIGHTHOUSE. Completed by the U.S. government as the U.S. Lighthouse Establishment, it marked the entrance to the Cape Fear River. It was begun in 1784 by the state with money raised by a tax on tonnage carried by ships using the river's ports. This structure is considered North Carolina's first lighthouse.

circa 1800   SHELL CASTLE ISLAND LIGHTHOUSE. Built on an islet near Ocracoke Island, also known as Old Rock Island, this was the first lighthouse to mark Ocracoke Inlet. Construction was overseen by Henry Dearborn, who also built the 1803 Cape Hatteras tower. It was destroyed by lightning in 1818.

1803   FIRST CAPE HATTERAS LIGHTHOUSE. Lighted with a whale-oil flame and tended by Keeper Adam Gaskins, who was appointed by President Jefferson, this first Cape Hatteras tower was 90 feet high. The first illumination was provided by a pan of whale oil with multiple "floating" wicks but could not be seen where it was needed, out beyond Diamond Shoals. The lighthouse was heightened to 150 feet in 1854.

1812   FIRST CAPE LOOKOUT LIGHTHOUSE. The 93-foot brick tower was covered with wood and painted red and white; in 1817 Winslow Lewis wrote that it "appears at a distance as a ship of war with her sails clewed up and was often taken for such during the late war [War of 1812]."

1816   FIRST FEDERAL POINT LIGHTHOUSE. Located on the east side
of the Cape Fear River in an area now part of Fort Fisher
State Park, this lighthouse was equipped with eight whale-
oil lamps. It marked the entrance to New Inlet.

1817–18   SECOND BALD HEAD ISLAND LIGHTHOUSE. Known affectionately as
Old Baldy, this tower rises 110 feet high over the Cape Fear River
and is the oldest standing lighthouse in North Carolina. It was
built to replace the first tower, which had been destroyed due to
erosion. It is listed on early light lists as the "Cape Fear Lighthouse."
The site was established in 1817 and the light exhibited 1818.

1823   OCRACOKE LIGHTHOUSE. Noah Porter of Massachusetts built this tower
to replace the burned Shell Castle Island Light. The inlet channel had
moved closer to Ocracoke Island, which made the island a better location.
This light holds the historic distinction of being the oldest continuously
operating lighthouse on the North Carolina coast. It has been lighted
every night since 1823 except for a short time when Confederates
removed its Fresnel lens. It is now owned by the National Park Service
and is within the boundaries of Cape Hatteras National Seashore.

1824   FIRST DIAMOND SHOALS LIGHTSHIP. This was considered one of
the toughest assignments for the U.S. Lighthouse Establishment
on the East Coast. The lightship was placed at the outer edge
of the dangerous shoals. The anchor did not hold in severe
storms. Three years later keeping a lightship at Diamond Shoals
was deemed impossible and the lightship was removed.

1825   LONG SHOAL LIGHT VESSEL. The "straw-colored" light vessel
marked the shoal across northern Pamlico Sound. Light vessels
or "light boats" were designed for inland waters and were
smaller than lightships. They were often unmanned and tended
by a keeper on the mainland. Each light vessel was painted a
color to help identify the station to which it was assigned.

ROYAL SHOAL LIGHT VESSEL. This "lead-colored" vessel was
placed on the southwest point of Royal Shoals in Pamlico Sound
and was anchored nine miles from the Ocracoke Light.

1826   WADE'S POINT SHOAL LIGHT VESSEL (aka Wade Point). A light vessel took up duty as early as this year. It was located on the west side of the entrance to the Pasquotank River in Albemarle Sound and marked the way to Elizabeth City.

1827   NINE FOOT SHOAL LIGHT VESSEL. Placed about four miles northwest of Ocracoke Lighthouse, it marked the northeast side of Royal Shoal in Pamlico Sound and was painted white.

1828   NEUSE RIVER LIGHT VESSEL. This light vessel was anchored off Marsh Point and painted a lead color. It marked the Neuse River entrance from Pamlico Sound.

circa 1828   PAMLICO POINT LIGHTHOUSE. Located on the east side of the shoal (aka Pamptico Point) it marked the channel out from Pamlico Point on the south side of the Pamlico River. It was a white frame structure with its light 37 feet above water. It was originally equipped with ten whale-oil-burning lamps that were replaced in 1856 with a fifth-order Fresnel lens.

1831   BRANT ISLAND SHOAL LIGHT VESSEL. The first small light boat here marked the point of the shoal in southern Pamlico Sound to guide vessels around the hazard until 1851, when it was replaced by a larger one.

1835   ROANOKE ISLAND OR CROATAN LIGHT VESSEL. Painted a lead color, it marked the channel between Pamlico and Albemarle Sounds.

ROANOKE RIVER LIGHT VESSEL. This "straw-colored" light vessel was stationed in Albemarle Sound and marked the entrance to the Roanoke River.

1836   HARBOR ISLAND LIGHT VESSEL (aka Harkers Island Light Vessel). This red vessel was on the bar and marked the channel between Pamlico and Core Sounds.

1837   SECOND FEDERAL POINT LIGHTHOUSE and brick keepers' quarters completed. This light, with its fourth-order Fresnel lens removed, was demolished by Confederates in 1863, and the bricks from the tower were incorporated into the building of Fort Fisher. The keeper's house became the fort's headquarters.

1845   WADE'S POINT LIGHT VESSEL (aka Wade Point). A heavier, 76-ton lightship took over watch here. The yellow vessel was anchored on the west side of the river entrance. It marked the passage into the Pasquotank River from Albemarle Sound.

Note: The light vessels placed in the sounds between 1825 and 1845 were later replaced by cottage-style lighthouses as technology made it possible to support them by pilings with metal screw-shaped ends driven into the sandy/muddy bottoms of the sounds and rivers entrances. The screwpile lights were phased out in the 1950s, either demolished or bought privately. Only one original survives, the 1887 Roanoke River Lighthouse, which was relocated to Edenton in 2012. It had been built on the foundation of its predecessor that had been destroyed by fire two years earlier. Sound and range lights were replaced by buoys and post lanterns mounted on simple platforms.

1847   FIRST BODY ISLAND LIGHTHOUSE (later spelled Bodie Island). The first of three lights at this location was a 57-foot white tower with a fixed white light varied by red and white flashes at "about" one-minute intervals, according to U.S. Lighthouse Service Light Lists. Shortly after being put into service the tower started to lean since a foundation had not been built to save on construction costs. Congress was not pleased with lighthouse construction, and it authorized U.S. Topographical Engineers and Army Corps of Engineers (merged in 1863) to build lighthouses and fortifications based on training at West Point Academy.

1849   OAK ISLAND RANGE LIGHTS. A pair of brick towers on Oak Island guided ships over the bar into the Cape Fear River. The rear tower was 37 feet and the front 27 feet high, and both were equipped with fifth-order Fresnel lenses. One report suggested that, after the lights were rebuilt in 1879, the front range light was a wooden structure mounted on rails so it could be moved as the Cape Fear River channel changed.

CAMPBELL'S ISLAND LIGHT. This was one of a series of lights built to guide ships up the Cape Fear River to the port of Wilmington. The light, a sixth-order Fresnel lens, was on the edge of a marshy point.

ORTON'S POINT LIGHT. On the Cape Fear River, it was located near Orton Plantation on the edge of the marsh.

1850   PRICE'S CREEK RANGE LIGHTS. This was another of the network of range lights along the Cape Fear River. Located on the west bank of the river at the entrance to Price's Creek near what is now the state ferry dock at Southport, the rear light was on the keeper's house and the front light was housed in a 25-foot-tall brick tower. Both structures held sixth-order Fresnel lenses. Only the front tower remains today; it is the last standing relic of the Cape Fear River lights. The tower was a Confederate signal station in 1864–65 and gave blockade-running ships information about Union ships' positions. It first appeared on the government official Light List in 1850.

1851   BRANT ISLAND SHOAL LIGHT VESSEL. A heavier lightship took over duty here. Painted a "straw color," this ship in southern Pamlico Sound marked the island and shoal.

HORSE SHOE SHOAL LIGHTSHIP. Located in the Cape Fear River after a failed attempt to build a lighthouse on the shoals, the lightship marked a channel at Horseshoe Bend between Price's Creek and New Inlet.

UPPER JETTY LIGHT VESSEL. Located in the Cape Fear River, it was the nearest light to the port of Wilmington; it was replaced with a lighthouse in 1855.

1852   A milestone year for the U.S. Lighthouse Service: Since the late 1840s, the service had been committed to update all old lighting systems with the Fresnel lenticular system that had been proven far superior in focusing a light's intensity and casting it farther out to sea where mariners needed guidance. Stephen Pleasonton was replaced as overseer of American lights by a professional, nine-member Lighthouse Board consisting of seven military men and two men with science expertise.

OCRACOKE CHANNEL LIGHT VESSEL. This light vessel marked Ocracoke Inlet and later served as a range light with the Beacon Island Light in Ocracoke Inlet.

1853   BEACON ISLAND LIGHTHOUSE. This light, inside the Ocracoke Inlet channel, was a brick keeper's house with the light mounted on the roof in a lantern room. Equipped with ten whale-oil lamps, it was later upgraded to a sixth-order Fresnel lens.

1854   FRYING PAN LIGHTSHIP. In ten fathoms (60 feet) of water off the outer end of Frying Pan Shoals, this lightship was located in the Atlantic Ocean off the entrance to the Cape Fear River. It was the second of the larger ocean-going lightships along the North Carolina coast. It was painted yellow, with the words "Frying Pan" painted in black on both sides.

1855   WADE'S POINT LIGHTHOUSE (aka Wade Point or Pasquotank River Light). The screwpile was at the point off the shoal, situated on the west side of the Pasquotank River, and marked the channel into the river and Elizabeth City docks. It was painted white, with a fifth-order Fresnel lens mounted in a lantern room on the roof.

BOGUE BANKS RANGE LIGHTS. These lights, located at Fort Macon at Beaufort Harbor Inlet (formerly called Old Topsail Inlet), marked the channel for this once-busy port. The main, rear range light was a brick 50-foot tower located outside and to the rear of Fort Macon with a fourth-order Fresnel lens. The front beacon was located on a 30-foot-high wooden platform near the beach that housed a sixth-order lens. Both lights were taken down by Confederates to clear a line of fire for the fort's guns. They were not rebuilt. Plans housed in the National Archives illustrate the main range as a conical tower; however, a drawing by a Union soldier depicts an octagonal-shaped lighthouse.

UPPER JETTY RANGE LIGHTS. These range lights were the final ones built for the Cape Fear River channel to the Wilmington docks. The front light was on the keeper's house, and the rear light was mounted on a wooden platform. Both were sixth-order Fresnel lenses.

1856   CAPE HATTERAS BEACON. The small wooden building was a modest 20-foot-high square structure situated about half-way between the Cape Hatteras Lighthouse and the tip of Cape Point. Its sixth-order Fresnel lens helped coasting (local) boaters to enter Pamlico Sound around the cape.

1857   NORTHWEST POINT ROYAL SHOAL. As a hexagonal screwpile lighthouse in 6 feet of water on the northwest point of Royal Shoal, this light was nine miles from the Ocracoke Lighthouse. It was equipped with a fourth-order Fresnel lens.

ROANOKE MARSHES LIGHTHOUSE. The screwpile lighthouse stood on iron pilings and was surmounted by a lantern room that housed a fourth-order Fresnel lens. It replaced the light vessel that marked the south entrance to the channel between Pamlico and Albemarle Sounds.

1859   SECOND BODIE ISLAND LIGHTHOUSE. Designed by Captain Lorenzo Sitgreaves of the U.S. Army Corps of Topographical Engineers, the tower replaced the leaning 1847 tower that had been built without a foundation. Regrettably, Confederates destroyed this new tower only two years later so it would not be of benefit to Union forces preparing an attack on Roanoke Island. The third-order Fresnel lens was saved.

CAPE LOOKOUT LIGHTHOUSE. The second light to mark this area, it was the first tall coastal lighthouse (at least 150 feet tall) to be built in North Carolina and sent a light beyond Lookout Shoals. Captain W. H. C. Whiting of the U.S. Army Corps of Engineers supervised and approved the design for the new 163-foot tall brick lighthouse equipped with a first-order Fresnel lens that became a model for other tall coastal lights on the Outer Banks. It still functions today.

1860   CROATAN LIGHTHOUSE (aka Caroon's Point, Roanoke Island, or Mashoes Creek). The screwpile structure marked the channel from Albemarle Sound into Croatan Sound. It was destroyed by a Confederate raiding party from the CSS *Albemarle* in 1864, and the keeper was taken prisoner.

1862   NEUSE RIVER LIGHTHOUSE. Standing in 5 feet of water, this square screwpile structure was situated on the western side of the river entrance from Pamlico Sound. The light was under construction when the war began, and it was finished after Union forces took control of the area early in the war.

1863   BRANT ISLAND SHOAL LIGHTHOUSE assumed the light vessel's duty when it was established as a square, white, cottage-style screwpile lighthouse in 7 feet of water and housed a fifth-order Fresnel lens. It marked the southerly approach to Pamlico River. It burned in 1876 and was rebuilt 1877.

1866   SECOND CROATAN LIGHTHOUSE. This screwpile was built to replace the first one burned by Confederates in 1864. It marked the entrance to Croatan Sound from Albemarle Sound and exhibited a fixed white light, and the building had green shutters and a brown roof. The Lighthouse Board resumed the job of rebuilding towers damaged or destroyed during the Civil War and building new, more efficient ones.

1866   FIRST ROANOKE RIVER LIGHTHOUSE. The square screwpile lighthouse stood in 7 feet of water in Albemarle Sound near the river entrance. Pilings were painted red, and the house white, and it displayed a light from a fourth-order Fresnel lens showing red. This light station was destroyed by fire in 1885 and was rebuilt in 1887.

THIRD FEDERAL POINT LIGHTHOUSE. As a marker for New Inlet leading into the Cape Fear River, the light was completed near the ruins of Fort Fisher to replace the second Federal Point Lighthouse destroyed by Confederates. It was a white structure 45 feet high, with the light in a lantern room mounted on top of the keepers' quarters. The U.S. Lighthouse Service Light List indicated one fixed "bright" light. It was discontinued when the Army Corps of Engineers purposely closed New Inlet in 1880.

OAK ISLAND RANGE LIGHTS are rebuilt. These range lights were square at the foundations rising to white pyramidal structures. They replaced the destroyed brick towers. The front light was 20 feet high and the rear 40 feet. Their warning lights varied over the years as red or white, with a two-story keeper's house nearby.

NORTH RIVER LIGHTHOUSE. The square white screwpile structure rested in 3.5 feet of water on the bar at the entrance to North River in Albemarle Sound. Pilings were painted brown, and the lantern black, and it exhibited a fixed red light from a fifth-order Fresnel lens.

1867   LONG SHOAL LIGHTHOUSE. The square screwpile stood in 9 feet of water in northern Pamlico Sound. It replaced the light vessel that marked Long Shoal and was equipped with a fourth-order Fresnel lens.

SOUTHWEST POINT ROYAL SHOAL LIGHTHOUSE. The square white screwpile was positioned on the southwest side of the shoal in Pamlico Sound about eight miles from the Ocracoke Lighthouse. Its supporting piles and roof were painted brown and the lantern black. It was discontinued in 1880 but relighted in 1887.

HARBOR ISLAND BAR LIGHTHOUSE. The square, white screwpile structure on the bar was in 6 feet of water and marked the entrance to Core Sound from Pamlico Sound. It displayed a flashing red light every ten seconds. Note: there are discrepancies on some of the river and sound lights, but the stated dates are from the official light lists published by the U.S. Lighthouse Service.

1870   CAPE HATTERAS LIGHTHOUSE. The second Cape Hatteras tower was completed and is still standing. It is the tallest brick lighthouse in North America, at 198 feet high. In 1999 the National Park Service moved it 2,900 feet away from the eroding shoreline to preserve it. It is within Cape Hatteras National Seashore and is open for climbing seasonally. Note: due to wear and tear on stairs not designed to take heavy foot traffic, all lighthouses open to the public must close periodically for repairs.

1872   THIRD BODIE ISLAND LIGHTHOUSE. This lighthouse still stands about forty miles north of Cape Hatteras. It is within Cape Hatteras National Seashore and is owned by the National Park Service It retains its original first-order Fresnel lens. Both the tower and lens have been restored.

1874   HATTERAS INLET LIGHTHOUSE (aka Oliver's Reef Lighthouse). This screwpile lighthouse stood in about 7 feet of water on the north side of the entrance to Hatteras Inlet from Pamlico Sound. It was a square white screwpile structure showing a flashing red light every thirty seconds.

1875   CURRITUCK BEACH LIGHTHOUSE. The lighthouse was the last of the tall coastal lights built by the U.S. Lighthouse Board in North Carolina. The same plans were used as for the third Bodie Island tower; however Currituck Beach retained its natural brick color as its daymark. It has been beautifully restored by a nonprofit the Outer Banks Conservationists, Inc. and is open for climbing from March through November.

1877   ROANOKE MARSHES LIGHTHOUSE. This was the second lighthouse built at this site to mark the south entrance of the Croatan Sound. It was given improvements that included a compressed-air siren fog signal. The white screwpile structure stood in 13 feet of water. The pilings were painted brown and the lantern black, with a fixed red light. A reproduction is located on the waterfront of Manteo.

1879   EDENTON HARBOR RANGE LIGHTS. A unique setup, one light was on a pole at the end of the county wharf, and the rear range was, according to the official U.S. Light List, "400 feet northward in a tree."

1880   LAUREL POINT LIGHTHOUSE. This screwpile was a white hexagonal lighthouse on brown pilings. It was unique at the time it was built because it was the only flashing light on Albemarle Sound. It marked the entrance to the Scuppernong River into Columbia. It flashed a white light for 4.3 seconds followed by an eclipse of 25.7 seconds, for two cycles each minute.

1891   DIAMOND SHOALS LIGHTHOUSE. The U.S. Lighthouse Board attempted to build a 148-foot-high lighthouse in the ocean on a caisson underpinning resting on the shoals. Shifting sands tilted the caisson, and the project was abandoned.

PAMLICO POINT LIGHTHOUSE. The U.S. Lighthouse Board rebuilt this screwpile lighthouse at the south side of the entrance to the Pamlico River leading to port at Washington, N.C.

GULL SHOAL LIGHTHOUSE. This white hexagonal screwpile lighthouse sat on brown pilings 44 feet above the water in 9 feet of water on the east end of Gull Shoal in Pamlico Sound. It exhibited a fixed red light that could be seen eleven miles away.

1897   DIAMOND SHOALS LIGHTSHIP. A more modern lightship, this vessel had the advantage of an extremely heavy mushroom anchor that kept it on station more successfully against storm winds and waves than its predecessor seventy years earlier. It was placed off the outer edge of the shoals. It was destroyed by a German U-boat in 1918, but its crew safely escaped to shore.

1903   CAPE FEAR LIGHTHOUSE. The Lighthouse Board constructed a tall, skeleton steel tower on the southeast point of Bald Head Island and mounted a first-order Fresnel lens in it—classic brick towers had given way to modern steel design. It satisfied the Lighthouse Board's desire to have a light tall and bright enough to warn of Frying Pan Shoals while serving river traffic. It was demolished in 1958.

LOOKOUT SHOALS LIGHT VESSEL. Placed off the outer edge of Lookout Shoals, a tragedy happened nearby in July 1913 when the steamer *City of Atlanta* inadvertently ran down the light vessel's whaleboat as it was picking up mail, drowning three of the crew. The lightship itself was a victim of the Great Depression, removed in the name of economy in 1933 and replaced by a buoy.

1958   OAK ISLAND LIGHTHOUSE. Not far from the original Oak Island Range Lights, the USCG built one of the last lighthouses, a 153-foot tower of concrete that has paint mixed in so it needs repainting only rarely, if at all. It was the last lighthouse built in the state, as global positioning satellites came to dominate the job of marine navigation.

1964   FRYING PAN SHOALS LIGHT STATION (later automated as Frying Pan Tower). This "Texas tower" station was a new kind of lighthouse seen on North Carolina's coast for the first time when the USCG lighted dangerous Frying Pan Shoals with a light 130 feet above the ocean, replacing the Frying Pan lightship. This light station looks more like a Texas oil rig platform, with pilings driven an incredible 293 feet into the ocean floor. Now privately owned, it operates as an off-the-grid bed-and-breakfast.

1966   DIAMOND SHOALS "TEXAS TOWER" LIGHT STATION. Modern technology was again put to work by the USCG to build a light on Diamond Shoals in 54 feet of water for the first time in history. It held a light that could be seen for seventeen miles. Now privately owned, its owner plans to repurpose it as an "on-ocean technology center."

21st century   No more lighthouses as official aids to navigation are planned, but reproductions have been built to portray what once existed at Roanoke Marshes and Roanoke River. A smaller-scale version of the Pamlico Point Light Station sits on Washington, N.C., docks. The challenge today is to preserve the ones still standing. Volunteers are welcome and needed at most light stations. With the number of boaters increasing, the USCG focuses on placement of buoys to warn of ever-changing channels due to shoaling. North Carolina's dynamic inland waters cause sand to accumulate and shift, continually creating new hazards.

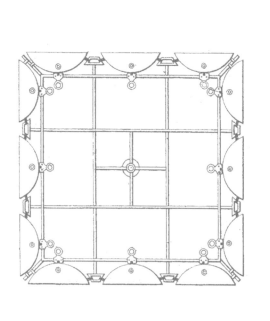
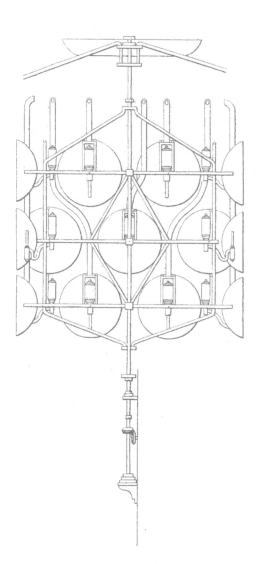

Bibliography

Anderson, Kraig. "North Carolina Lighthouses." Accessed January 20, 2018. http://www.light housefriends.com/pull-state.asp?state=NC.

Appletons' Annual Cyclopædia and Register of Important Events of the Year 1880. New Series, Vol. 5. New York: D. Appleton, 1888.

Barrett, John G. *The Civil War in North Carolina.* Chapel Hill: University of North Carolina Press, 1963.

Binkley, Cameron. *The Creation and Establishment of Cape Hatteras National Seashore: The Great Depression through Mission 66.* Atlanta: National Park Service Southeast Regional Office, Cultural Resource Division, 2007.

Blunt, Edmund. *The American Coast Pilot.* New York: E. G. W. Blunt, 1842.

Branch, Paul, "Subtlety and Subterfuge: Bombing the Lights." *Maritime Magazine,* October 28, 1986.

Bureau of Lighthouses. *U.S. Lighthouse Service Bulletin.* Washington, D.C.: Government Printing Office, 1912–39.

Carr, Dawson. *Gray Phantoms of the Cape Fear: Running the Civil War Blockade.* Winston-Salem, N.C.: John R. Blair, 1998.

Chenery, Richard L., III. *Old Coast Guard Stations,* Vol. 2: *North Carolina.* Glen Allen, Va.: Station Books, 2000.

Childers, Lloyd D. "Leasing a Lighthouse Complex." *North Carolina Historic Preservation Office Newsletter* (Winter 1995): 10–11.

Claudy, C. H. "The Floating Lighthouses." *Yachting,* November 1907, 262–65.

Clifford, Candace, Project Manager. *Finding Aid for Lighthouse Records in the National Archives.* Cypress Communications. Accessed February 9, 2017. https://lighthousehistory.info/research/uslhs /#USLHB.

———. *Inventory of Historic Light Stations.* National Maritime Initiative. Washington, D.C.: History Division, National Park Service, 1994.

Cloud, Ellen Fulcher. *Ocracoke Lighthouse.* Spartanburg, S.C.: Reprint Company, 1993.

———. *Portsmouth: The Way It Was.* Island History 3. Ocracoke, N.C.: Live Oak Publications, 1996.

Crawford, Captain William P. *Mariner's Notebook: A Guide to Boating Fundamentals.* 3rd ed. San Francisco: Miller Freeman, 1971.

Dominique, Jessie Lee (Babb). Information compiled from interviews by the author in Beaufort, N.C., and on Portsmouth Island, N.C., March 2003–May 2004.

Duffus, Kevin. *The Lost Light: The Mystery of the Missing Cape Hatteras Fresnel Lens.* Raleigh, N.C.: Looking Glass, 2003.

Elizabeth, Norma, and Bruce Roberts. *Shipwrecks, Disasters and Rescues of the Graveyard of the Atlantic and Cape Fear.* Morehead City, N.C.: Lighthouse Publications, 2001.

Fatorić, S., and E. Seekamp. "Assessing Historical Significance and Use Potential of Buildings within Historic Districts: An Overview of a Measurement Framework Developed for Climate Adaptation Planning." AG-832. Raleigh: N.C. State Extension. Accessed February 2018. https://content.ces.ncsu .edu/assessing-historical-significance-and-use -potential-of-buildings.

Fonvielle, Chris E., Jr. *The Wilmington Campaign: Last Rays of Departing Hope.* Campbell, Calif.: Savas, 1997.

———. *The Faces of Fort Fisher, 1861–1864.* Carolina Beach, N.C.: SlapDash Publishing, 2014.

Fresnel, M. Augustin. *Mémoire sur un nouveau système d'éclairage des phares.* Paris: L'Imprimerie Royale, 1822. Translation by Thomas A. Tag. Dayton, Ohio: Self-published, 2004.

Fulcher, Susan. "Reclaiming Its Shining Past: The

Restoration of the Currituck Beach Lighthouse Property." *Lighthouse News* 3, no. 2 (1997).

Garrish, Ruby Austin. Information compiled from interviews by the author at her home on Ocracoke Island, N.C., 1997.

Goree, John A. "Price and Strother, Joshua Potts, and the Evolution of 'A Map of Cape Fear River and Its Vicinity.'" *North Carolina Historical Review* 76, no. 4 (1999), 391–409. https://www.jstor.org/stable /23522307.

Halbrook, Stephen P., and David B. Kopel. "Tench Coxe and the Right to Keep and Bear Arms, 1787–1823." *William and Mary Bill of Rights Journal* 7, no. 2 (1999): article 3. http://scholarship.law.wm .edu/cgi/viewcontent.cgi?article=1421&context =wmborj.

Herring, Ethel. *Cap'n Charlie and Lights of the Lower Cape Fear.* Winston-Salem, N.C.: Hunter, 1967.

Hickam, Homer, Jr. *Torpedo Junction.* Annapolis, Md.: U.S. Naval Institute Press, 1989.

Historical Society of Pennsylvania. "Coxe Family Mining Papers," 2001. Accessed April 19, 2004. http://www.hsp.org/collections/coxe/family.html.

Hitchcock, Susan. *Ocracoke Light Station: Cultural Landscape Report.* Atlanta: Cultural Resources, Partnerships and Science Southeast Region, National Park Service, 2016.

Hobbs, Helen. "Framers of Freedom: Henry Dearborn." *NH: Years of Revolution, Profiles Publications and the NH Bicentennial Commission (1976 and 2005).* Accessed March 3, 2018. http:// www.seacoastnh.com/Famous-People/framers-of -freedom/henry-dearborn/.

Holland, F. Ross, Jr. *America's Lighthouses: An Illustrated History.* New York: Dover Publications, 1981.

———. *Great American Lighthouses.* Washington, D.C.: Preservation Press, 1994.

———. *A History of the Bodie Island Light Station.* Washington, D.C.: Division of History, National Park Service, 1967.

———. *A History of the Cape Hatteras Light Station.* Washington, D.C.: Division of History, National Park Service, 1968.

———. *A Survey History of Cape Lookout National Seashore.* Washington, D.C.: Division of History, Office of Archeology and Historic Preservation, 1968.

Horan, Jack. "People and Places: Diamond Shoals and Frying Pan: Offshore Light Towers Beckon New Missions." Winter 2013. Accessed January 30, 2018. https://ncseagrant.ncsu.edu/coastwatch/previous -issues/2013-2/winter-2013/people-and-places -diamond-shoals-and-frying-pan-offshore-light -towers-beckon-new-missions/.

Howard, Phillip. "Captain Joe Burrus, August 24, 2007." *Ocracoke Newsletter,* May 9, 2017.

Jones, Ray. *The Encyclopedia of Lighthouses: The Definitive Reference.* Old Saybrook, Conn.: Globe Pequot Press, 2004.

Kendall, Connie Jo, "Let There Be Light: The History of Lighthouse Illuminants." *The Log* 13, no. 3 (1997): 22–29.

Khoury, Angel Ellis. *National Historic Lighthouse Preservation Act Application to Obtain Light Station Property.* Outer Banks Conservationists, Inc., February 7, 2003.

Kochel, Kenneth G. *America's Atlantic Coast Lighthouses: A Traveler's Guide.* Rev. ed. Clearwater, Fla.: Betken Publications, 1996.

Mobley, Joe A. *Ship Ashore! The U.S. Lifesavers of Coastal North Carolina.* Chapel Hill: North Carolina Division of Archives and History, 1996.

National Archives Records Administration (Washington, D.C.), Record Group 26: U.S. Coast Guard. Entry 3, NC-63, "Letters to Fifth District Inspectors, 1851–1912," Cape Lookout, 1904–5.

———. Letters from District Engineers: Reports of Physical Condition of Lighthouses, 1870–76, 1885–88, Entry 72, NC-31.

———. Letters Received from District Engineers and Inspectors to Light House-Board, Entry 23, NC-31, vols. 2, 8, and 16, February 1853.

———. Records of the Fifth Light-House District (Baltimore), 1851–1912, Entry 3, NC-63, Lamberton, Entry 24, vol. 1173, box 197, p. 256.

———. "Site Description Files," "Clipping Files," "Letter Index," North Carolina Lighthouses, Entry 63, NC-31.

National Archives Records Administration (College Park, Md.), Record Group 365: Treasury Department Collection of Confederate Records. States Lighthouse Bureau Records, Entry 79: Lighthouse Bureau, letters box 2 on North Carolina, 1862. Transcribed by Sandra MacLean Clunies, 2002.

National Park Service. *Cape Hatteras.* Accessed December 2017. https://www.nps.gov/caha/.

———. *Cape Lookout.* Accessed December 2017. https://www.nps.gov/calo/.

———. National Historic Landmark Nomination: Cape Hatteras Light Station. U.S. Department of the Interior, Washington, D.C.: National Park Service, 1998.

National Register of Historic Places, Bodie Island Light Station, Nags Head, Dare County, N.C., National Register #03000607, 2003.

National Register of Historic Places. *Bodie Island.* Washington, D.C.: Department of the Interior, 2003.

North Carolina Museum of History. "North Carolina American Indian History Timeline." Accessed January 2018. https://www.ncmuseumofhistory .org/american-indian/handouts/timeline.

O'Connor, William D. *Heroes of the Storm.* Boston: Houghton, Mifflin, 1904.

O'Neal, Earl W., Jr. *Ocracoke Island: Its People, the U.S. Coast Guard and Navy Base during World War II.* Ocracoke, N.C.: Self-published, 2001.

Oppermann, Joseph K. *Cape Lookout Lighthouse Historic Structure Report.* Winston-Salem, N.C.: Cultural Resources Division, Southeast Region, National Park Service, 2008.

Oxford, Lee Thomas. *The Civil War on Hatteras: The Chicamacomico Affair and the Capture of the US Gunboat Fanny.* Charleston, S.C.: History Press, 2013.

Payne, Roger L. *Place Names of the Outer Banks.* Washington, N.C.: Thomas A. Williams, 1985.

Powell, William S. *North Carolina through Four Centuries.* Chapel Hill: University of North Carolina Press, 1989.

Putman, George R. "Beacons of the Sea; Lighting the Coast of the United States." *National Geographic Magazine,* January 1913.

———. *Lighthouses and Lightships of the United States.* Boston: Houghton Mifflin, 1917.

———. *Sentinel of the Coasts: The Log of a Lighthouse Engineer.* New York: Norton, 1937.

Reese, David, and Robert Browning, "Lighthouse Management: A Balancing Act by the U.S. Coast Guard." *Cultural Resource Management* 20, no. 8 (1997).

Roberts, Bruce, and Ray Jones. *Southern Lighthouses.* Old Saybrook, Conn.: Globe Pequot Press, 1994.

Roberts, Bruce, Cheryl Shelton-Roberts, and Ray Jones. *American Lighthouses,* 3rd ed. Old Saybrook, Conn.: Globe Pequot Press, 2012.

Rowlett, Russ. "Early Federal Octagonals." *The Lighthouse Directory,* University of North Carolina at Chapel Hill, 2000. https://www.unc.edu/~rowlett /lighthouse/types/octagonals.html.

Satterwaith, Sheafe. "Notes on Bald Head Island," David Stick Collection, Outer Banks History Center, Manteo, N.C., 1964.

Schubert, Frank N., ed. *The Nation Builders: A Sesquicentennial History of the Corps of Topographical Engineers 1839–1863.* Honolulu: University Press of the Pacific, 2005.

Shelton-Roberts, Cheryl. "Fresnel Defies Napoleon, Newton and Death to Design Revolutionary Lens." *Lighthouse News* 2, no. 3 (1996).

———. *Lighthouse Families.* Birmingham, Ala.: Crane Hill Press, 1990.

———. "Light Years Away." *Lighthouse News* 2, no. 1 (1996).

Shelton-Roberts, Cheryl, and Bruce Roberts. *Moving Hatteras: Relocating the Cape Hatteras Light Station to Safety.* Morehead City, N.C.: Lighthouse Publications, 1999.

———. *North Carolina Lighthouses.* Morehead City, N.C.: Lighthouse Publications, 2000.

Shelton-Roberts, Cheryl, ed., and Sandra MacLean Clunies, certified genealogist. *Bodie Island Keepers Oral and Family Histories.* Morehead City, N.C.: Outer Banks Lighthouse Society, 2013.

———. *Hatteras Keepers Oral and Family Histories.* Morehead City, N.C.: Outer Banks Lighthouse Society, 2001.

Sprunt, James. *Chronicles of the Cape Fear River.* 1916. Spartanburg, S.C.: Reprint Company, 1973.

Stanford, Herbert W., III. *A Look into Carteret County, North Carolina: History, Economics, Politics and Culture: 1607–2030.* Morehead City, N.C.: Self-published, 2014.

Stick, David. *Bald Head: A History of Smith Island and Cape Fear.* Wendell, N.C.: Broadfoot Publishing, 1985.

———. *Dare County: A Brief History.* Raleigh: North Carolina Division of Archives and History, 1970.

———. *Graveyard of the Atlantic: Shipwrecks of the North Carolina Coast.* Chapel Hill: University of North Carolina Press, 1952.

———. *North Carolina Lighthouses*. Raleigh: Division of Archives and History, North Carolina Department of Cultural Resources, 1980.

———. Notes on Bald Head Island and interviews with island families, Outer Banks History Center, Manteo, N.C. Research concluded March 1984.

———. *The Outer Banks of North Carolina*. Chapel Hill: University of North Carolina Press, 1958.

———, ed. *An Outer Banks Reader*. Chapel Hill: University of North Carolina Press, 1998.

Tag, Thomas. *From Braziers and Bougies to Xenon*. Dayton, Ohio: Self-published, 2004.

———. *The Genius and the Mentor*. Dayton, Ohio: Self-published, 2004.

———. "Lighting Cape Hatteras." *Lighthouse News* 5, no. 4 (2000).

University of Missouri–Kansas City School of Law. "Alexander Hamilton (1755–1804)." Accessed August 14, 2018. http://law2.umkc.edu/Faculty /projects/ftrials/conlaw/marrynewyork.html.

U.S. Army Corps of Engineers. "The Corps' Connection to the Washington, D.C., Tidal." Office of History Vignettes no. 48. Accessed June 2011. https://www.usace.army.mil/About/History /Historical-Vignettes/Parks-and-Monuments/048 -Cherry-Tree/.

U.S. Department of the Treasury. "Albert Gallitin (1801–1814)." Accessed 2013. https://www.treasury .gov/about/history/pages/agallatin.aspx.

———. "Alexander Hamilton (1789–1795)." Accessed June 2016. https://www.treasury.gov/about/history /pages/ahamilton.aspx.

U.S. Light-House Board. Annual Reports, 1872, 1890, 1903, 1914, Lighthouse Site Files. In author's possession.

———. *Laws of the United States Relating to the Establishment, Support, and Management of the Light- houses, Light-vessels, Monuments, Beacons, Spindles, Buoys, and Public Piers of the United States from August 7, 1789, to March 3, 1855*. Washington, D.C.: A. O. P. Nicholson, June 1855.

U.S. Light-House Service. *List of Beacons, Buoys and Day-Marks in the Fifth Light-House District*. Washington, D.C.: Government Printing Office, 1839–39.

Wallace, David H. *Principal Keeper's Quarters Cape Hatteras Light Station*. Harpers Ferry, W.Va.: Harpers Ferry Center, National Park Service, 1991.

Weiss, George. *The Lighthouse Service: Its History, Activities and Organization*. Baltimore: Johns Hopkins University Press, 1926.

Wheeler, Wayne. "The 1838 Inspection of America's Light Stations: Stephen Pleasonton and the Blunt Brothers." *The Log* 33, no. 2 (2017): 8–13.

———. "History of the Administration of the Lighthouses in America." Accessed June 3, 2017. http://uslhs.org/history-administration-lighthouses -america.

Wilkinson, John. *Narrative of a Blockade-Runner*. New York: Sheldon, 1877.

Wolfram, Walt. *Ocracoke Speaks* (audio CD): recordings of native islanders' brogues; accompanying booklet compiled by Ellen Marie Cloud, Ocracoke Preservation Society. Raleigh: North Carolina Language and Life Project, N.C. State University, 1992–99.

Index

Page numbers in italics refer to illustrations and illustration captions.

About the Authors

North Carolina native, University of North Carolina–Greensboro graduate, and lighthouse historian Cheryl Shelton-Roberts is the editor of *Hatteras Keepers Oral and Family Histories* and *Bodie Island Oral and Family Histories*, compilations of dozens of stories from the families of Cape Hatteras and Bodie Island Lighthouse keepers. She researched and penned *Lighthouse Families*, a touching chronicle of the lives of U.S. lighthouse keepers' families and winner of the U.S. Coast Guard's outstanding history book for 2007. Other works include *Moving Hatteras: Relocating the Cape Hatteras Light Stations to Safety* and *Cape Hatteras: America's Lighthouse*. She has created numerous publications for the National Park Service.

Nationally acclaimed photographer Bruce Roberts served as the first director of photography and senior photographer for *Southern Living* magazine. His lighthouse photographs have appeared in hundreds of books and magazines, including *Our State* magazine, *Time*, *Life*, *Time-Life Books*, *Southern Lighthouses*, and *American Lighthouses*.

In 1994, the couple cofounded the Outer Banks Lighthouse Society, an organization dedicated to the preservation of North Carolina lighthouses, the history of the women and men who saved countless lives from the capricious Graveyard of the Atlantic, and the history of the U.S. Lighthouse Service. They have published the society's newsletters for a quarter century. Both have been awarded the prestigious Keeper of the Light award from the American Lighthouse Foundation for their preservation efforts, including the part they played in the successful 1999 move of the Cape Hatteras Lighthouse to safer ground. They live in Morehead City, North Carolina.